Weird Maryland

Sterling Publishing Co., Inc.
New York

WEIRD MARYLAND

MARYLAND

Your Travel Guide to Maryland's Local Legends and Best Kept Secrets

BY MATT LAKE

Mark Sceurman and Mark Moran, Executive Editors

WEIRD MARYLAND

Published by Sterling Publishing Co., Inc.
387 Park Avenue South, New York, NY 10016
© 2006 Mark Sceurman and Mark Moran
Distributed in Canada by Sterling Publishing
c/o Canadian Manda Group, 165 Dufferin Street
Toronto, Ontario, Canada M6K 3H6
Distributed in Great Britain by Chrysalis Books Group PLC
The Chrysalis Building, Bramley Road, London W10 6SP, England
Distributed in Australia by Capricorn Link (Australia) Pty. Ltd.
P. O. Box 704, Windsor, NSW 2756, Australia

10 9 8 7 6 5 4 3 2 1

Manufactured in the United States of America

Photography and illustration credits are found on page 254
and constitute an extension of this copyright page.

Sterling ISBN 13: 978-1-4027-3906-4
Sterling ISBN 10: 1-4027-3906-0

For information about custom editions, special sales, premium
and corporate purchases, please contact Sterling Special Sales
Department at 800-805-5489 or specialsales@sterlingpub.com.

Design: Richard J. Berenson
      Berenson Design & Books, LLC, New York, NY

Weird Maryland is intended as entertainment to present a historical record of local legends, folklore, and sites throughout Maryland. Many of these legends and stories cannot be independently confirmed or corroborated, and the authors and publisher make no representation as to their factual accuracy. The reader should be advised that many of the sites described in *Weird Maryland* are located on private property and should not be visited, or you may face prosecution for trespassing.

CONTENTS

DEDICATION

This book is dedicated to a large family of people named Lake, a couple of guys named Mark, and my wife, Mrs. Not-Lake, a mysterious character known as Caroline, whom many people have heard about but few have actually seen.

Foreword: A Note from the Marks

Our weird journey began a long, long time ago in a far-off land called New Jersey. Once a year or so we'd compile a homespun newsletter called *Weird N.J.*, then pass it on to our friends. The pamphlet was a collection of odd news clippings, bizarre facts, little-known historical anecdotes, and anomalous encounters from our home state. The newsletter also included the kinds of localized legends that were often whispered around a particular town but seldom heard outside the boundaries of the community where they originated.

We had started *Weird N.J.* on the simple theory that every town in the state had at least one good tale to tell. The publication soon became a full-fledged magazine, and we made the decision to actually do our own investigating to see if we could track down where all of these seemingly unbelievable stories were coming from. Was there, we wondered, any factual basis for the fantastic local legends people were telling us about? Armed with not much more than a camera and a notepad, we set off on a mystical journey of discovery. Much to our surprise and amazement, a lot of what we had initially presumed to be nothing more than urban legends turned out to be real—or at least to contain a grain of truth, which had sparked the lore to begin with.

After a dozen years of documenting the bizarre, we were asked to write a book about our adventures, and so *Weird N.J.: Your Travel Guide to New Jersey's Local Legends and Best Kept Secrets* was published in 2003. Soon people from all over the country began writing to us, telling us strange tales from their home states. As it turned out, what we had perceived to be something of very local interest was actually just a small part of a larger and more universal phenomenon.

When our publisher asked us what we wanted to do next, the answer was simple: "We'd like to do a book called *Weird U.S.*, in which we could document the local legends and strangest stories from all over the country." So for the next twelve months, we set out in search of weirdness wherever it might be found in the fifty states. And indeed, we found plenty of it!

After *Weird U.S.* was published, we came to the conclusion that this country had more great tales than could be contained in just one book. Everywhere we looked, we found unwritten folklore, creepy cemeteries, cursed locations, and outlandish roadside oddities. With this in mind, we told our publisher that we wanted to document it ALL and to do it in a series of books, each focusing on the peculiarities of a particular state.

One of the first states we decided to tackle was one about which we had already collected the greatest volume of material—Pennsylvania. When it came time to decide on which author we wanted to be our eyes and ears in the Quaker State, we were fortunate to have a ready cohort. Matt Lake was our editor for the *Weird N.J.* and *Weird U.S.* books. And we could tell right from the beginning of our association with him that Matt "got it." He was like a kindred spirit in weirdness. It was clear to us that he possessed what we refer to as the "Weird Eye." The Weird Eye is what is needed to search out the sort of stories we were looking for. It requires one to see the world in a different way, with a renewed sense of wonder. And once you have it, there is no going back—you'll never see things the same way again. All of a sudden you begin to reexamine your own environs, noticing your everyday surroundings as if for the first time. And you begin to ask yourself questions like, "What the heck is *that* thing all about, anyway?" and "Doesn't anybody else think that's kinda *weird?*"

After collaborating with Matt for a couple of years, we had not only cultivated a great professional relationship, we had become good friends. We'd get together from time to time and swap stories of our weird travels over pints of Guinness at pubs in Philly and NJ. Aside from being an intrepid researcher and evocative storyteller, it was obvious that Matt really relishes his weird work. With the Pennsylvania book completed, we could hardly bear the thought of ending our partnership with him. Then it occurred to us—from his home in southern PA, it was just a stone's throw to the border of Maryland! We knew from our research that the Free State was a hotbed of weirdness, and who better to explore it, we reasoned, than our man on the

Mason-Dixon line? So we gave Matt the assignment of spending the next year of his life tracking down all the strange legends, peculiar people, and oddball sites that the Old Line State had to offer. And, being a bit odd himself, Matt was more than happy to rise to the challenge.

Contained in these pages are a vast array of unique places, sites, and stories that make Maryland the fascinating and just downright weird place that it is. So come with us now and let Matt be your tour guide through one of the most intriguing and bewildering states of them all. It's a place we like to call *Weird Maryland.*

–Mark Moran and Mark Sceurman

Introduction

It was a dark and stormy night at the beginning of a particularly cold winter. The freezing northern wind whipped the ocean's surface into a froth as I parked the car near the boardwalk. If I hadn't taken this assignment, I would never have come out on this wretched night to this desolate place. But I had, and now I was here. I rechecked the card in my hand and took another look at my watch. Yes, this was the right place and the right time.

I pushed my way through the door, bellied up to the bar, and ordered my favorite cocktail, a virgin kamikaze. Out of the corner of my eye, I saw a heavily bandaged man with bloodstains on his shirt sitting on the seat next to me. He nudged me. It was only then that I recognized him.

"Mark? What happened to you?"

"Nothing. I'm in disguise."

"Where's the other Mark?"

"He's sitting right next to me."

I looked over to the next stool, but the only thing I could see next to Mark was a large book of matches. The other Mark is a master of disguise.

"Your next assignment is on the CD you're resting your drink on," said the Mark in bandages. "See you next year."

And with that, he disappeared into the crowd. I picked up the CD case and flipped it open. Neatly written on the top half of the CD was the word Background. Beneath it were two words that would send me on the road for twelve months, camera and notebook in hand. They were two words that would ultimately be responsible for the death by exhaustion of two computers, and several serious injuries to the transmission and fenders of my car. Seldom have two words been a portent of so much. Those two words were *Weird Maryland*.

I make no apologies for calling Maryland weird. If you take issue with the description, just grab a map and look at the outline of the state. It's geometrically perfect along two sides (courtesy of Mason and Dixon), and the rest of it consists of six thousand miles of squiggles (courtesy of Mother Nature's mountains and coastline). And there's a little square notch carved out of Maryland to accommodate the only chunk of the United States that isn't a state—the District of Columbia. I'd say that's weird enough for most people.

If you disagree, consider these little facts. Maryland is one of the few states

that adopted a state sport and a state beverage. There's nothing too strange about that until you consider what those official choices are. The drink is hardly a common bar order among Maryland's maritime tipplers: The official state beverage is milk. And its official sport is jousting.

It's small wonder that Maryland likes to think of itself as America in Miniature. It has everything a country could want, packed into a state you can drive across in less than a day. Thousands of miles of gorgeous coastline. A bay that's a mecca for sailors the world over. Rolling mountains, fertile farmland, vibrant cities, beautiful small towns—it's all part of the Maryland experience. And so, of course, is the strong vein of strangeness passing through it all. Because Maryland is one weird state.

They call this the Old Line State because of the disciplined militias that defended it against the Tories. They also call it the Free State, but not for the same reason. That nickname came about much later, in the early 1920s, when Maryland caught criticism for not issuing its own state law in support of Prohibition. When politicians from other states began denouncing Maryland for not taking a stand along with the rest of the states, newspaper editorials and people on the streets insisted they were free to make that decision for themselves—or in this case, not to. It doesn't make any difference whether Maryland took this stand because it's a state that likes its booze or because it doesn't like being bossed around. It's the fierce independence of the place that makes it such a haven of weird.

And lest we forget, let's be quite clear about one thing: There's nothing wrong with being weird. Weird is a good thing. It's the opposite of everything that's dull and ordinary and dominated by the uniform strip mall mentality. And thankfully, although nowhere in the twenty-first-century world can we completely sidestep the march of prefabricated blandness, Maryland has held on to more than its fair share of old weirdness and is doing a good job of manufacturing new examples.

I had only one reservation about writing a book called *Weird Maryland*. It wouldn't take long for the people I encountered along the way to realize that I wasn't a local. In fact, before I'd make my way three words into any sentence, they'd realize I was from a different country. And not just any country: The one that had tried to invade Baltimore's Fort McHenry the night before Francis Scott Key wrote the United States's national anthem. In short, they'd peg me for a Limey and associate me with the people who tried to break the lines of the Old Line State and take away the freedom of the Free State. That was my reservation, and it was a big one.

Fortunately, I could not have been more wrong. I discovered that the good people of Maryland (and they are many) are rightly proud of their state and are happy to share it with anyone who appreciates it as much as they do. And with all the good weird that permeates Maryland . . . what's not to appreciate about the place?

—*Matt Lake*

Local Legends

*Legend. n. Any story from the past,
but not verifiable by historical record.*

The word *"legend"* has been given a bad rap over the past few centuries. If you describe a story as a legend, you are dismissing the events in it as works of imagination, just too incredible to accept as truth. This isn't a bad thing when you're describing the plot line of a movie, but somehow people hold legends to a higher standard. The fact that legends are told as if they are accurate descriptions of real-life events means that they're often dismissed out of hand when a few of the details in them turn out to have never happened.

We at *Weird* never throw out a legend just because it contains a few facts we can't verify. Far from it. Legends aren't meant to be cross-checked with three independent sources before going to press. They are stories told for entertainment and perhaps a little edification, and they often contain truths that go beyond mere historical accuracy. Compared to glossy and synthetic forms of modern entertainment, tales of dark doings and long-dead characters have some substance. Even if it's a debased form of legend, like the urban tales of the hook-handed man who disturbs couples parked in cars, we contend that it's a far more important kind of entertainment than whatever's playing at the local Cineplex. That's how they got the name legend—at its root, the word means "something that must be read."

Local legends are even more significant than classic legends of King Arthur or the lost city of Atlantis. The legends of Maryland may not have the pedigree or symbolism of ancient tales, but you can get into your car and zoom off to visit the location where a local legend is supposed to have taken place. Whether you choose to go out to suburban Baltimore or DC or the swamps of Delmarva to track down the tales of local tradition, at least give them a try. Whether these stories are real history or not, there is something compelling about them.

Echoes of the Bunnyman

Unless you've seen the killer bunny scene in the movie *Monty Python and the Holy Grail,* it's hard to imagine getting worked up about the horrors of being attacked by a rabbit. Even if the rabbit in question is a full-grown man dressed up in a white, furry costume with floppy ears, it's hardly the stuff of nightmares. Yet for decades, the towns around Washington, DC, have buzzed with tales of a hatchet-wielding man in a furry costume. He kills. He hacks private property with his axe. He threatens small children in their schools. And he's universally known as the Bunnyman.

Though the Bunnyman is most closely associated with Fairfax County, Virginia, his stomping ground stretches across DC and reaches into at least a dozen Maryland towns. If, of course, he really does exist. Even the true believers and witnesses concede that it's likely that many sightings could be of copycats, scaremongers, or regular guys in Halloween costumes.

The only solid documentary evidence of the Bunnyman comes from two *Washington Post* articles that ran in late October 1970. They were based on a heavily edited police report. The opening paragraph of the first article in the *Post* set the tone for the investigation.

"Fairfax County police said yesterday they are looking for a man who likes to wear a 'white bunny rabbit costume' and throw hatchets through car windows. Honest." The article goes on to describe how an air force cadet in the area for the Air Force–Navy football game was parked in his car at the 5400 block of Guinea Road when a man "dressed in a white suit with long bunny ears" ran from the bushes and shouted, "You're on private property and I have your tag number." This strange creature then lobbed a hatchet at the couple through the open car window. The occupants of the car, Cadet Robert Bennett and his fiancée, were unharmed.

Later that month, in the Halloween issue of the *Washington Post,* the story continued with another tale of a hatchet-wielding bunny-costumed maniac, this time chopping away at the frame of a new house in Fairfax County. A security guard saw a man with a long-handled axe who appeared to be about five feet eight, one hundred and sixty pounds, and in his early twenties. When the guard approached, the Bunnyman complained about trespassers and threatened to knock him on the head, then beat a hasty retreat when the guard went for his weapon.

After five months, in March 1971, the local police department investigator in charge of the case, William L. Johnson, marked it as "inactive." The few leads that he had received were largely traced back to schoolyard gossip. The only promising lead came from a local landowner who had received a phone call from the "Axe Man," who

wanted to meet with him and air his grievances about alleged dumping. The police staked out the meeting, but the Axe Man didn't show.

That should have been the end of the story, except that the whispering chain of local legend made it grow to massive proportions. Over the next few years, a bunny-clad man was sighted and talked about in schools and youth groups in Washington, DC, and the Maryland towns of Greenbelt, Hyattsville, Landover, New Carrollton, Palmer Park, Seabrook, Silver Spring, and Upper Marlboro. True, it's entirely possible that many of these cases were a copycat or a hoax or a wild rumor, but the Bunnyman legend had taken hold and wasn't about to relax its grip.

In 1973, as part of a folklore project for her English class, a University of Maryland student named Patricia Johnson interviewed almost three dozen teenagers from Prince Georges County about their Bunnyman stories. Her paper eventually found its way into the Maryland Folklore Archive, where the *Weird* research team found it. It's easy to dismiss some of Johnson's interviews as schoolyard nonsense, but others make compelling reading. Johnson herself was clearly not won over as a true believer, and many of her sources were also skeptical.

The following text is the words of some of Johnson's more convinced sources, along with some letters sent to the *Weird* headquarters. But when you deal with folklore, what's important is not whether you believe it's documentary truth or not. It's whether you want to hear about it. And really, who wouldn't want to hear tales of an axe-wielding man in a rabbit costume?

The Bunny Hits Below the Greenbelt

Back in the Seventies, the sign in front of the Community Church in Greenbelt was smashed up, and everyone said that this weird old man had done it. He was supposed to hang out in the woods there, and he once dashed past and threw a hatchet at the sign. They say he had a white beard and wore women's hose all over his face. He didn't talk, but would make yelling and screaming noises.—*Anonymous*

Banging on the Door

In 1971, a friend of mine lived in Hyattsville on Edmonston Road. What happened was he said about 11 o'clock at night a knock came at the door. It kept getting louder and louder. So he went to the door and he opened it. There was a strange looking white character sitting outside. So he slammed the door and was yelling for his father. All of a sudden, there was the door, being hacked down with a hatchet. He could see it coming through the door itself. So his father got up . . . then called the police. They had two pillars in front of their house coming up to the door and the Bunnyman chopped them down, chopped the door down, and ran off. The neighbors say they saw him.

About seven blocks away he struck again at someone else's house. It was really freaky what happened. He was at another person's house and he must have made some noise. When the guy opened the door, he said he saw a six-foot tall creature completely dressed in white. He didn't know if it was a Bunnyman or someone in a white jacket, but he had a hatchet in his hand.—*Ralph Spaulding*

The Bunny Hops to Riverdale

I first heard about the Bunnyman, who's also called the Goatman, when I was in tenth grade at Parkdale High School in Prince Georges County. There was a cut-through road between George Palmer Highway and Landover Road. They said that the Bunnyman would be up there. Some boys went by and he had an ax or something and chased them away. I also heard that he didn't look like a bunny but he looked like a goat. Everybody said he was up there almost every night. You could hear him running through the woods and see him running past sometimes.—*Name withheld*

The Legend of Black Aggie

Imagine a chart of the biggest hits in the wonderful world of scary supernatural phenomena. In some seasons, ghosts would top the chart. In others, it would be invisible demons or flying points of light in the night sky. But over the years, you will find one enduring presence: The statue that comes to life.

Whether it's the man-shaped, man-made clay monster called the Golem or the massive bronze statue of the Talos from Greek legend (and Ray Harryhausen's *Jason and the Argonauts*), there's something about inanimate objects coming to life to attack people that taps a nerve in the human psyche. And it's just this fear that forms the focal point of Maryland's most popular legend: Black Aggie.

Black Aggie is a cemetery sculpture that is dark in both color and mood. It is a seated woman draped in a shroud. Her head is bowed, perhaps from the burden of tales of abuse, merciless killing, and revenge from beyond the grave. Like all good folk stories, that of Black Aggie is actually many tales, often contradictory ones. As in all word-of-mouth stories, details vary wildly until someone tries to write them down into a coherent narrative, and even then, the tales become embellished and different themes emerge in the retelling.

Some say that Black Aggie was a grotesquely creepy statue erected as a cruel joke by a husband who had killed his wife or who had treated her so contemptuously that she lost the will to live. Others say that the statue was typical Victorian cemetery art and dedicated to a well-loved wife, but that the grave site was haunted because disrespectful visitors had disturbed the spirit of the woman. Still others said that the statue was erected to commemorate a black woman murdered by white men.

But no matter who the woman was in life or how she died, the tales say she would punish anyone who disrespected her. Legend has it that if you sat in her lap at

night, she would wrap her arms around you and crush you to death, or stab you. If you stared in her face, her eyes would glow menacingly and strike you blind. Pregnant women would miscarry. Unmarried women would become pregnant. People's hearts would stop at the very sight of her by moonlight. It's hardly surprising that fraternities would routinely haze their pledges with a nocturnal visit to Black Aggie. Even the name of the burial ground, Druid Ridge Cemetery, was enough to conjure images of dark and mysterious rituals.

The actual history of the dark statue is in many ways just as interesting as the legends that surround it. After the Civil War, a rising star of the Union army, General Felix Agnus, married Annie Fulton, the nurse who had tended his wounds during the war. The couple settled in her hometown of Baltimore. His distinguished military record won him a successful government career, from which he eventually retired to take over as publisher of his father-in-law's newspaper, the *Baltimore American.*

In 1905, at the age of sixty-five, Agnus purchased a bronze statue called *Grief* from a local artist named Eduard Pausch and installed it at the family plot he had just bought at Druid Ridge Cemetery, a few miles outside Pikesville. The first person to be buried in the shadow of this dark statue of a grieving angel was his mother.

Then, a year later, the widow of the famous sculptor Augustus St. Gaudens accused Agnus of being a "barbarian" for so poorly copying her husband's work. Agnus was indignant at the accusation, but he soon discovered that the woman was right: His statue was an unauthorized casting of a famous statue by Augustus St. Gaudens, which stood in Washington, DC's Rock Creek Cemetery. This statue had been commissioned twenty years earlier by Henry Adams, the grandson of John Quincy Adams, to commemorate his wife Marian Adams, who had poisoned herself during a bout of depression. It

stood near Marian's plot, but it was unmarked, and Henry Adams never spoke about it or his beloved wife.

Agnus sued the sculptor Pausch, who had advertised the statue as an original work. Although Agnus won his suit, he chose to keep the statue where it was.

Within twenty years, Felix and Annie Agnus were buried in the shadow of the statue. Some time later the legends began. For years, a visit to the grieving angel meant all but taking your life in your hands—just ask the thousands of thrill seekers who went to check Aggie out. Then, in 1967, after countless cases of vandalism and disturbances, she was removed from the cemetery and eventually donated to the Smithsonian Institution. She went missing for decades but has surfaced again. She is now in the courtyard of the Dolley Madison House in the Federal Courts complex, at the corner of Madison and H streets, near the White House.

All that remains at the Agnus family plot is the granite platform she once sat on, with scars where the workmen chipped her off her mounting. But visitors still keep coming to the spot where she once sat. Some legends, it seems, don't even need the physical feature that spawned them.

Another Aggie?

Not all the Black Aggie legends seem to point to the Agnus statue: The details just don't fit its features. Some tales mention Aggie's victims being enveloped by her open arms or stabbed by her shears. One celebrated story from 1962 tells how one of the statue's arms had been cut off and discovered in the trunk of a sheet metal worker's car. He told the judge at his trial that Aggie had cut off her own arm in a fit of grief and given it to him, though others say that he witnessed Aggie killing another victim and cut the arm off himself.

But this doesn't sound like the Agnus memorial. These details fit a statue one block over from where Aggie used to be in Druid Ridge Cemetery. While this statue is also dark (both were made out of the same menacing bronze), this one is measuring out a garland of flowers and cutting them with a large pair of scissors—a classic Victorian symbol for youth cut down in its prime. The garland has been broken near the statue's left arm, which has a discolored line on its bicep that could be where a repair took place. Perhaps the Aggie of legend hasn't altogether abandoned Druid Ridge after all. Maybe she's just at a different address.

Red-eyed Aggie

She has eyes made of rubies, so at night it looks as if her eyes are bleeding. The husband killed her and erected this statue as a joke. They never caught him for it, though, and they only found out about it after he died. She will kill any couple that goes out there, in payback for what her husband did. She's sitting on a rock and has a pair of scissors in her hand. If you sit on her lap, she will kill you with the scissors. They found one girl stabbed to death one morning in her lap.—*BH*

Green-eyed Aggie

She used to have marbles in her eyes that light up green, but they were stolen. If you sit in her lap at night, her arms will come around and squeeze you to death. It happened to a boy named Steve Bledsoe during Fraternity Hell Night. Before it happened, he cried out "It's moving, it's moving."—*Taylor*

The Ducks Should Duck

You're okay if you go alone, or just with friends of the same sex. But if a boy goes there with a girl, Black Aggie will kill you. That's because of a couple who went out there one night and did something they shouldn't have, right on her lap. Oh, and at midnight she sometimes gets up and wanders around the cemetery. There's a lake around there and she strangles all the white ducks that live in it.—*Stewart*

Her Deadly Gaze

No plant life will grow anywhere around her. At midnight when there is a full moon, she will roll her eyes and raise her hands in anger. People who have returned the gaze of Black Aggie's red eyes have been struck blind instantly. If you are pregnant, do not go out and see her at night or your child will be stillborn.—*Barb Z.*

Give Her a Hand

Back in the 1960s, a man cut her hand off because of a girl they found stabbed through her heart. People say that the man saw Black Aggie murder the girl, and he wanted to make sure that she never killed again. When her hand was off, Aggie was harmless. But when the judge ordered them to put it back, Aggie got some of her evil power back again.—*Anonymous*

Black Aggie Hazing

They say that if you sit in her lap at midnight, you can hear her heart beating and see her move. For a fraternity hazing ritual, they made a pledge sit on her lap, but then they snuck around behind the statue and dropped a piece of raw liver down the kid's back. He died of fright. —*Anonymous*

Perry Hall

Perry Hall is a small community just outside Baltimore that contained only a few dozen houses until the Second World War suburban housing boom expanded the area. Nestled away in the woods are the remains of the original Perry Hall Mansion, a colonial plantation house built in the 1770s by a wealthy Baltimore businessman; it now lies empty and surrounded by fences, and perhaps more thickly by rumor and legend.

The prevailing story is that the owners of the mansion died there on Halloween night back in the eighteenth century. Many members of the household, more than fifty by some accounts, subsequently died there under mysterious circumstances. They say that people visiting the house see lights go on even though there is no electricity hooked up. If you try to video the mansion, you will not see anything on the tape, but you will hear a soundtrack. And most people who feel sensitive to paranormal activity get a vibe about the place that they just don't feel comfortable with.

There's not much in the actual history of the place to support these legends, though. The house was already built on a thousand-acre estate when one of the wealthiest Baltimore businessmen of the 1770s, Harry Dorsey Gough, bought it and renamed it Perry Hall after his family's estate in Staffordshire, England. Gough was a bit of a rogue, prone to drinking and gambling on horse races, but through a religious friend he saw the light and converted to Methodism. As the most influential man in the area, he became a mover and shaker in the Methodist movement. His beliefs led him to some political strife later on, as Methodists were pacifists who opposed the

Revolutionary War. (He didn't toe the party line on slavery, however, and throughout his life maintained a household of more than fifty slaves.) But after the Revolution, he supported the Federalist movement and various philanthropic ventures, and eventually served in the Maryland House of Delegates. He died in the Perry Hall Mansion in 1808 at the age of sixty-three, and his wife survived him by fourteen years. The place remained in the family for decades, gradually declining through neglect. In 1875, two Philadelphia businessmen, William M. Meredith and Eli Slifer, bought the estate, subdivided its land into small farming plots, and sold them to German and Irish immigrant families. The mansion fell into further neglect, and except for occasional structural work to keep it from collapse, it has stood empty for many years.

Clearly, there was nothing outwardly eerie about the lives or deaths of the Methodist family that took care of Perry Hall Mansion in its heyday. But who knows what may have gone on in their household among the dozens of slaves the family owned? Perhaps the degradation bound up in the institution of slavery, or some abuses we don't know about, could be at the root of the legends surrounding this once stately home. But whatever the cause, the abandoned hulk of a building certainly has a creepy air to it. Look at it sometime through the chain-link fence and see if you agree.

Don't Get Fenced In

Ever since I moved to Perry Hall in Baltimore County, I have heard stories of the Perry Hall Mansion. Supposedly, the house was built on an old slave plantation, and more than fifty residents died of supernatural causes. The house was shut down, and its windows and doors are all boarded up. I heard they put up a fence because teenagers who went up to the house died or went missing soon after. Outside of the fenced-in area, there is a well in the back, and legend has it that there is also a shed that contains tools that a ghost will use to kill you. Teenagers usually go there at night, trying to see a ghost. I am a huge believer of the supernatural, so of course I went with a group of friends. I felt like someone was watching us the entire time. If you are ever in the Perry Hall area, come and see it for yourself! If you travel on Belair Road, near the Gunpowder River area, it's off of Perry Hall Road. You will pass a barn that looks like the one from the movie *Children of the Corn*; it's on the left, a few blocks up. *–Abbey*

The Ghost of Big Liz

Marshes provide some of the most fertile land imaginable for growing legends. Something about misty, flat, sparsely populated land that's perilous to walk through at night spawns the creepiest legends. And that's exactly what happened in Dorchester County with the legend of Big Liz. She's sometimes called Bigg Lizz, as if six letters are simply not enough to describe this big-boned woman from the Delmarva Peninsula.

Liz was a large and muscular slave who came to an unfortunate end at the hands of her master. Some versions of the story are set during the Revolutionary War, while others say it happened during the Civil War. There's no definitive version of the tale, and although the events in most of the stories are the same, the significance of the story is quite different depending on how it is told. Whichever account you prefer, there's no solid historical evidence to back it up. This is one tale that's told just for the fun of it. We'll stick to the Civil War version of the story here, and follow it up with another example set in the Revolutionary War.

A certain plantation owner was a member of the army of the Confederate States of America, and President Jefferson Davis made him responsible for a substantial war chest. Around that time, he discovered that one of his slaves was acting as a spy for the Union. He well knew the punishment for treason and dreaded what might happen if his household would be found responsible for it. So he determined to put a permanent stop to the security risk, which meant putting a permanent stop to the life of the slave in question. She was much too big for him to handle by himself, so he had her drag the war chest out into the swamp and dig a hole for it. She worked for hours at the task, until she was too exhausted to defend herself. At that point, her master drew a sword and beheaded her. Her body fell on top of the chest in the hole, and he covered it up with the freshly dug swamp dirt.

Only when he was finished did he realize that he had buried only her body. Her head had rolled off and was lost. He assumed that wild animals would deal with it, and that as a traitor, she deserved no better.

The following day his body was discovered lying on the ground beneath his bedroom window with a look of horror on his face. Some believed that the ghost of the woman he had killed rose from the grave, found her head, and came after the man responsible. Now, they say, she still roams around the area by night, making sure that nobody touches the gold in the chest. She paid with her own life for the right to keep it, and nobody's going to take it away from her in death.

The Big Liz Revolution

Just outside of Cambridge lies the Greenbriar Swamp. Around the start of the Revolutionary War, the Bucktown Plantation lay on the outskirts of the swamp, owned by a greedy slave driver whose name is lost to history. He was afraid that his money would be stolen by British soldiers, so he hatched a plan to keep the bulk of it safe. He put gold in a chest and took it into the swampland with one of his strongest slaves, a huge woman named Big Liz. He commanded her to dig the hole, and watched her do it as he sat back and ate his lunch. When she was done, he commanded her to put the chest in the hole. While she was distracted at this task, he took a yard-long tobacco knife and swung it towards Big Liz, slicing her head clean off.

He buried her body on top of the chest, at one stroke ensuring that the secret location of the chest was safe, and turning the place into a grave to deter anyone who might be digging in the area anyway. But his plan backfired. He served in the army during the war, and boasted about his plan to his fellow soldiers. And after he died in battle, some tried to look for the chest. But everyone who did try backed off when they visited the Greenbriar Swamp. By night, they could hear howling from the undergrowth. Some people say they could see a large headless figure wandering around with something tucked under her arm, something that turned out to be her head.
—*Brendan*

Summoning Big Liz

There's a local legend you hear at scout camp and other places that you can call up the spirit of Big Liz. You drive up to the cemetery and flash your lights three times over the graves, honk your horn three times, and shout out her name three times. You reverse out and drive to the bridge. With your front tires on the bridge, you do the same thing: Flash, honk, and call out three times. Then you roll down the windows, cut the engine, and wait.

If it works, they say the wind will pick up and you'll hear a gate open. You may see a light coming towards you across the marsh. The light will take the shape of a large headless woman. At this point, you'd better hope you don't look like Big Liz's master, because she's had hundreds of years to get even and she may try to turn your car over and kill you.

This has never worked for me, but it may be because I picked the wrong cemetery. There are three of them around Cambridge, all of them old, so it's not clear which is the right one.—*Shelley*

College Tales

Institutions of higher learning are all too often also institutions of higher storytelling. Anywhere you find masses of young adults in a new neighborhood, relishing their newfound liberation from high school, you'll find folklore on a whole new level. Traditions and lore are passed down on an accelerated schedule, handed down from sophomore to freshman instead of generation to generation.

UMD's Point of Failure

Since it was established in 1896 as an agricultural college, the University of Maryland has undergone many changes, not the least of which was a fire that destroyed most of the original main buildings in 1912. The sixteen-year-old college caught fire on the night before Thanksgiving, and by the time it was over, twelve buildings were either destroyed outright or damaged beyond repair. The student records and other college paperwork had gone up in smoke, and so had the dormitories. There's a map of the original buildings in the quadrangle called the Acropolis, showing the only building that survived intact: Morrill Hall. The fact that this hall housed the cadavers used by its medical students added a mysterious quality to its survival. It's a favorite story to say it's haunted, but that's not the legend we're focusing on here.

The most abiding legend is a superstition about the map of the old buildings in the Acropolis—specifically about the Point of Failure—with lines from the destroyed buildings converging to a single focal point. Those lines also appear on the quadrangle's floor, scored into the pavement where they meet in a single point in what was then the middle of the square. They call this the Point of Failure and say that the curse of the fire is concentrated into this point. Any student who steps on the Point of Failure will not graduate. Prospective students who step on it scotch their chances of getting admitted. And more horrifically, parents who step on it will not win financial aid.

Fortunately, all is not lost if you do tread on the Point of Failure. You can always rub the nose of the university's mascot, Testudo the terrapin, whose 1933 bronze statue stands in front of the McKeldin Library. Testudo seems to carry all the luck needed to defuse the curse. Even when he was kidnapped by rival students from Johns Hopkins in 1947, the UMD students who managed to retrieve him and then have a party were able to avoid capture by two hundred Baltimore police officers who were called in to break up the riot. Now that's a curse antidote of legendary proportions.

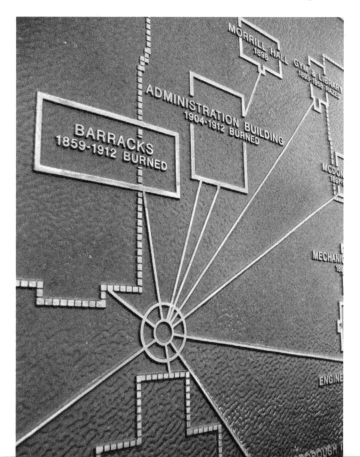

Curse You!

During the Colonial days in the late 1600s, witches and their curses were a fact of life in most of the Western world. Whether you believe in witchcraft or not, at the time, strict laws called for the execution of anyone suspected of atheism or witchcraft. This was bad news for any hermits or herbalists. During any time of tribulation, it's human nature to look for someone to blame. So in those days, whenever crops failed, people fell ill, or any other misfortunes struck, a witch trial was sure to follow. You need only look a few hundred miles north to Salem, Massachusetts, to see how hairy things could get.

According to historians working in the 1930s for the WPA Writers Project, only five people in Maryland were ever accused of witchcraft in a court of law. Some authorities put the number at twelve, but account for the discrepancy because seven were tried and punished on board ship en route to the colony. Of the five who were formally accused, only two were found guilty and only one, Rebecca Fowler, was executed for the crime. But that doesn't mean that other witches weren't placing curses or being subjected to frontier justice elsewhere in Maryland. We know of several high-profile stories, some of which may actually have some truth to them.

Legend of Moll Dyer

In the late 1600s and early 1700s, the area around Leonardtown in Saint Marys County was a terrible place to live. At least, it was if your name happened to be Moll Dyer. She couldn't go out picking herbs for remedies or cooking without someone staring and mouthing the word "witch." Anytime someone's cow went dry or crops withered or a person woke up with a hangover, they'd mumble that the witch was placing another curse on them. Yep, Leonardtown was definitely not the most hospitable place for Moll, but getting the cold shoulder from her neighbors was nothing compared to what was in store for her when the epidemic hit town.

The illness that swept through Leonardtown struck young and old alike, but the youngsters fell particularly hard, and that was the final straw for the townsfolk. It was then that the mob got up in arms and went into the woods to dispose of the witch once and for all. It has to be said that their attempt, though it ended in the death of Mistress Dyer, could hardly have failed more spectacularly. The day she was put to death by the mob was the day that put her name in the history of

Maryland, carved as it were into stone.
Because, according to the legend, the mob
chased Moll Dyer through the woods until she came to a
large rock. Holding on to the rock with one hand, she
raised her other hand to the skies and prayed for
deliverance or mercy or at very least a fair trial. None of
her prayers were answered. After the mob killed her,
though, they noticed something strange and disturbing
about that rock. It bore a handprint right where Moll
Dyer had touched it.

This rock does indeed bear a hand-shaped
indentation that fits a woman's hand. And there are
other indentations—two that could fit a pair of knees.
It's easy to check it out, because over the centuries it
became so celebrated that in 1975 a large section of the
rock containing the prints was moved from the woods
into town. It now stands near the courthouse, outside the
St. Mary's Historical Society in Leonardtown.

There are a few variants of the Moll Dyer story,
including one in which she was driven out into the cold
winter's night when the mob torched her house and was
found frozen to the stone some days later. Some
say that she cursed the spot where she was killed
and the people who killed her. They also say that
the people who hunted her down all met their
ends in gruesome ways.

In fact, this legend proved particularly thorny
to research. Nobody seems to know who Moll
Dyer was. Nor does anyone know where she
came from, though she is widely acknowledged to
have emigrated from Ireland, where she was well-
to-do; she left her home country for mysterious
reasons. There's a large folder of information on
the rock at the historical society, but the audit trail
of official genealogical records is not there. You
won't find any real estate transactions, birth,
baptismal, or burial records mentioning her name.

However, this doesn't necessarily prove that she
never lived or died here. The circumstances of her death
would probably preclude her being buried in a parish
churchyard, and the details of the story do fit the history
of the area. The witchcraft hysteria of the time makes this
tale plausible (at least, right up to the bit about the
handprint in the rock). There was indeed an outbreak of
"pestilence" in the area in the winter of 1697, probably a
nasty strain of influenza, that killed many people. It was
so severe that when it abated by the middle of 1698, the
governor of the colony declared a day of thanksgiving and
ordered that a hospital be built at Coole Springs, some
fifteen miles from Leonardtown.

None of this, however, accounts for the symptoms
people feel when they approach or touch the rock itself.
Waves of nausea are common among the more sensitive
folk who get near it. And out in the woods where she used
to live, an area called Moll Dyer's Run with a Moll Dyer
Road in it, they say her ghost still walks . . . or actually
runs, as if being chased.

Ancient and Unsolved Mysteries

Of all the strange tales that we hear and read, the ones that appeal to us most are those we just can't explain. Whether it's some strange geographic feature whose origins are shrouded in obscurity or a modern day marvel, there's nothing we love more than a mystery.

Maryland is full of mysteries. For a state that has so many universities and scientific research facilities, it's rather encouraging to know that there are still hundreds of things here that remain unexplained. In a world that's all too often simplified to the point of sound bites, something that makes you pause and think is a rare thing indeed. And if you end up throwing up your hands in frustration and saying, "I don't know what to think!" then you can join the rest of us. Because in cases like these, there are no easy explanations.

Written in Stone

Ancient civilizations carved messages in stone. The trouble for us is that we don't know what their messages mean. Somewhere between five hundred and one thousand years ago, the tribes that lived in Maryland sent their messages down the ages to us. Now we can only scratch our heads and wonder. Assuming, that is, that we can find those messages. While rock carvings usually can withstand centuries of weathering, in the past one hundred years many have been eradicated, thanks to vandalism, land development, and other hallmarks of the progress of civilization. But some stone carvings do remain. . . .

The Bald Friar Petroglyphs

The massive hydroelectric project that gave us the Conowingo Dam on the Susquehanna River also took something away. Before the dam was built, alongside the river there was a massive rock called Bald Friar that was covered with native rock carvings. Like many messages carved in stone by different cultures, the meaning of these carvings was obscure. They had been observed for centuries (one story told of William Penn asking a native about them and being told the carvings had been there since before their grandfathers were born). Sadly, they had been wrecked by settlers chipping away at the big rock for raw materials. The rockface was smashed still further to make a straight ferry path. And finally, when the dam came, it was dynamited and what was left was buried under the dam water.

Fortunately, before the flooding began, members of the Academy of Natural Sciences photographed and drew images for future study. Then they did what few archaeologists do to preserve the historic record: They used dynamite to blow the rock into sizable chunks they could haul out. Bits of those carved rocks found their way to museums and historical sites all across Maryland. It's possible to hunt them down now, but only if you know where to look.

The historical societies of Cecil and Harford counties have some. Harford County's are in the foyer of its historical society building in Bel Air; Cecil's are in the garden of its historical society in Elkton. Thirteen stones were donated by a private collector to the Jefferson Patterson Park and Museum in Calvert County. And there's a group of stones in Druid Hill Park.

The carvings on these stones are remarkable and mysterious. Deep grooves display striking images of . . . who knows what? One common symbol that the rocks share is a carved concentric circle, a prehistoric sign that may represent the world or the cycles of life through birth, death, and reproduction. There are also diamond shapes with little arrows at one apex that some people believe are fish, perhaps indicating good fishing spots in the river or alluding to some legend we don't know. And then there's the bizarre stylized face image that various scholars have called the head of a serpent, a fish, or a human: three different images and no solid facts.

Our favorite interpretation, though, involves the human head, which could very well be False Face, a character in an Iroquois legend in which a stranger confronts the Spirit Medicine Man in a valley and challenges him to a contest of power. The origins of the

stranger's power are unknown, but he tried to use it to move the mountain. He succeeded only in making it tremble in an earthquake. The Spirit Medicine Man acknowledged that the stranger's power was strong, but he lacked faith. Spirit Man moved the mountain behind the stranger's back, and when the stranger wheeled around to look at it, he smashed his face against the rock. To make amends for his injury, the Spirit Medicine Man taught the stranger (henceforth called Old Broken Nose or Crooked Face) the powers of healing.

The Iroquois celebrate the legend to this day with crooked-nosed masks. If the odd face shapes in the Bald Friar petroglyphs also represent the story, then perhaps these rock carvings were, as some experts believe, used in myth telling and shamanism.

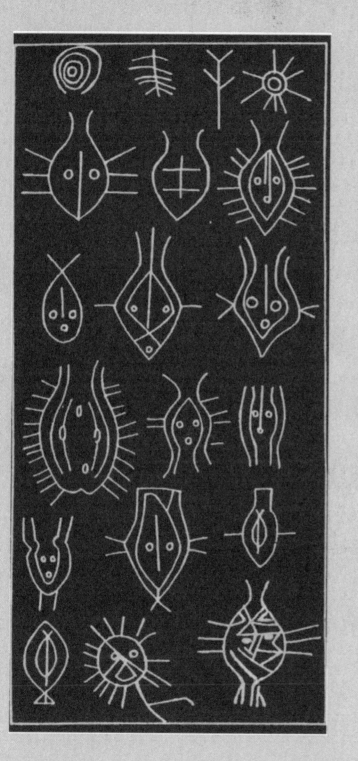

A Volcano in Our Midst

Garrett Island is pretty well known to bass fishermen and environmentalists, but to most of us, it's little more than a bridge support for traffic crossing the river between Perryville and Havre de Grace. It's not always been that way; four hundred years ago, John Smith of Pocahontas fame sailed there, and found a thriving meeting place for local tribes. The mile-long forested island is now a wilderness. It almost became a luxury development in the 1990s, but it's now part of the Blackwater National Wildlife Refuge. It's also an ancient volcano.

A buddy of mine took a canoe trip there with the Lower Susquehanna Heritage Greenway and learned that this chunk of granite at the mouth of the Susquehanna River was thrown up by volcanic activity. A geologist on the trip pointed out a huge black basalt rock which marks where one of the lava vents used to be. Now every time I drive along Route 40 across the river towards Havre de Grace, I take a quick look at the island and imagine it spewing lava millions of years ago. It's completely dormant, of course, probably completely dead as far as volcanic activity goes, but anyway, it's a neat piece of geological history.–*The Green Man*

Glyph on Garrett Island

There's a strange carving in the rock at Garrett Island—a deep hole about wide enough to stick your finger in, surrounded by a square. Is it a symbol of some kind? A place to mount a staff or pole? Nobody's sure, and very few people have seen it. If you have any ideas or evidence, pass them on. This is something we want to know more about.

King and Queen Seats

The White Trail through the woods of Rocks State Park in northern Harford County climbs steeply, too steeply for the *Weird* research team to handle on a steamy Sunday morning in July. Taking advantage of the cool rocks that litter the trail, we took several sit-down breaks for water and trail mix. But our seats were not the reason this park got its name. That honor goes to the enormous rocks of gray grit stone at the summit that are thronelike recesses. For centuries, these piles of huge flattened boulders have been called the King and Queen Seats.

Even though it overlooks a daunting 190-foot drop to Deer Creek, this stunning weathered outcropping at the top

of the white trail is a favorite hiking destination of guitar-playing young adults, families, and pagans. And some trekkers like to clamber to the top and sit in one of the twin recesses carved into the topmost rock.

Except for one iffy legend, nobody really knows how the rocks came to be called the King and Queen Seats. The earliest written record about them is from Thomas T. Wysong, in his 1879 book *The Rocks of Deer Creek*. Wysong repeats a three-hundred-year-old legend that touches on the rock thrones. Before European settlers appeared there, the Deer Creek area was inhabited by three separate tribes of Susquehannock Indians, who lived less than five miles apart from each other, and who operated a kind of confederacy to protect the valley from any possible aggressors. While the tribes were autonomous, there was a supreme leader who oversaw their alliance.

Onto this background, Wysong repeated a legend of love and rivalry, featuring two heads of the three tribes, especially Lone Wolf of the lower village. While traveling, Lone Wolf visited a New York Iroquois tribe and there met a girl named Fern-Shaken-by-the-Wind. He tried to court her in an elaborate ritual that involved bringing her back to the valley with her brother as chaperone and lavishing her with gifts. Unfortunately, during tribal councils held at the rocks, Wolf discovered there was a rival for Fern's affections: Bird-that-Flies-High, the son of the alliance's supreme leader, had already given the girl his own gifts. Trouble soon began. After slights and insults between the two rivals, they held an archery contest to be judged by Fern. When Lone Wolf won, Bird was infuriated. The two warriors got into a fistfight, and Lone Wolf ended up falling off the cliff.

This act would have automatically consigned Bird to a death sentence, but Fern gave two jewels to Lone Wolf's family as a blood offering, and Bird's life was spared. In the end, the two married and sat as joint rulers on the King and Queen Seats. They were the last members of the tribes to do so, since shortly afterward, European settlers drove the Susquehannocks out of the valley.

This is a pretty enough tale, but it's hard to tell how much of it is true. In his book's preface, Wysong admitted that the stories in his book are "the interweaving of fact and fancy."

Certainly, some of the ideas he writes about do have a ring of truth. The idea of an alliance between neighboring villages makes sense, especially among the aggressive Susquehannocks, who were often at war and would relish the opportunity of some peace in the neighborhood, especially if it meant they could rely on their neighbors as reinforcements.

But the notion of appointing a king and queen of the alliance remains a sticking point. The idea of twin thrones for a royal couple seems so European that it may be one of the fancies that Wysong warned about in his book's preface. Then again some historians believe the Susquehannocks were a matriarchal society, so having a throne of power may be a possibility. But all too often the term *matriarchy* means only that the tribe traced their ancestry through the mother's line, not that the women held significant political power.

Whatever the actual significance of the seats may be, the place remains exciting and awe-inspiring—and not just because of the spectacular view and the danger of falling nearly two hundred feet off the precipice to the river below. Some people insist that there's more to the place. They say that either Bird or Wolf, possibly both, still haunt the area around the rocks. Others say that the place was chosen for tribal councils because it was a sacred place and that it remains sacred to this day. Still others wonder at the way the rocks look—deeply grooved and apparently stacked in piles of flattish boulders—but that's no mystery. It's an erosion pattern that's common with this kind of rock. Whatever the reason, the seats still offer a glorious view across the valley to another wooded slope topped with gray rocks. Who knows what those rocks mean?

Watch the Skies! Keep Watching!

Strange objects in the sky have been the stuff of Maryland legend since well before *The Day the Earth Stood Still* (a movie that coincidentally took place in a little town to the south surrounded on three sides by Maryland). Talk to anybody who believes in UFOs (and trust us, we have), and you'll find that Maryland is a hotbed of UFO sightings, especially in the area around Washington, DC.

There were so many sightings that the air force got involved and tracked and investigated UFO sightings between 1948 and 1969 in an exercise called Project Blue Book. And they were aided by the Ground Observer Corps (GOC), a volunteer civil defense league that watched the skies for enemy attack and reported their sightings. A great many of those were filed away as weather balloons, recognizable aircraft, astronomical, or hoaxes, but just over seven hundred were classified as Unknown. Here are the top thirteen cases in the Maryland region in date order, followed by some stories from the files of Project Blue Book.

Case 1011, November 18, 1951	Andrews AFB, Washington, DC
Case 1074, March 20, 1952	Queen Anne's County, Maryland
Case 1431, July 12, 1952	Annapolis, Maryland
Case 1661, July 26, 1952	Andrews AFB, Washington, DC
Case 2077, September 12, 1952	Allen, Maryland
Case 2253, November 30, 1952	Washington, DC
Case 2997, May 11, 1954	Washington, DC
Case 3427, February 10, 1955	Bethesda, Maryland
Case 3750, September 7, 1955	Washington, DC
Case 3810, October 11, 1955	Point Lookout, Maryland
Case 6148, October 27, 1958	Loch Raven Dam, Maryland
Case 7754, December 13, 1961	Washington, DC
Case 9305, March 8, 1965	Mount Airy, Maryland

UFOlogy's Big Year

Nineteen fifty-two was a banner year for UFO sightings in the United States as a whole, as well as in Maryland and DC, when there were five investigated sightings. During the hot July of 1952, UFOs buzzed the nation's capital in one of the most widely witnessed and reported cases on record. On four separate occasions, flying disks were seen zooming over the White House, the Capitol building, and the Pentagon. A little before midnight on July 19, radar from Andrews Air Force Base in Prince Georges County and Washington National Airport picked up objects that had suddenly appeared in restricted airspace. Andrews dispatched jet fighters to take care of what appeared to be a hostile act on the seat of government, but the saucers evaded them. In fact, they outran them, changed direction more quickly than the military could, and generally put them to shame. Then they vanished. And a week later, it happened again.

These 1952 sightings came only a year after a giant robot had walked out of an alien spacecraft in Washington, DC, and greeted the world with the words "Klaatu barata nikto." And although *The Day the Earth Stood Still* was only a movie, it tapped deep into the paranoia that permeated the cold

war. Newspaper reports of the lights, radar blips, and interceptor jets over Washington stoked those fears some more. The air force issued its statement through Major General John Samford and blamed it on weird weather. However, many people didn't buy it. They couldn't understand how temperature inversions might cause bright orange lights in the air and fast-moving blips on radar screens. But they could certainly wrap their imaginations around an alien invasion force, especially since a few months later the crew of Capital Airlines flight 610 flying out of DC on November 30, 1952, at three twenty in the morning observed an object with several lights following the DC-4 airplane for twenty minutes before turning away. Tom Selby, a senior air traffic controller at Andrews Air Force Base, also observed the mystery aircraft.

In the years that followed, flying saucer paranoia took hold. It was partly fueled by science fiction: *It Came From Outer Space* and *War of the Worlds* hit the silver screen in 1953. But unsatisfied curiosity also played its part. People heard that the pilots and air traffic controllers who tracked the objects were told to forget the whole thing and not talk about it to anybody. People naturally suspected a cover-up.

What actually caused the events that July is still a mystery, but more details have come to light as information became declassified. In 1977, a special study group within the air force, the Office of Scientific Intelligence, investigated the reports of those air traffic controllers who had years of experience and had logged several hours of bizarre readings in July 1952. The controllers were utterly convinced that they had had a "very good target" in their scopes. After all, the sightings came from radarscopes at Washington National Airport and Andrews Air Force Base, which had twenty-four-inch radarscopes with a hundred-mile range.

According to the observations of the night shift controllers, there were seven sharp blips that suddenly appeared on the Andrews scope. The arm of the scope swept a circuit once every ten seconds. The blips had not been there on the last rotation; they blipped into sight at eleven forty p.m. sharp. Their location was just southeast of Andrews AFB. Senior Controller Harry G. Barnes at National buzzed the tower, where Howard Cocklin confirmed their scope had the same targets and said that he could actually see one of them from the window, glowing bright orange. It got worse: As the radar swept around, the cluster of targets stopped and fanned out, flying into restricted airspace. When two flew over the White House and another approached the Capitol, Barnes contacted Andrews Air Force Base and interception jets were ordered up. Unfortunately, the jets were coming from Newcastle, Delaware, because the runway at Andrews was being repaired.

Meanwhile, an airplane was approaching one of the objects. Its pilot, Captain Casey Pierman, saw something suddenly pick up speed from a leisurely 130 mph and streak out of sight in a few seconds. Back at the control tower, the radar blip track showed another object suddenly stop on a dime and veer off at right angles to its original path. A special ASR (Airport Surveillance Radar) designed to track fast objects saw another weird bogey traveling at about two miles a second zipping past Andrews AFB toward Riverdale.

The air force jets finally arrived around two a.m., by which time the UFOs had vanished. The jets left, and five minutes later the UFOs were back. The operators at Andrews' radio range station saw a "huge fiery-orange sphere" directly over their station, and a radio engineer at the Washington Radio Control transmitter station saw five disks in a loose formation

long enough that two F-94s were dispatched from Newcastle County AFB in Delaware. One of the mystery objects was still visible when they arrived, but when the F-94 gave chase at 600 mph, the UFO left it in the dust. With no targets left, the F-94s returned to base, and a few minutes later the UFOs reappeared. They were tracked by Washington, Andrews, and even Langley AFB in Virginia. When the UFOs were locked in over Washington, the fighter planes were ordered to turn around and engage them as targets. They did, but the targets were no longer there. The jets stayed as long as they could, but finally ran too low on fuel and had to return.

circling around, then tilting up and ascending into the sky.

A week later, beginning just after nine p.m., the whole scenario repeated itself, but this time with some additional witnesses. The Pentagon's UFO investigator, Major Dewey Fournet, a radar expert named Lieutenant Holcomb, and the air force's press man Albert Chop, were all on hand. By midnight, a handful of blips were consistently seen for

The blips did not reappear, and in the years that followed, people looking for a comfortable explanation of what happened have blamed it either on equipment malfunction (unlikely, given that three separate bases tracked the objects with multiple radar scopes) or obscure meteorological conditions. Other more paranoid explanations abound. Some people hold that hostile forces (perhaps from the Eastern bloc) were spying on us. And then, of course, there is the last option: aliens from another planet. Most of us . . . well, we're still wondering.

Viva Loch Raven

In the card file for case number 6148, dated October 27, 1958, the Air Force Project Blue Book noted an event that took place at Loch Raven Dam in Maryland. Apparently, two young men observed an egg-shaped object hovering above Bridge No. 1 over the reservoir. It was one hundred feet long, one hundred twenty-five feet in altitude, and glowing a dim white. Their car went dead seventy-five to eighty feet from the bridge, or about two hundred to three hundred feet from the UFO. After leaving the car and watching for another forty-five seconds, they saw the UFO flash brilliantly white, shoot straight up, and disappear from view in five to ten seconds. There was a loud noise as the object left, as well as an increased sensation of heat. The witnesses later noticed that their skin had been reddened on the side facing the object.

In the words of the witnesses, who were not named in the report but have subsequently been identified as Philip Small and Alvin Cohen, this is how it happened:

B-115—Loch Raven Dam and Spillway near Baltimore, Md.

After you pass the dam the bridge looms up in front of you at 200 to 250 yards away. We saw from that distance what happened to be a large, flat sort of egg-shaped object hanging between 100 to 150 feet off the top of the superstructure of the bridge over the lake.

When we got to within 80 feet of the bridge, the car went completely dead on us. It seemed as though the electrical system was affected: the dash lights went out, the headlights went out, the motor went dead.

It seemed to flash a brilliant flash of white light, and we both felt heat on our faces.

Concurrently there was a loud noise, which I interpreted as a dull explosion. The object started to rise vertically. It didn't change its position, as far as we could tell, during the rising. It was very bright and the edge became diffused so that we couldn't make out the shape as it rose. It took from five to ten seconds to disappear from view completely. We were very frightened.

We got back to a phone booth in approximately 15 minutes and called the Ground Observer Corps, with no result. Our story elicited only complete disbelief.

Interview with a UFO Investigator

When people catch sight of something mysterious in the sky, whom do they call? There are several networks of UFO investigators with field operatives in various states. The best bet for Marylanders is MUFON (the Mutual UFO Network). *Weird* caught up with MUFON's man in Maryland, George Reynolds of Elk Mills. George has been investigating UFO sightings for more than fifty years, and in that time he's got it down to a fine art.

What got you interested in UFOs in the first place?
I saw my first UFO in 1945 very shortly after the war was over. I was still in the navy, and our ship was at anchor in Buckner Bay near Okinawa. I was working in the engine room, and it was very hot. So I went up top to cool off and look at the sky and think, Well, the war's over, and I've made it, and I'm gonna go home.

As I looked up, I saw a bright star. It just gleamed, and as I looked at it, it took off and moved down to the south, made a right turn, and went over and stopped. I couldn't figure out what it was; it didn't move fast, it moved slowly and just stopped. I can still close my eyes and see that night in Okinawa on the submarine deck of the U.S.S. *Beaver.*

What did you do when you got home after the war?
When I left the service, I went to college — got my prerequisites at the University of Delaware and went on to study at M.I.T. in Cambridge, Massachusetts, over five summers. Then I went to study at the University of Arizona as it was then, Arizona State University, at Tempe, Arizona. The next summer they sent me off to the University of Michigan at Ann Arbor to study under a Dr. Cooke, who put the first strain gauges on airplanes. I took many courses at the Ballistic Institute at the Aberdeen Proving Grounds.

How did you get into researching UFOs?
In 1953 in October, I sat down and wrote up my résumé and mailed it to a group called the Aerial Phenomena Research Organization, APRO, in Tucson, Arizona. Right away they called me up on the telephone and said, "We'd like you to be a field investigator for us, with your background in instrumentation with the government," so I agreed to be a field investigator. In 1983 or 1984, they started to fold up and I got a call from Mutual UFO Network, so I took the job as Maryland State sectional director for UFO investigations. My director is Dr. Bruce Maccabee, spelled like in the Bible. We have research scientists in MUFON in almost three hundred fields of science. We have a manual for training people how to go about it. You can take a written examination to show you've examined the book. If you pass the exam, you become a field investigator.

Have you found a way to predict when a UFO might show up?
We've noticed that when a UFO is in the area, there seems to be a distortion in the magnetic field. We had hundreds and hundreds of reports, maybe thousands, of cases of magnetic deviance when UFOs are around. So I started playing around with it. I have a good friend in Denver, Pennsylvania, Ed Stork, who is an electrical engineer. He's worked in laboratories doing experimental research for all the transfer switches and electronics for a phone company, so he's pretty good electronically. Ed has an idea to use a flux gate compass to look at the magnetic fields. On an airplane, particularly the old-type planes with a lot of metal, you couldn't have your compass on the dashboard, because it would pull the compass off base. They put the compass on the wing or the tail; they still do this, and the flux gate compass has wires coming to the dashboard and you have a repeater, so where the compass

is pointing, the repeater on the dashboard is pointing in synchronous motion.

Ed took this flux gate compass thing, and we put operational amplifiers up with a chart recorder on it, so I could have a recording of what's going on. You'd get an ambient reading, then all of a sudden you'd get lots of activity.

Have you personally picked up any UFOs with this rig?
I've had two right here in my backyard. I had a table with three different types of UFO detectors—magnetic detectors for magnetic field deviation. Some of them were simple, a go/no-go detector like a burglar alarm on a window. Well, Ed built these and set them up all nice and sensitive so that when something came and upset the magnetic field in the area, it would go.

It was 9:49 in the evening on a Wednesday, and all the alarms went off there. I ran to the table because it was the first time this had happened. I thought I had a malfunction, maybe one of the wires had come off, but the pen on the chart recorder was banging a full hundred percent in both directions—bang bang bang—spilling ink, and flopping all over the place. And looking at this, I said, "Oh, I'm supposed to run outside and look in the air!" So I ran out the door and looked up, and it was overcast and I didn't see anything.

Two weeks and two minutes later, at 9:51 p.m. on a Wednesday night, it happened again. I ran outside, and I looked up. And this is what I saw. I saw four red lights, sort of in the form of a cross, outside the periphery of something. It was only a couple or three hundred feet up, again it was real overcast, and it was down below the ceiling right above me. Going along about like a Piper Cub plane, maybe one hundred miles an hour. Just sliding along. These were white lights, front back east west, there was no strobe lights, no red lights, no green lights, no running lights. Somewheres near the front, there was a red light. It was strobing, pulsing about twice a second, maybe once a second, going pulse, pulse pulse pulse. It made no noise at all, and I watched it go over me, northeast towards Wilmington.

Apart from the lights, what did this thing actually look like?
It was only a couple of hundred feet away, but I couldn't make out any shape. I was in the house, and your eyes are adjusted to the light indoors. When I was on submarine duty in World War II, we'd get ready to go topside, they'd put us in a room with a red light for half an hour and your irises would adjust for night vision.

So are the chances of just catching sight of a UFO remote, or is there hope for anyone who doesn't have equipment like yours?
A good friend took me over to a meeting, and we're walking home near ten o'clock in October, around 1998, I think. All of a sudden John starts screaming my name at the top of his voice, saying, "George, George, look!" It sounded like something had him. Maybe two hundred to

lights focused on the cloud bank . . . it looked like two UFOs going away from us. So that was my second time.

Did you ever see any evidence of a government cover-up? Any mysterious men in black hanging around these sites?
People think I'm a government agent. I have a blue shirt, makes me look like a military man. And I shine my shoes, and that scares people. [laughing] I'm just an ex-navy man. But when NASA first got started, they hired the Brookings Institute to figure out what we should do if we find some kind of alien life or alien artifacts out in space. What should we tell the people? Margaret Mead, the great anthropologist, and some others got together to figure this out, and this was the answer: Don't tell 'em. When an advanced civilization comes in contact with a lesser civilization you get acculturation — that's the disintegration of the lesser culture. You need twenty-five to thirty years of subliminal education (exposure to the idea of aliens) to bring the people up to a level where they can stand this and survive. We've had more than thirty years of subliminal education up to today. We could be ready for it now.

three hundred feet from me, there was something eighteen to twenty-two feet getting up off the ground. It had two big lights I'd estimate a couple of feet across, and these white lights were set at an angle. The ground looked like it was covered with snow, it was so white. It got up slowly and flew directly over the top of us moving to the southwest and then went into a cloudbank . . . the two

Lots of people dismiss the whole business of UFOs. How do you get them to come around to your way of thinking?
You don't argue. If a guy says, "This is a bunch of garbage," I'll say, "That's your opinion, I got mine. Let's talk about something else."

A Wild Gray Goose Chase

Even before the 1940s were over, the air force was well under way with its investigations of low-flying mystery craft. The now legendary incidents at Roswell, New Mexico, took place in 1947, and in 1948 the first issue of *Fate* magazine featured flying saucers on its cover. Pilots in the war were so used to dealing with aircraft that they couldn't identify that the armed forces gave them a name—foo fighters—and treated them like any other wartime enemy. When the war was over, the air force continued the campaign to find the enemy.

In May 1949, the quest led a unit to a tobacco shed on a farm near Glen Burnie, eleven miles south of Baltimore. There they discovered the weather-beaten wrecks of two circular flying machines. One of them was a sort of helicopter, featuring a small cockpit with a reinforced frame of rotors to lift the whole shebang above the ground. The other looked like some kind of spool with two circular steel-reinforced frames designed to rotate in opposite directions. The farm was abandoned, and nobody knew where the owner was.

So why does Roswell get all the glory and Glen Burnie remain a footnote in the annals of UFOlogy? Because the investigators knew exactly who was behind these bizarre aircraft. They just couldn't find him. Jonathan Caldwell, a carpenter and self-taught aircraft maker, had been designing and building experimental autogyros and "disk rotor planes" since 1923, when he filed a patent for the Cyclogyro that was granted to him in 1927. Other strange designs followed, including the Ornithopter. He built these and other bizarre craft first in Denver, CO, then subsequently in Orangeburg, NY, and Madison, NJ.

Caldwell's frequent changes of address had less to do with making the most of enterprise zones than keeping out of jail. His company, Gray Goose Airways, was constantly in financial trouble. Caldwell was a terrible

businessman, selling bogus stock certificates whenever he ran short of cash. Naturally, this meant that some investors sued him for fraud. He jumped states when things got too hot, and ended up in 1939 in Glen Burnie, issuing stock in a company called Rotor Planes, Inc.

Ten years later a disgruntled investor had written to the air force explaining how similar Caldwell's designs had been to these flying saucers he had been reading about lately. But although the aircraft in the Glen Burnie shed had been flying saucers at one point, they were in ruins by 1949. Caldwell was long gone, and the only reliable witness to the Gray Goose aircraft was a test pilot who had kept the disk-shaped helicopter aloft for a few minutes in 1939. It had reached an altitude of forty feet but then flew straight down to the ground.

Clearly, the Gray Goose investigation had been a wild goose chase. And with that avenue closed to them, the military had to trot out the old standby of temperature inversions.

How Close Was That Encounter?

If you ever watched Spielberg's magnum opus *Close Encounters of the Third Kind*, there are three types of UFO sightings. The third is the most interesting because it involves actually meeting aliens. Well, UFO aficionados have a different take on things. They actually subdivide close encounters in completely different ways, including Type G encounters that involve direct interaction with humanoids and Type E's that involve sighting at a distance. But that's more detailed than most people need to get. The important thing to know is that people in Maryland believe they have actually encountered "people" from inside UFOs. And some of them have gone on the record with their beliefs.

The most celebrated case of a close encounter involved a man known only as Michael who died a decade ago. *Weird Maryland* spoke with a close friend of his on condition that we not reveal any details that would point to the man's real identity. Before his death, Michael lived and worked in the northeastern part of the state. He was a well-respected professional in a responsible position (and so was the friend *Weird Maryland* spoke with). Here's what the friend told us: Michael believed that he had been abducted by aliens frequently since his early childhood. He grew up on a farm, and as a child, he would be visited at night by creatures that came through the walls. He thought of them as ghosts, but they did things that ghosts typically don't.

"These things would come through the wall and git him," our source told us. "Take him off the farm and sometimes let him outside the door of the house instead of put him in the bedroom. And he would bang on the door, and after a while, he'd lay stones there to throw up the wall to get his daddy up."

These visitations happened to Michael even into adulthood. And when he was in the care of these creatures, they left some physical evidence on his body.

"Michael had an implant in the roof of his mouth. I had a good nurse I worked with (I won't mention her name because she works up at the Christiana Hospital). She used a light to check him out, and we saw there was a bump at the top of his throat."

Michael is no longer with us, and because he kept his story secret, he took all the evidence with him to the grave. But he isn't the only person to have encountered alien creatures in the Free State.

According to a report filed with the National Investigations Committee on Aerial Phenomena (NICAP), one night in August 1952 there was another close encounter with a UFO. This time in Seat Pleasant, Prince Georges County. A young mother named Suzanne Knight saw a UFO at close range with an occupant on board. The

whole thing started with a buzzing noise outside her kitchen window. She looked out and saw a bright object descending rapidly at a forty-five-degree angle and stopping suddenly three hundred feet off the ground, about half a block away from her. The dull silver, wingless aircraft was smoking from the rear and, with yellow light streaming from a row of square windows in its side, looked like the gondola underneath a zeppelin. In her report to NICAP, Mrs. Knight wrote, "There was a man in front looking straight ahead towards the front. I couldn't understand what he was looking at so intently." She reported that the creature looked yellow in the light, and "around his arm and the side of his helmet, next to his face, there seemed to be a shadow or a dark line."

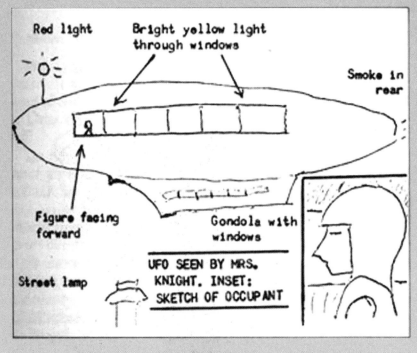

A little more than twenty years later, according to a report in an early issue of *Strange Magazine*, in the summer of 1973, welterweight boxer Butch Dory and several other witnesses caught sight of a large figure emerging from a lake. The article, written by one of Maryland's most recognized reporters of the weird, Mark Opsasnick, described the scene in College Park of a creature with a large round head, which the witnesses shot at. (Didn't anybody pay attention during *The Day the Earth Stood Still?*)

There were more sightings in Maryland. In his book *1973: The Year of the Humanoids,* David F. Webb described a scene that summer in Pikesville, Baltimore County, in which a woman was awakened by an explosion and kept awake by a loud humming. She walked out onto her porch and saw a red transparent object about six feet high and fifteen feet long. There was a bubble on top of it with a human figure standing up inside. Webb gave no further details.

Fast forward almost thirty years, and the Anomaly News Syndicate reported that a strange creature was roaming around Ellicott City near the intersection of routes 29 and 40 during the spring of 2004. A truck driver taking a detour off the highway to grab breakfast around ten in the morning found himself in a residential area. He startled a pedestrian in a gray, hooded sweatshirt walking a dog. The pedestrian looked around and startled the driver right back—its face was rectangular, with a sunken nose and pale creamy skin. Its eyes were large and all black. Its mouth was tiny. When the driver stopped half a block later to get a better look, the figure had vanished.

Whether you believe any of these tales or not, be warned: There are people in this great state who do. And that's just one more example of how this place embraces the unusual. Long may it continue (as long as they keep their probes and implants to themselves).

It Fell From the Sky

UFO spotters aren't the only people who see strange things in the sky. Some of the most bizarre sights up aloft aren't aircraft at all. In fact, some of the reports we've read at historical societies and library archives predate manned flight by decades . . . even centuries. We can't explain what these things are, but we know they were up there. And sometimes they fell down to earth.

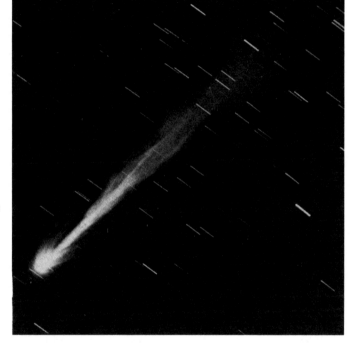

The earliest report we could find came from more than three centuries ago. In a speech delivered to the Maryland Historical Society in 1856, historian S. F. Streeter quoted an earlier unnamed source about some curious phenomena that occurred near the Virginia border a hundred years before the Revolutionary War. Streeter went on to explain that these three events were taken as portents of disaster . . . in his opinion, the events that led to the fall of the Susquehannock tribe. Here is how Streeter's speech began:

> About the year 1675, appeared three prodigies. . . .
> The one was a large comet, every evening, for a week or more, streaming, like a horse-tail, westward until it almost reached the horizon, and setting towards the northwest; another was the appearance of swarms of flies, about an inch long and as big as the top of a man's little finger, rising out of spigot holes in the earth, and eating the new sprouted leaves; and the third, flights of pigeons, in breadth nigh a quarter of the mid-hemisphere, and of whose length was no visible end; whose weights break down the limbs of large trees, whereon they rested at night, and of which the fowlers shot abundance, and eat 'em.

The next reports came from the father of weird studies, Charles Hoy Fort, who collected strange stories from newspapers and historical records all over the world. In the first half of the twentieth century, he dug up thousands of reports and collected the best in a series of books. In his book *New Lands*, Fort quotes from a story—based on newspaper reports from Maryland, Delaware, and Virginia—in the November 1881 issue of *Scientific American* about "black bodies and the dark rabbles of the sky." The *Scientific American* writer dismissed the vision as an aurora—a luminous light phenomenon that occasionally brightens the sky. But Fort delved a little deeper. He scoped out the official meteorological reports in the *Monthly Weather Review*, October 1881, and discovered only one aurora in Maryland on September 23 and "all other auroras far north of the three states in which it was said phenomena were seen." What caused the strange dark images to swirl in the sky remains a mystery.

Crop Circles

When you're looking for the truly out of the ordinary in Maryland, you need to look beneath the surface of people and at the very land itself. The ground beneath your feet has done some pretty weird stuff over the centuries. Consider this: Maryland is home to quite a few crop circles—those weird geometric designs in farmers' fields. Various sites in Harford County were hit with random patches of crop damage in the 1990s. Farmers in Blue Ball, Cherry Hill, Churchville, and their neighboring towns found mashed-down patches of barley and other crops in their fields. Some people blamed it on human pranksters or animals rolling around on the crops; others said the circles were due to wind damage and too tall crops that could not support their own weight. But researchers analyzed the situation more closely and said none of those explanations fit. They came to a different conclusion.

It all started in 1996, when a Pennsylvania-based investigator named Linda Moulton Howe and local archaeologist and investigator of anomalies George Reynolds closely inspected a rash of "sloppy circles" that had appeared in a few sites around Elkton. They sent stalk samples to a team of researchers who specialize in the subject, namely BLT Research, a nonprofit group, which is not named for the sandwich. The B is for the New York businessman John Burke, Michigan biophysicist Dr. William Leavengood is the L, and a research assistant from Harvard and the University of Maryland, Nancy Talbott, brings the T.

This research group shed some light on these samples, but raised a lot more questions. They found that the circles were definitely not hoaxes. For one thing, they were not quaint designs that a prankster could boast about. And for another, the stalks were not broken as they would have been by trampling or pressing under boards. They had bent over because of structural damage to the nodes along the stalks. (Nodes are thick bulbous knuckles of fiber that keep a stalk straight if some of its cells are cracked from wind or other damage.) The BLT group found that the cells at the nodes were shattered from within, causing the stalks to fold in on themselves. It was the kind of damage you'd get from microwaving them. (Microwaves excite water molecules into heat, and nodes have higher levels of water than elsewhere in a stalk.) But where would such microwave energy come from? The BLT had no ready answers.

Other strange forces seem to have been at play in these sites. Reynolds and Moulton Howe noted that they would experience numbness in their limbs when walking around the circles. Reynolds took some physicists from the University of Delaware around two large circles in fields near the Mount Aviat Academy. The compasses they brought went haywire. The poles tilted and began to spin around as if pulled by an electromagnetic tornado.

Reynolds also witnessed something comical when passers-by tried to take photographs of the circles. "They would step into the circles, and their batteries would die out. I warned them, but they thought they were smart city folk and didn't take the warning seriously. Their batteries died right away."

More eerily, Reynolds observed a strange silence when he stood in the circles. "No insects or birds came anywhere near," he told *Weird*. Weeks later, after the area was harvested, Reynolds noticed that although weeds had begun to grow in the harvested stubble, nothing grew in the crop circle sites.

Strange things were clearly happening in those fields. They may still be happening to this day, but the farmers didn't seemed concerned. If they lose a few square yards to crop circle action, they'll take it in their stride. But they're much less easygoing about researchers tramping over their fields. So perhaps we'll never know what happened there or if it's still going on. But it's fun to speculate.

Cape Henlopen's Corpse Light

The so-called Corpse Light off Cape Henlopen on the Delmarva Peninsula has been blamed for shipwrecks going back to the mid-1600s, including the celebrated Christmas Day sinking of the *Devonshireman* in 1655. The captain apparently steered this ship around what he assumed was a lighthouse, and it foundered on the rocks, killing almost two hundred people. (It's also been implicated in the sinking of the British brig-sloop H.M.S. *DeBraak* in 1798, the remnants of which are now in the Zwaanendael Museum in Delaware. This is less likely, since the *DeBraak* went down in a sudden afternoon squall.)

Some of the rangers who host school trips in Cape Henlopen believe that there's something to the tales, and insist that they're not saying that just to add a little supernatural interest to their night nature walks. A couple of them told us that they had seen lights they couldn't explain in the bay (and these are people who can explain almost anything about the cape). But like any lightly studied phenomenon this old, the legends outweigh the actual sightings. The legends say that the Corpse Light is a phantom lighthouse conjured by an old Lenni Lenape curse specifically to punish the British for a massacre they perpetrated during a wedding ceremony. This tale got some traction when pleasure cruisers in 1800 swore they saw a lone Indian on a rock, just before their barge smashed against the rocks.

Take this back story with however much salt you like, but be aware that some dark nights around the cape aren't quite as dark as they should be.

The Hebron Light

The mysterious yellow ball of light that raced around the dark roads in Wicomico County in the 1950s is one of the best-documented cases of a light we can't explain. Several police and newspaper reports described how the luminous ball played a game of cat and mouse with two police officers in their cruiser around Church Road in Hebron. And at least one of the reports commented that the phenomenon had been well known to locals at least fifty years earlier.

The light has been covered second-hand in several books, including *Mysterious Fires and Lights* (Vincent Gaddis, Mackay, 1967), but the newspaper records of the time provide a much more vivid account of the tale. The story opens in early July 1952, in a front-page report in the local town newspaper, *The Salisbury*.

Trooper Robert Burkhardt had seen a ball of light as bright as a headlight on Church Street near Route 50, about a mile west of Hebron, the previous week and arranged for others to witness it too. He took the barracks commander of the Maryland State Police, Lieutenant Serman, and two other troopers to the spot, and about twenty carloads of people also traveled the road that night and witnessed the phenomenon. In the article, Lieutenant Serman said the light "has a sheen like a neon light," and Trooper Burkhardt said it was "about the size of a wash basin, about the height of an automobile light, and the same color as a headlight." The phantom light danced around the wooded road, never going higher than about five feet, bounced into the woods on one side, and crossed

Several police and newspaper reports described how the luminous ball played a game of cat and mouse with two police officers in their cruiser around Church Road in Hebron.

into the nearby field, he said. On the night of July 9, it was visible for a couple of hours.

The light was already well known at this point and apparently seen by hundreds of people that year. There was an old legend attached to it. They said the road was haunted by either a black maid who had been hanged there or a low-life gambler who died in a knife fight.

Unfortunately, the light did not reappear the following night, when about three hundred people showed up to see it, complete with flashlights. Lieutenant Serman clucked that "you couldn't have seen the light because the area was as bright as Main Street." Another man who came out to see the sights had another explanation. Ocean City resident Sam Todd had grown up in Tennessee and explained that he had seen ghost lights out there and that they were caused by gases coming out of the ground. (There is a strange but scientific phenomenon called will-o'-the-wisp, in which marsh gases spontaneously ignite.) His opinion was reported in stories in the Associated Press and *Baltimore Evening Sun* over the following few days. A Johns Hopkins professor confirmed the will-o'-the-wisp idea. "There must be a marsh out there, or perhaps a peat bog. . . . The gas is generated by decaying vegetable matter, seeps up to the surface, gathers in a sort of pocket and is moved around by gusts of wind."

While the professor's right, the Hebron light had some unusual qualities. It accelerated up to around fifty miles per hour and dodged about in swift changes of direction, something will-o'-the-wisp light doesn't do. So what is the story behind the Hebron light? Nobody knows for sure, and with a lack of photographic or videotaped evidence, it's going to be hard to figure it out. Sightings tailed off as the area became more developed, and most people think that the light has been missing in action since the mid-1960s. But if anybody knows differently, be sure to set us straight.

Some sorry souls live in a world that is increasingly filled with cookie-cutter architecture, identical strip malls, and soulless chain stores. The people who walk this world might as well be animated characters in a video game. With five hundred channels to fill, even the televised world they look at is populated by prefabricated characters with cut-and-paste dialogue. It's a world slapped together quickly and efficiently and with the single goal of getting things done so that its designers can move on to the next project.

Thank goodness that the rest of us live in the REAL world, the wide WEIRD world where people celebrate the strange and marvelous, like the fabled people of Maryland. Some are mythic characters like the ancient Greek Argonauts. Others are flesh and blood folks you can walk past on the street without batting an eye. The way some of them look, of course, may force you to bat an eye.

Fabled People and Places

The storied places where Maryland's off-the-grid people live may also be as legendary as the lost city of Atlantis or as real as a Baltimore suburb. One thing's for sure: They have history, depth, and if there is any justice in the world, a future.

Can any single chapter do justice to the infinite variety that is Maryland? Of course not. For a sampler of our state's beautifully bizarre variety, turn the page and open your mind.

The Pig Woman of Cecil County

Of all the bizarre characters of Cecil County folklore, the Pig Woman stands apart from the rest. For one thing, her story is not a single story at all, and the only common factor in the tales is her name and the deformities that earned her that name. The tales of Maryland's Pig Woman focus on a seriously deformed woman who stalks a couple of towns not far from Elkton. Depending on who's telling the story (and which story it is), she inhabits the woods and riversides around North East, especially around an old bridge just south of town, or alternatively around a garbage dump near Rising Sun, farther north and near the Pennsylvania border.

In the Elkton tales of the Pig Woman, several people hiking through the woods came to a burning farmhouse and saw a flaming figure jump to the ground from an upper-story window. Rushing forward to see if they could be of assistance, the passers-by saw the smoldering figure get to her feet and face them. Her charred face was deformed and glowering, and so hideous that the witnesses turned tail and fled. From that point on, they say, the deformed creature stalked the woods at twilight, ambushing unsuspecting travelers, especially children, in her quest for human flesh to feast upon.

Other versions of the tale take place in that most popular setting of urban folktales: the car at night. Couples who drive to the distinctly unromantic setting of the Rising Sun town dump are likely to have their tryst interrupted by a snout-faced old woman who bangs the side of the car until the couple leaves. And those who try to drive across a wooden bridge in the forests south of North East are likely to stall and hear scraping sounds from the fenders and body of the car. When the terrified victims of this assault manage to turn the engine over and speed away, they have a souvenir of their encounter with the Pig Woman: hooflike indentations all over the body of the car.

The very name Pig Woman is enough to conjure tales of mystery and horror, and it seems that that is exactly what has happened. There was a rash of pig-woman stories in London in 1814, in which breathless witnesses spoke of seeing the silhouette of a pig's head flickering in darkened carriages by the light of the gas-powered streetlights. Some even claimed to have seen a snout emerge from the carriage window. These stories appeared on the Letters page of newspapers at the time, and there was some talk that the woman in question was the daughter of an upper-class family in the fashionable district of Manchester Square. Similar themes emerge in the Maryland tales, with rumors that the Cecil County Pig Woman is a member of the du Pont family, which once owned a lot of land in northern Maryland and whose cousin-marrying ways spawned more than one rumor of inbred monsters.

Back in London in the early 1800s, a number of sideshows at St. Bartholomew's Fair in London would tout the Pig Woman as an attraction. According to Christopher Hudson's book *The Great Pig Woman Fraud*, this was a cruel scam involving a shaved bear dressed in women's clothing and doped up to prevent any violent outbursts. Such degrading shows were not unusual in the fairs of the time. From such beginnings, the tale of Pig Woman could easily pass into folklore and travel across the ocean to the New World. But why such a legend would settle in Cecil County and attach itself to two towns there is a mystery. Of course, what's a good folktale without an element of mystery?

The Swine-faced Horror of Elkton

Now, as for the Pig Lady, this local legend is on the stupid side, but that's why I love it. It involves a bridge in Elkton. If you drive your car onto the bridge and stop in the middle, one of two things is said to happen: (a) The Pig Lady or her ghost magically makes your car stall, you are stuck there, and she comes out and kills you, or (b) You stop the car on your own, honk the horn, and she comes out and kills you.

Of course, there have been no deaths reported on that bridge in the last fifty years, but plenty of teenagers honking their horns. She is supposedly a du Pont (oh, you du Ponts and your rampant inbreeding!) who has been shunned by the family for her deformities. So, instead of living in a Brandywine Valley mansion like the rest of the du Ponts, she is forced to dwell under this bridge. And she's not at all happy about it.—*Dena*

Swine Fever!

I have been out to the Pig Lady's bridge in Elkton. Like most, I approached it thinking it was nothing more than a dumb way to waste a weekend night. What I found was far from dumb. It was one of the most seriously frightening situations I've ever found myself in.

Two friends and I had been hanging out one Saturday, and we found ourselves bored as usual. One of the friends said he had been out to see the Pig Lady with his older brother a couple years before and remembered how to get out there. We decided to go and made our way to the bridge, remembering that when we got there we were supposed to yell for her and honk our horns. I wish we had even had the chance. Before we could get that far, we were already scared off.

The bridge is shady and quiet and foreboding. We rolled up to it with all of our windows down. The entire trip we had been joking around about it, mocking the legend, mocking the deformed Pig Lady herself. But when we got there, all of us shut up. Something just seemed completely off about the place. It felt too quiet, too still—which is why, I'm sure you'll understand, all three of us nearly lost it when a high-pitched scream split the night from below the bridge.

My friend Cal, who was driving, froze in fear when he heard the screams. Me and Victor did as well, but it mattered more that he did, since he was driving and thenceforth, not hitting the gas and getting us the heck out of there. None of us yelled in response or said anything. It was much more basic than that. As soon as we heard it, all of us went stiff, our bodies frozen. Cal's hand instinctively reached out and slapped Vic hard in the chest. He was so scared he didn't even make a noise in response.

The sound I heard that night is hard to describe. When it was farther off, it sounded like a woman yelling. But as it got closer and closer, it got deeper and deeper and less and less human. It was a distinct squeal—a full on, rumbling, nasty pig squeal.

Like I said, it was coming up from under the bridge, getting closer, louder, and more menacing. I was in the backseat staring straight ahead. All three of us saw the same thing—nothing. But we did hear the sound of gravel crunching under feet, mixed in with the pig squeal and that was enough. Cal's flight or fight instinct kicked in and he peeled out of there. We pulled a quick U-turn and sped away faster than you can even imagine.

As we did, I spun around and looked back to see if I could pinpoint what had been making that terrifying sound. I couldn't see anything definitive in the darkness, but it did look like a figure was moving around on top of the bridge.

Call me crazy, or say I have an overactive imagination. Even I'm not sure of what I saw that night, but I'm certainly sure of what I heard—the screams of the Pig Lady, who is more real than any of us ever imagined.—*Billy Miles*

A Tale o' the Hon

Imagine if you will, a creature approaching you in lurid clothes. Bright paisley-pattern pedal pushers with an animal-print top stretched across its body. Its feet are in sling-back sandals with heels that make it teeter on the brink of a fall. Its head seems to be preternaturally large, thrusting up into a helmet-shaped dome. As it approaches you, you can smell a peculiar acrid odor that reminds you of something . . . could it be Aqua Net hairspray? It could, and the creature that totters toward you could have been in the 1988 movie *Hairspray,* like a middle-aged version of Ricki Lake's character and a female version of Divine.

The creature you are imagining is a Hon, and her native habitat is Baltimore. The name comes from what a Hon calls everyone she meets, and the look comes straight from the flamboyant

harbor town fashions that were in vogue back in the '60s, when local filmmaker John Waters was at his most impressionable. The look gelled into something iconographic in Waters's movies and around town in good ol' Bawlmer.

Sure, the beehive hairdo, the cat's-eye spectacles, the gaudy spandex clothing, and the fun-trashy attitude aren't unique to Baltimore. The singers of the renowned band B-52's from Athens, Georgia, namely Kate Pierson and Cindy Wilson, aced the look, but it was the Baltimore Hons who spawned an annual summer festival more than a decade ago. Centered around the Café Hon on the Avenue in Hampden, HonFest is partly an inverse fashion show contest, partly an excuse for games, music, and a get-together, and mostly a reflection of Denise Whiting's sense of humor. Whiting, the proprietor of Café Hon, thought that a backyard variation on a beauty pageant would be a good lark, which it was, but throughout the '90s it grew into a monster street party drawing thousands of visitors. There are divisions for Honettes, age seven to fourteen, and Li'l Miss Hons, who are even younger. Despite Glenn Milstead's pioneering work in the Hon look in his alter ego of Divine, Honfest is a women's festival. Here's a rule to live by: Never underestimate the power of brightly colored spandex and ozone-melting quantities of hair spray. The Hon look is still going strong. We just can't quite figure out why.

Backward Talkers of Smith Island

Talk for long enough about Maryland's peculiar people, and sooner or later someone will mention an island in the Chesapeake Bay where people speak like Shakespeare. The story goes that it was populated in the 1600s by boatmen who sustained themselves by catching and selling shellfish. Because of the huge demand for soft-shell crabs, oysters, and in earlier years, terrapins (Maryland's famed turtles), the island population worked hard to provide them. The work was difficult and isolated; it didn't attract too many outsiders over the centuries. Not to mention there was no regular ferry to the island for three hundred years. It is not surprising that the islanders kept the distinctive vocabulary, accent, and speech patterns of the time and place from which they came. In short, they talk like the British used to back in the seventeenth century, but with their own quirks.

When someone from Smith Island says, "It wouldn't be no fun to do that," they mean it literally. The double negatives cancel each other out to make a positive statement, "It would be fun to do that." But that would be much too thrusting and dynamic a statement for an islander to make. They're much more comfortable backing into their declarations. In fact, when they do make even a modest statement, like saying it's a fair morning, they often back it up with "I swagger," as if such a declaration is too bold to go unqualified. Among the islanders, in fact, the verb

"swagger" is about as powerful as "I believe" to the rest of the English-speaking world.

There could be many reasons for this quirky use of language: The powerful influence of the island's nonconformist Methodist religion, for example, tends to foster modesty in its adherents, and despite the fish stories of weekend anglers, the meticulous and patient waterway work of the professional fishermen doesn't lend itself to bold speech. But many students of language attribute it to a centuries-old undiluted strain of British understatement and irony. Saying something like "shame you had to come barefoot" is a dig at someone's fancy footwear.

There are other little language quirks among Smith Islanders that hearken back to Shakespeare's day. Flying in the face of standard grammar, they might say, "I weren't there," much as do farm folk in England. And they use the pronoun "it" in several eccentric ways, such as "It's nothing to do here in winter" and "It was terr'pins seen there today." They also use archaic terms like "nary" and "yon" and "of a night" (for "at night") without affectation.

The weird thing is that if anything, the eccentricities of speech are getting more pronounced as time goes by. The population of the island declined severely through the twentieth century, starting with a 1933 hurricane that changed the lay of the land, a severe dip in the crab population over the following ten years, and the call to arms and mainland manufacturing during the Second World War. According to *An Island Out of Time* by Tom Horton, a onetime resident of the island, the island's population was 153 in 1980. In 1987, it dipped to 124. By 1994, only 90 people called the island home. But just when the trend seemed relentless, out came the 2000 census figures, which show a startling six-year rise to 364. Such a leap can only be a result of immigration. And that, if anything, has fueled the strange language pattern of the islanders. Linguists have noticed that as a population declines, their distinctive patterns of speech become more pronounced, as if to emphasize "us and them" differences.

That could be the reason behind their distinctive accent, which, like that of many American actors who try to sound English, jumps wildly between different regional quirks. It's not unusual to hear a hint of the English Gloucestershire yokel at the beginning of a sentence, a distinctly Australian twang in the middle, and a soupçon of Appalachian banjo dueler at the end. But then again, they say that Aussies and various Virginia communities also have time capsule accents that preserve how the English spoke in their hometowns the year they emigrated.

So before the wave of newcomers and tourists washes away the distinctive language of the Smith Islanders, it's probably a good idea to listen to them talk. And the best way to do that is by listening in on marine radio as they converse among themselves: In Tangier Sound, tune in to channel 66 and the neighboring bands to hear the boatmen carry on conversations as they harvest their own territories. It's not Shakespeare, but it makes intriguing listening nonetheless.

Tales of Zoobieville and Midgetville

When people in the northeastern part of Maryland and western Delaware began submitting their tales of the mysterious Zoobieville to us at *Weird*, they assumed that the scaled-down suburb full of tiny people was unique. Not quite. We've heard similar stories from folks in Washington, DC, and Baltimore, and in the town of Pasadena in Anne Arundel County. The details are remarkably similar in all these areas, but more often than not the community described in these tales goes by the descriptive name of Midgetville.

There's an odd streak that runs through us regular-sized folk. We can quite easily take the presence of small children in our stride, but we often get the urge to stare at child-sized adults. So the possibility of a tiny town somewhere nearby with houses, mailboxes, street lamps, and a population that's somewhere between one-third to one-half normal size is very compelling. And that's where the tales of Midgetville come in.

It seems as though the mythical town of Midgetville is the very essence of weird. There's at least one in every state and sometimes several spread across different counties. But only Maryland has three clusters of Midgetville lore: Up in the northeast in Cecil County, around Baltimore and Anne Arundel counties, and along the Potomac west of DC. In most cases the evidence is scanty, but that's no reason to ignore the tales.

Here's an outline of the Midgetville story. A group of circus folk retired from the Big Tent and used their show business earnings to build a town to suit them. The houses were said to be perfectly proportioned but tiny. The streets were built to a small person's scale. While Midgetville is always located on the outskirts of a regular town, hidden so that the locals couldn't disturb them, someone always seems to know someone who's been there. And on a dull night, groups of people always decide they want to go there to check it out.

But take caution. When you drive to the outskirts of the settlement, they say, a car (often described as a white or black pickup) will chase you and attempt to run you off the road. Or worse, crowds of tiny people armed with rocks and baseball bats and shotguns will come after you, hell-bent on doing you and your car some serious damage.

It's easy to see how residents of such a place would become hostile. Once a place gets a reputation for being Midgetville, it gets lots of rowdy traffic. The residents, whether they are little folk or not, are not going to enjoy the horn-honking and trash talk that's part of the Midgetville road-trip experience. Who could blame them? So if you're tempted to scope out a Midgetville, be considerate, quiet, and don't spoil it for everybody.

Tiny Tales

We don't want to contribute to any neighborhood scuffles, so we're not giving away precise directions to the Midgetvilles we've heard about. Actually, we've never been given accurate enough directions to find the places—with one exception. In fact, it was at the center of a zoning controversy covered in the *Washington Post* in 2005.

Small Wonder

My story is about a little place called Midgetville, or Zoobieville as it's sometimes called around here. The site is common knowledge among younger kids and teens. I kept hearing about it all throughout junior high and high school, how there were these midgets who lived all together in a little community, with little mailboxes all in a row at the entrance.

I have ridden by there a few times, but I really didn't see much. However, my friend had an experience that scared the wits out of her. She was in a Jeep with a bunch of people one night and they decided to check out Midgetville. When they got there, they actually pulled off the road and onto the grass to get out and walk around. No one else I've known had ever done this. As they came closer to the entrance, they saw those little mailboxes and made their way to the entrance. All of a sudden a male midget comes running from the back yard of one of the houses, yelling and carrying a shotgun! My friend and her group ran back to the jeep and got inside. They were trying to pull away, but the car was stuck in a ditch. Then they heard gunshots—the guy had shot at them! Finally after much pushing on the gas pedal, the jeep was free of the ditch and they sped away with the guy still yelling and shooting. Needless to say, after my friend told me her experience, I didn't go back there again. I didn't want to deal with vigilante midgets.—*Jennifer*

Mini Frisbees over Zoobieville

Word has it that some very small people live just north of Smith Bridge Road near Route 202, across the border in Delaware. The location is hidden and difficult to find. Back when it was legal to smoke in restaurants and bars in the First State, whenever those aluminum ashtrays went missing, people would say that the Zoobies stole them to use in their games of Frisbee. The village itself seems like a quaint early 20th century town with wooden frame houses surrounding a town square and parks for socializing and playing Ashtray Frisbee.—*LucySkyye*

Midgetville East

In high school, we all knew about Midgetville. It was supposed to be somewhere in Eastern Maryland where a bunch of rich, retired midget actors from *The Wizard of Oz* built a completely scaled down neighborhood of suburban excellence. But since the town was built in an isolated, hard to find place, the residents went insane, and their inbred children had insatiable desires for mischief and blood. They wait in the trees in front of their homes and jump down on lost motorists and bite their eyes.—*Dyna Moe*

Trying to Find Her Way Back to Midgetville

When I was in high school in the mid-eighties, a friend from Glen Burnie drove me to this remote town of little houses and little people. I was able to find my way back and show other people. But now, 20 years later, I remembered this place one day and have tried to tell my fiancé and a friend who now lives in Glen Burnie and they all think I'm crazy. I'd love to find proof that this little town exists.—*Kimberly Crockett*

Devil's Backbone

Stretching along Antietam Creek off Route 68 near Boonsboro in Washington County is an ominously named park. The locals say that the Devil's Backbone County Park got its name from a geological feature: the twisted rocky ridge that rises up near the creek. But nobody's exactly sure why anybody brought the devil into the equation. Perhaps the superstitious equate the abrupt twists and turns of the ridge with a hideously deformed demon. Perhaps the rocky terrain felt grim and foreboding.

On the surface, this is a beautiful area for hiking, bass and trout fishing, and camping. Outdoorsmen can while away many happy hours in the park. But people who feel sensitive to presences they can't explain say there's something there that causes the hairs on the scalp to stick up. Perhaps it's knowing that only a few miles away is the site of the greatest single day of bloodshed in U.S. history, the battlefield at Antietam.

A few alarming stories circulate about the site. They say that the abrupt twists and turns have led to horrible accidents. One particularly grim tale tells of a man whose spooked horse threw him at a curve in the road and galloped off, leaving him paralyzed at the roadside in the dark. Apparently, all the traffic for the rest of the night ran over him without ever seeing him.

None of these stories appear in written histories of the state, so it's hard to know what to believe. If you're in the mood to walk along Satan's spine, exit Boonsboro westward and turn left on Route 68. About four miles down the road, you'll see an old mill on your left: The park entrance is opposite. Just drive carefully around the bends, especially when you cross the bridge. We don't believe there's a devil hanging around there, but there's no harm in acting with caution just in case.

Troubled at the Mill

I used to visit Devil's Backbone Park often, but I'd go past the Old Mill across the road from the entrance just as fast as I could. I don't know what it was about the place, but it sent cold chills down my own backbone.—*Bill*

Devil's Back Brace

When you walk along the ridge that gives the Devil's Backbone County Park its name, you notice one thing: The top of the ridge is blocked off with a long and overgrown chain link fence. Perhaps the authorities don't want you to give the Devil a backache for fear of repercussions. You just end up trampling his rib cage instead.—*Chris*

Spirited Performance

I heard that the spirit of a wolf possessed a man who was camping around the Devil's Backbone. His friends saw that he was in a daze and led him back to the campsite. A huge gust of wind blew and sent everything around them flying, and then he came back to his senses.—*Anonymous*

Devil of a Fuss

There's a lot of fuss about the Devil's Backbone, but I think it's just overactive imaginations fired up by the name. It's just a ridge near a twisty stretch of road and despite that fact, it's been the site of too many accidents in my time. Now, the Antietam Bridge just up the road up alternate route 40 is a different story. There's no devil there, but they say that a young Indian girl haunts that bridge.—*TheWalker*

Devil's Island and the Damned Quarter

Forget what you learned in the Steve McQueen prison movie *Papillon*. Devil's Island isn't a French penal colony. It's a Chesapeake Bay shellfish zone in Tangier Sound. Or at least it used to be, until fainthearted cartographers edited the name to the more family-friendly Deal Island. The marshy area nearby that's now called Dame's Quarter once had a darker name too: It used to be called the Damned Quarter.

It's anybody's guess why these places earned their devilish and damned descriptors. The pat answer is that they used to be a hotbed of pirate activity. No doubt picaroons did hop in and out of the island's waterways, but it's too small to have been a serious base of operations—it's only three miles long—and none of the big names of piracy frequented it. And the boggy Damned Quarter was hardly suitable for buccaneers to navigate through or weigh anchor in. Some local historians speculate that Devil's Island earned its name first, and Damned Quarter was so dubbed to acknowledge it as Satan's suburb.

But there are no hard facts about the origin of the name, and where fact leaves a vacuum, fantasy floods in. Amateur folklorists swear that the original names of Devil's Island and Damned Quarter were given because the original settlers in the area believed the devil lived there. They used to see him and his minions in the water around the island, and in the boggy marshland,

and gave cursed names to the area to warn people off.

But there's another explanation with a ring of truth to it: They picked those names because they had a robust sense of humor. While the idealistic religious colonies up north in Pennsylvania were routinely calling their new towns Paradise and Providence and Bethlehem, the gritty longshoremen and their hardscrabble fishwives were more realistic about the mosquito-infested, humid summers and fierce stormy winters. Without any false modesty, these names could be saying, "It's a terrible place really, but it's home."

However inhospitable it may once have been, the area was good to its early settlers. Like other islands in the sound, Deal Island became a huge exporter of soft-shell crabs. It also became the base of operations of the Methodist minister Joshua Thomas, the "Parson of the Islands," who held religious camps and meetings behind St. John's Methodist Episcopal Church that were attended by residents of nearby Smith and Tangier islands. Perhaps Reverend Thomas's influence drove out the devil from the place-names as well as the souls of his flock, or perhaps the crustacean harvest was easier to market with the name Deal on it instead of Devil. Whatever the reason, the maps now label the place Deal Island. But all the residents still acknowledge the original names.

The Frederick Shoe House

Back in the 1960s and early 1970s, the folks of Frederick would tell the tale of the house that nobody would pull down. The story dates back to the 1930s and tells a strange tale about a widow who lived in a huge house that was once luxurious and stately but over time suffered from neglect. The old dowager loved the place, though, and refused to yield to pressure from her grown daughter, who also lived there, to sell it. The issue caused a rift between the two. The daughter knew that she would eventually have her way, even if she had to wait until nature took its course, so she waited.

One night her mother complained of pains down her left side, and the daughter realized that she was having a heart attack. She insisted her mother should go to the emergency room,

but the mother insisted that first she needed to change into a new pair of shoes. She left her old shoes by the hearth and made her way out of the house for the last time. She died that night.

Soon after the funeral, the daughter began to clear the place, getting it ready to put on the market. But when she came to the hearth, she found that her mother's shoes wouldn't budge. They were rooted to the spot, and no amount of pulling or hacking at them would help. It was as if they had fused to the hearth tiles.

As the old folks in the town would tell the story thirty-five, forty years ago, the shoes remained stuck to the spot. Despite the value of the property, the bewitched footwear kept prospective buyers away. Nobody dared to bring in the wrecking ball either, so the house remained empty and decaying. But it was still occupied. Even though the doors and windows were boarded up, you could sometimes see a figure entering the house at twilight. And although there was no electricity, you could see lights burning behind the boards. Surely, it was the ghost of the old woman who once lived there, who refused to move out even though she was no longer living at all.

Nobody today appears to know where the house is. It may still be standing empty, but no house in town seems to fit the description. It may have been torn down. Or perhaps it always was just a good story. Even so, it's one that's worth retelling.

The Legend of the Delmarva Moors

Like the Wesorts of Prince Georges County, the Delmarva Moors have been described as "triracial isolates." The term describes the group's African-American, European, and Native American roots and that their community developed in isolation from the dominant European culture.

C. A. Weslager, in his book *Delaware's Forgotten Folk*, 1943, describes the "Moors" he met in Delaware as follows: "Certain facial characteristics . . . set them apart from both whites and Negroes. The darkest have brown skins and the lightest resemble their white neighbors in complexion. Blonde, red and sandy hair may be seen, but the majority have brown or black hair, either wavy or straight and coarse like that of the full blooded American Indian." To many, they look a lot like the dark haired swarthy Moors from Spain.

So who are the Moors and how did they come to settle on the Delmarva Peninsula? When asked this question by researchers, the Moors' typical response was one of three amazing legends.

The first legend of the Moors' origins, as found in the article "The Moors of Delaware: A Look at a Tri-Racial Group" (author unknown), is that "the Moors originated sometime before the Revolutionary War through the founding of a colony along . . . the Delmarva Peninsula by a group of dark skinned Spanish Moors. Through intermarriage with the local Indians come the people called Moors. . . ."

This legend has some historical support in that it is known that Sir Frances Drake had several hundred Muslims from Morocco and the Ottoman Empire on board when he stopped for a few months in Roanoke, Virginia. These Moors could have mingled with the Native Americans in Virginia and eventually made their way to Delaware and New Jersey, if not in person, then in offspring.

A story is also told of an expedition of Charles II to Tangiers in North Africa. When this expedition disbanded in 1684, the crew, who were Moors, set sail for America. They supposedly arrived on an island in the Chesapeake Bay and named it Tangier Island. From here, they mixed with the Native Americans and spread to Delmarva.

The second origin legend is that the Moors are descendants of Spanish or Moorish pirates who came ashore and intermarried with the Nanticoke and Lenape people in the area.

This story is more likely than the first because of the well-documented history of piracy around the shores of the area during the "Golden Age" of piracy (ca. 1660–1720).

The last story is a romantic legend where a beautiful, wealthy woman, who was either Spanish or Irish, bought a male slave who was a Moor. They fell in love and had children of "Moorish" complexion. C. A. Weslager found some evidence of a wealthy Irish widow living in the Cheswold area of Delaware (Moor country) but nothing definitive.–*Brian Carrol*

W hen people feel like getting scared, they turn first to ghost stories. But when they want to get really good and scared, they turn to a good old-fashioned monster. You just can't beat an enormous winged creature with talons, threatening to rip you apart with its beak. Unless it's with the threat of a huge furry creature that could rip your limbs off and throw you up a tree. Or perhaps a giant slithering thing that poses no threat at all, but looks so creepy it doesn't have to.

And guess what? Maryland has them all. Sea serpents have made their appearance here over the centuries, and so have monstrous flying creatures, four-footed fiends, and, of course, Bigfoot himself. People love to pooh-pooh the idea of creatures that aren't recognized by science. They've seen enough hoaxes to be skeptical. But skepticism counts only if you know something about the

Bizarre Beasts

creatures you want to dismiss. And we aren't prepared to dismiss Maryland's hidden creatures just yet.

After all, science doesn't know everything. People wrote off tales of huge ape-men in the mountains of the Congo until mountain gorillas were discovered early in the last century. Most people believed the giant squid was an ancient legend on a par with dragons until one of them washed up in Tasmania. So until Maryland's bizarre beasts march forward into the annals of official zoology, we'll be content to stick with cryptozoology, the study of hidden animals. And we'll hope they don't stay hidden long.

Chessie—The Chesapeake Bay Sea Serpent

Let there be no doubt about it: The giant marine serpent is everybody's favorite not-officially-discovered species. If you harbor any doubts about this, think of the world's most famous sea creature, Nessie, the Loch Ness monster. Then sail three thousand miles west and consider Maryland's own maritime monster, the Chesapeake Bay creature known as Chessie.

There have been reports of serpentine creatures in and around the waters of the Chesapeake since at least 1846, when a Captain Lawson reported a small-headed creature between Cape Charles and Cape Henry. But it was only in the following century that Chessie got her name. According to a collection of reports assembled by researcher Dave Elberti in the Maryland Folklore Archive, detailed sightings of Chessie started coming in from the 1930s onward. In 1934, two perch fishermen spotted something coming up for air near Baltimore. In news reports, the shaken fishermen, Francis Klarrman and Edward J. Ward, described what they saw:

> This thing was about 75 yards away, at right angles from our boat. At first it looked like something floating on the water. It was black and the part of it that was out of the water seemed about 12 feet long. It has a head about as big as a football and shaped somewhat like a horse's head. It turned its head around several times—almost all the way around.

In 1963, another sighting took place, this time from a helicopter pilot named Walter L. Myers. He wrote to Senator George W. Della, claiming he saw Chessie while flying over the lower Bush River area. "I assure you that Chessie exists," he wrote, "or my eyes were deceiving me."

Once the newspapers get on it, people begin actively looking for Chessie, which often leads to imaginary or exaggerated reports, making reliable data harder to pin down. "Big fish" stories are all too common. But in the late 1970s, retired CIA employee Donald Kyker and his neighbors, the Smoot family, spotted four of these creatures about seventy-five yards offshore. The creatures were between twenty-five and forty feet long, about a foot across, oval-headed, and free of any distinguishing marks or limbs. It was not until Memorial Day in 1982 that anybody captured Chessie on film. At around seven thirty p.m., Robert and Karen Frew were watching a group of swimmers in the bay from their home at Love Point, at the northernmost tip of Kent Island just east of Annapolis. A short distance from the group, they caught side of a dark serpentine form cruising toward the humans. Frew grabbed his video camera and filmed the path of the creature as it dived near the unsuspecting swimmers and reappeared at the other side of them.

Frew was trained in wildlife management at the University of Maine, but he didn't recognize the species. "What we saw is not a run-of-the-mill animal," Frew claimed. It moved from side to side like a snake and at one point swam in water only four or five feet deep. It appears to be unafraid of people, but not much interested in them either. "It seemingly doesn't eat people," he said, "because it swam within fifty feet of them."

The footage Frew recorded lasted less than five minutes, with only about two minutes' worth of the creature, but it has been the subject of much scrutiny. At about the same time, a resident of Reistertown in Baltimore County, Mike Frizzell, was actively investigating Chessie. Mike Frizzell's Enigma Project got hold of Frew's tape and showed it to scientists at the Smithsonian Institution's Museum of Natural History later that summer. The quality of the tape was not good enough for zoologist George Zug and his colleagues to draw any definite conclusions about

APL Computer Enhancement (1982)

Video taken by Robert Frew. Courtesy of The Enigma Project

the creature. "Animate but unidentifiable" was one recorded comment; the scientists were reported as being "basically noncommittal but not skeptical."

A laboratory in Laurel, Prince Georges County, offered to enhance the tape. Johns Hopkins Applied Physics Laboratory used graphical computer enhancement to resolve details that were unclear on the original footage. A definite serpentine form emerged from the blurry tape. It's a brownish, snakelike or eel-like aquatic animal, round as a telephone pole, with humps along its back and a football-shaped head. It seems to spend too long out of the water to have gills and apparently eats bluefish, since it's mainly spotted between April and the end of summer during the bluefish runs. Soon afterward, the project's funding ran out and work on the tape ended. For more than twenty-two years, the tape has remained in limbo.

So we're left with some relatively solid data about the creature and much conjecture.

What is Chessie? Various reports and artists' impressions seemed to point in the direction of a prehistoric creature called the Zeuglodon. *The Washington Post,* when it covered Chessie, touted a mutant eel theory. With a lightheartedness typical of serious newspapers covering these matters, they suggested the comic-book notion that the Calvert Cliffs Nuclear Power Plant may have accelerated mutations on the native species of water snake.

Another theory sounds a little more solid. The Chessies (remember, they have been spotted in groups) may have descended from giant South American anacondas that escaped from ships abandoned in Baltimore. Some people say that snakes were placed in the holds of eighteenth- and nineteenth-century sailing ships to control rats. As the hulls of the decommissioned ships decayed in the shipyards, these slithering pest controllers could have escaped and thrived on the abundant wildlife in the estuaries. But how could equatorial creatures survive the bleak Maryland winters? Some believe that the outfall pipes of the city's water system could have provided shelter or that a few survived by sheer brute strength, and, due to natural selection, later generations were able to tolerate the cold.

Whatever the origins or current prospects of the Chesapeake Bay serpent, some people in high places have taken the matter seriously. State senator George W. Della of Baltimore, a member of the Senate Economics and Environmental Affairs Committee, drafted a resolution during the Maryland state legislature session of 1984 to "encourage serious scientific inquiry by the State into Chessie and other unusual animals in the Chesapeake Bay." Although widely ridiculed for the measure, Della insisted that for more than twenty years he had been receiving letters about Chessie from concerned citizens, ranging from grade schoolers to research directors, which, as far as he was concerned, constituted a significant enough interest to pursue the matter. We're inclined to agree with the senator.

The Fish That Ate Maryland

Not all aquatic monsters in Maryland are treated with skepticism by the scientific community. Some are treated much more badly. In fact, there's one species that's been suffocated and poisoned by scientists who encourage others to behead and bleed them to death.

In June 2002, the Maryland Department of Natural Resources Fisheries Service received two separate reports of a strange fish from anglers who were line fishing in a pond in Crofton, Anne Arundel County. The fish were smallish in size but from the dorsal fin forward looked more like snakes than fish. By September, these two isolated findings had blown into a full-on panic when scientists realized what they were dealing with—a voracious fish that can breathe air! Thanks to its snakehead and predatory ways, it acquired the nickname Frankenfish. This species originated in China and is divided into twenty-eight subspecies, some of which grow to massive size and readily attack humans with their sharp teeth. They easily devour other species of fish, and to make matters worse, they are extremely fertile. Adults can breed five times a year; they protect their eggs and fry by carrying them around in their mouths. Once the spawn are out in the water, the adults defend them fiercely, attacking and killing anything that gets near the young

ones—including humans and any other species they happen upon.

Most snakehead subspecies can breathe air from a very young age, making them well adapted to survival in stagnant water. During a drought, they dig into mud to stay moist. And most dangerous of all, they are migratory and, if necessary, can slide across land, eating just about everything in their path, to find more viable water to live in. In fact, the Frankenfish is so well adapted to survival that it poses a huge threat to native species, including those on the state's endangered list (which include 16 amphibians, 115 fish, and 5 federally protected freshwater crustaceans).

How did the snakehead get into Maryland's waterways? Presumably, they came through the exotic fish trade. Dealers sell them to enthusiasts, who perhaps set them free when the creatures grow to a yard long and start slithering around on the carpet, biting anything that threatens them.

The attempts to contain the species in Crofton failed. That year, a twenty-two-inch giant snakehead was captured by a crabber in the Fells Point district of Baltimore. This is small by giant snakehead standards; they can grow up to forty inches long. The fisheries department took no chances: They dumped two

---

**Northern Snakehead
Distinguishing Features**
Long dorsal fin • small head • large mouth • big teeth •
length up to 40 inches • weight up to 15 pounds

HAVE YOU SEEN THIS FISH?

The northern snakehead from China is not native to
Maryland waters and could cause serious problems if
introduced into our ecosystem.

If you come across this fish,
PLEASE DO NOT RELEASE.
Please KILL this fish by cutting/bleeding
as it can survive out
of water for several days and REPORT all catches to
Maryland Department of Natural Resources
Fisheries Service. Thank you.

Phone: 410 260 8320
TTY: 410 260 8835
Toll Free: 1 877 620 8DNR (8367) Ext 8320
E-mail: customerservice@dnr.state.md.us

herbicides
into the
Crofton pond
to eliminate
aquatic
vegetation,
thereby starving
the water of
oxygen, and then
sprayed a fish-killing
agent called Rotenone
into the water. This killed
more than one hundred and
twenty snakeheads, most of
them juveniles, with the
collateral damage of "60 pounds
of other varieties of fish." After
scooping out all the fish, they applied
potassium permanganate to clean the
poisons out of the water.

But the snakehead had already taken hold. By the
following year, wanted posters were put up advising
fishermen to behead or bleed to death any snakeheads
they caught, instead of returning them to the water. Soon
catching snakeheads had become a macho competition
along the Potomac, where seventeen were caught in the
summer of 2004; lumberjack Cliff Magnus caught the
largest (a six-pounder more than two feet long), and
retired racecar driver Tom "Snakehead Slayer" Woo
caught the most: three.

By that summer, the invasive creature had captured
the popular
imagination so much that it
joined the shark and the giant squid as the subject of a
horror movie. The Sci-Fi channel released an eighty-four-
minute gorefest featuring genetically engineered mutant
snakefish picking off humans in the Louisiana bayou.
The movie's name: *Frankenfish*. You know you've made it
as a monster when the Sci-Fi channel creates an original
movie about you.

What Is the Snallygaster?

Spend enough time around north-central Maryland, and you'll hear about the Snallygaster. He's spoken of and written about in a cluster of towns in Frederick, Montgomery, and Carroll counties, most prominently in Middletown, Rockville, and Sykesville. The trouble is, he's almost never described the same way twice. Sometimes he's part reptile, part bird, with octopus tentacles. Sometimes he has razor-sharp teeth. Other times he has a shiny metallic beak. Sometimes the creature tears the flesh of its victims. Other times it sucks on the veins of its victims until they're bled white. And lately the term Snallygaster seems to be used interchangeably with Maryland sightings of Bigfoot.

So where did the Snallygaster come from, and how did his name come to be applied to such radically different creatures? Ah, now there's a story. The creature's name comes from the German term *schneller Geist*—a fast-moving spirit or ghost whose rapid movement causes doors to slam and items to scatter. In north-central Maryland in the early eighteenth century, the German *schneller Geist* turned into the Snallygaster, a creature with overtones of European dragon lore and the thunderbird myths of Native American tribes. This monstrous bird of prey would whisk away chickens and small barnyard animals in the South Mountain region.

Occasionally a tale would surface of a child being carried

off. One branch of local lore stated that the seven-sided hex patterns painted on houses and barns were a charm to ward off the beast. (Few of these still exist in Maryland, though hex signs are still prevalent a little farther north in the old German settlements in Pennsylvania.) And so the stories continued for more than a century, firmly rooted in local folklore.

Written records of the creature don't appear until 1909, when the *Middletown Valley Register* published an account from Ohio of a flying creature some twenty feet long, heading toward Maryland. A later issue described a similar creature in Maryland's northern mountains, sleeping on a kiln. It woke with a horrible screech and flew off.

Fired by these tales, more reports came in, with witnesses describing an eagle-winged but fur-clad creature snatching farm animals, or tearing them apart and drinking their blood. Tales from out of state—mostly West Virginia and Ohio—described children being dragged off in broad daylight. Reports that cannot now be verified appeared, alleging that the Smithsonian Institution offered a substantial reward for the creature and that Teddy Roosevelt planned a hunting trip to find it. The whole story soon died down, with a final report from hunters in Emmitsburg who mortally wounded the beast and watched it disappear into the night.

The authenticity of these tales is seriously in question, especially because of the creature's convenient disappearance—that is, of course, until it suddenly reappeared two decades later during Prohibition. Stories began to circulate of thunderous explosions and loud screeching sounds from the mountain's illegal stills, along with reports of a winged creature with huge tentacles. Hard to believe, but the monster carried people off who were getting too close to the mountain and left their bodies scorched and bled white. The *Valley Register* ran reports theorizing that the creature had probably hatched from an

Between 'Dwayyo' and Snallygaster'

Sykesville 'thing' sought

Sykesville — Maryland State Police are continuing a search in this rural Carroll county community for a huge, hairy monster described by residents as a cross between a "Dwayyo" and a "Snallygaster."

Police pressed a helicopter and searchlights into service last week after Anthony Norris reported finding footprints in his backyard measuring 13½ inches long and almost 6 inches wide.

At the same time, several residents reported sighting the beast, described variously as 7- to 10 feet tall and ...

... tall, with a big bushy tail and black hair."

A person identified as John Becker told State Police at that time that he had battled the beast—which he called a "Dwayyo"—in his backyard, located near Gambrills State Park.

An Ellerton woman said she had heard it "cry like a baby and then scream like a woman."

"Like the Frederick creature monster, the Sykesville creature is ... to have killed seven ... a cow. ...

... reports indicate the creature came into being to scare moonshiners around the Middletown area.

Snallygaster tales continued to flourish through the early 1930's, but the sightings finally stopped when a Middletown newspaper published a story saying the winged creature had drowned in a moonshine mash barrel in the ... west of Mid...

egg mentioned in the paper twenty years earlier. Sightings increased exponentially, and other newspapers including the *Baltimore Sun* began to cover the story. In some cases, the tales were intentionally ridiculous, featuring the Snallygaster swooping down from the clouds on an antique bicycle, wearing water wings and shouting, "Balance the budget!" More newspapers were trying to get coverage on it when the *Valley Register* reported the Snallygaster's death by drowning in a vat of whiskey. The creature's death probably had something to do with

the fact that Prohibition was about to end and the moonshiners didn't need the Snallygaster's protection from prying revenue agents.

Sightings of Snallygasters still occur. At some point, the Snallygaster appears to have become a generic term for a bogeyman and lost its teeth (or beak or tentacles) for good. Any reports of a bipedal mammal called Snallygaster should instantly be filed under Sasquatch. The Snallygaster himself has been killed twice over and should be respectfully laid to rest.

Four-footed Fiends

Hungry quadrupeds crawl across Maryland in search of prey every day. Farmers have known about coyotes and wolves for centuries. Foxhunters have reveled in the fact that their prey of choice thrives in fields. But there are more four-footed creatures creeping around the Free State than these.

The Hyote of Glyndon and Joppa

It all started during the summer of 2004.

Everyone from housewives to hunters started reporting sightings of a strange creature prowling backyards and raiding pet food in central Maryland. These sightings were definitely different from the occasional report of a rabid raccoon or meandering bear. This animal couldn't be so easily identified—until the beast was discovered lurking in the woods behind a home in Glyndon, Baltimore County, in July 2004. The homeowners came up with a way to use a portable motion detector and secretly videotape the animal as it moved through the yard. The tape showed a low slung, apparently canine animal loping through the grass with very large ears, a long tail, and a shaggy mane of long fur. The video was an instant smash hit.

The creature became a regular on the nightly news and in the neighborhood, where some residents even reported it would come up out of the woods to feed on cat food left outside. The Glyndon community not only captured the beast on film, they named it—

the Hyote, so dubbed because it resembled a curious combination of hyena and coyote.

As the reality began to sink in that some sort of hybrid hyena-wolf-coyote was roaming through suburbia, a level of anxiety descended upon the public at large. While most were intrigued by the possibility of some exotic or unknown animal prowling the area, others were afraid the beast would quickly move from cat food to children.

The Glyndon community was not the first to discover the mystery beast, however. A year earlier a family living on a rural farm in Joppa, Harford County, reported seeing the animal. One morning the Mathis family awoke and looked out their window, only to spot a strange creature drinking from a pony trough behind their house. Family members were upset by the animal, which they were unable to identify, but they took pictures.

They held onto the photographs of the strange creature for a year—until the exposure of the Glyndon beast began to hit the airwaves and added to the frenzy.

While the popularity of the Hyote was picking up steam and new monikers like the Jersey Devil and the Creature from *The Lord of the Rings*, natural resources officials were busy putting a more scientific and less supernatural spin on things. The Maryland Department of Natural Resources issued a hypothesis that the

animal was most likely a common red fox that had come down with sarcoptic mange—a skin parasite that causes weight loss, fur to be easily rubbed off, and weak loping movements. While they were nearly certain the mystery beast was a mangy fox, the scientists left the door open to another possibility—that it was some sort of strange, exotic mammal that had been kept as a pet by a Maryland resident who released it when not able to properly care for it.

It didn't take long before the Glyndon Hyote was making national news, which in turn elicited reports of

similar creatures all over the country and the world. A farmer in Elmendorf, Texas, shot a twenty-pound, strangely blue-colored beast after it killed thirty-five of his chickens in one day. The eerie photos of that hideous animal only fueled the mystery behind the creature's identity—and also added a new candidate to the mix.

After the Texas creature was shot, locals began referring to it as El Chupacabra, a legendary monster deep-rooted in Mexican folklore that supposedly kills other animals by sucking their blood. At this point in the saga, the mystery beast was alternately described as a razorback hog, a hyena, an aardwolf, a coyote, a capybara, a Mexican hairless dog, a warthog, a wolf, an African wild dog, the previously believed extinct Tasmanian Wolf, the Jersey Devil and now—El Chupacabra.

Alleged sightings were also popping up everywhere from North Carolina to England, but in early August 2004 the mystery took a mighty blow when the Glyndon man who initially videotaped the beast was able to capture it in a cage trap he set in his backyard. Veterinarians from the nearby Falls Road Animal Hospital were able to conclusively identify the animal as a male red fox with sarcoptic mange—but there came one last twist in this tale.

Instead of solving the mystery, capturing the animal only added to the intrigue, when the man who caught the creature claimed that the animal he had trapped in his backyard was much smaller than the beast he had first seen. But with an animal captured, the case was satisfactorily solved for the media, which quickly dropped its nightly coverage of the mystery beasts. For those who saw the creature with their own eyes, however, questions linger, and there are many who stand firm that the small, sickly fox snared in a Glyndon backyard was not the mighty mystery beast—which they believe still roams Maryland's woods.—*Brian Goodman*

Goat Man of Prince Georges County

There exists a creature in Maryland known as the Goat Man. Whether it is Maryland legend or Maryland reality, there are enough witnesses and circumstantial evidence to keep the Goat Man's name alive.

So what the heck is the Goat Man? Some have claimed that he has a human body with a goat's head, like the popular portrayal of Satan. Some insist that he has a goat's lower body with the torso and head of a human, like the satyr of Greek mythology. Other observers say simply that he is an exceptionally hairy humanoid creature roughly six feet in height.

Since the late 1950s, the Goat Man's territory has included several localities in Prince Georges County, with an acute focus on the Bowie area, which is largely forest with a number of main highways running through it to other, more populous, parts of the state. At the heart of the matter is the bridge known as Crybaby Bridge on Governor's Bridge Road, where motorists can hear the shrill cry of an infant ghost—or the Goat Man. The Goat Man also frequents Lottsford Road and Fletchertown Road and the locale around Lottsford–Vista Road and Admore–Ardwick Road.

Some have claimed that the Goat Man was bold enough to break into their homes while they were out and they startled the belligerent creature on their return. The Goat Man also shoulders the blame for attacking cars left near the woods, often with an axe. This facet of the Goat Man myth has for many decades been blended with the urban legend of the Hook, in which two teens park on lovers' lane, the boyfriend gets out and does not return, then the girlfriend hears his blood dripping onto the car.

In this region, the Goat Man is the culprit.

More often than not, the Goat Man's origins are attributed to mankind's greedy quest for knowledge. At the center lies the United States Agricultural Research Center of Beltsville. Two common variations of the myth involve a scientist working with goats at the facility. In one story, the scientist goes mad for reasons often improvised by the storyteller and runs off screaming into the woods, where he stalks to this day with an axe. The second and more fantastic version claims that the scientist's experiments went horribly wrong and mutated him into a goatlike creature, whereupon he fled to the relative peace of the woods with an axe and a chip on his shoulder. There is a third assertion involving a botched attempt at creating a cure for cancer.

Another theory involves a mental health facility located in the Goat Man's known territory—the Glendale State Asylum between Lottsford Road and Fletchertown Road. Some locals speculated about experimentation on inmates or that "regular" insane persons may have escaped to commit the crimes blamed on the Goat Man. And finally, there is the assertion that the Goat Man is the embodiment of none other than the archfiend himself, summoned to this earth from time to time by the rituals of satanists.

Cryptozoologists, who study so-called extinct or non-existent animals, have been drawn to the story in droves.

The most persistent accusation against the Goat Man is that it assaults pets. The area has suffered several rashes of mutilated or missing animals, including several instances reported in 1971 in the *Washington Post* that mentioned the Goat Man. In some instances, the decapitated corpses of

the missing animals have been found, but there are other circumstances to consider (such as the fact that one of the dogs was found next to frequently used railroad tracks). Some even claim to have witnessed the Goat Man throwing dogs off Interstate 495 overpasses near secluded areas. And as recently as August 2000 a group of construction workers sighted a Sasquatch-like creature that in their estimation stood twelve feet in stature, traversing an area of Washington's suburbs.

Until the myths can be proved or disproved, the Goat Man will continue to be the object of both ridicule and fear for residents outside Washington, DC.–*John Lawson*

The Goat Man in Summerfield

A friend of mine lived in Summerfield, the off-base military housing in Prince Georges County. Summerfield is also quite wooded, with many nature trails, a stream, and a rather large swamp. My friend lived with the woods to the back of his house. Quite often, his children would go down to the stream running through the woods to play. One afternoon as he was preparing supper and getting ready for work (he worked nights), he went outside to call for his two oldest daughters to come in to eat. When he got outside he saw the younger one was already back in the yard. He asked where her sister was, and she replied, "Still down at the stream." That's when he heard her scream.

Knowing the kind of crazies that could have been in the area, a million possibilities ran through his head as he ran to her. A million possibilities—but never would he have thought of this. He found his daughter by the edge of the bank huddled up and crying. He tried to calm her down, but to no avail. All she would do is point to the other side. So he scooped her up and carried her back to the house to make sure she was okay. Finally, he got her to tell him what had made her scream. She said it looked like a goat at first because it was on all fours. Then it stood up on its hind legs and walked on two legs up over the bank, and disappeared into the brush.

At first he totally dismissed her story, but she had never lied or made up stories before. Being a good dad, he went to the stream to see if it had left any signs behind. All he found was some hoofed footprints that led up over the bank, and he followed them till they disappeared into the underbrush. Shaking his head, he walked back to the house to tell his wife of his findings. He left for work shortly thereafter and couldn't get this goat man out of his head. When he got to his desk, he typed in "Goat Man" and "Prince Georges County" on the computer to see what would come up. Never before in all his life had he been so shocked. He found web pages, tons of them, about the Goat Man of Prince Georges County. Well, if his daughter had seen what she claimed she had seen, it was the elusive Goat Man who has been stalking PG County for many, many years now.—*thestereogod*

Goat Man Plays Chicken

When I was studying Maryland folklore, I read about a Goat Man who frequented a stretch of the Beltway around Largo. He is a man with the legs and hooves of a goat, and he is tremendously aggressive. He can also run tremendously fast. He keeps pace with cars driving at speeds up to 60 mph and throws himself onto their hoods to run them off the road. The cars usually lose control and crash. That's a reason that some people give for the unusually high number of crashes in this stretch of road.—*Dolores*

Peeping Tom Goat Man

Out around some of the old back roads in Oxon Hill where couples would go for some privacy, there were lots of stories about people who saw a creature with the body of a goat and the torso, arms, and head of a man. They would hear scuffling noises on the dirt road and they would see this hoof-footed creature outside the car.—*Anonymous*

Not Your Grandma's Goat Man

My grandmother used to hear about the Goat Man when she was a girl. But the story she heard was different: In her version, the Goat Man wanders around the fields at night with a sickle or a shotgun. He doesn't live in a house anymore, but roams in the wild and hunts animals to eat raw. He hates people, so if he catches you around "his" fields, he will kill you. They say that the man was deranged after an accident that crushed his head at the temples. He survived, but the bulges looked like two horns and the deformity and brain damage he suffered drove him mad. I think this tale comes from around Annapolis and was current during the Depression. —*Enzo*

Goat Man Vacations in Kentucky

As a kid growing up, I heard of the Goat Man. He was half-human and half-goat with a human torso and a goat head. The stories my grandfather told were of this screaming devil jumping a fence, grabbing two full-grown pigs and jumping off with them. There are stories of him that are over sixty years old.—*Doug Oller, Paducah, KY*

Bigfoot Stalks the Free State

When you say the name Bigfoot, most people think of the wilderness in the Pacific Northwest, and of a cone-headed hairy creature loping along in a famous 16-mm film made in 1967 by Roger Patterson and Robert Gimlin in Bluff Creek, California. And they consider it to be a bit of a joke or a hoax. But the one thing people rarely think of when they think of Bigfoot is the great state of Maryland. And that's just plain wrong.

Hairy bipeds have been spotted in Maryland for many, many years. Too often newspapers have attributed the sightings to the Goat Man and the Snallygaster, two local legends that bear no resemblance to Sasquatch. Even such august journals as *The Washington Post* have made that mistake. An article in the *Post* dated November 30, 1971, describes a creature responsible for the death of a dog in Prince Georges County. Two men found the dog's head on Fletcher Road and associated it with a story told by a third man, who saw a hairy creature six feet tall walking across a field nearby. The creature made a squealing sound. The story used the name of another beast of local legend, the Goat Man, but the description is Bigfoot all over.

He goes by many names—Bigfoot or Sasquatch or the Skunk Ape, or the regional favorite Appalachian Ape Man or the affectionate Ol' Red Eyes. Whatever his name, this great hairy beast seems to spend a fair amount of time in the Free State. The woods, rivers, and wilderness areas in Harford, Frederick, Carroll, and Washington counties provide ample coverage for a shy creature to hide, and plenty of hunters and outdoorsmen bring back reports of him. Not surprisingly, news of sightings prompts a few dedicated people to investigate.

A collection of oral histories and research papers in the Maryland Folklore Archive shows some interesting Sasquatch stories. In May 1973, a Baltimore County resident, Tony Dorsey, heard his dog barking at the woods near his home. "I walked into the woods and something came charging at me and stopped," Dorsey said. "There was no sound, just a thumping noise. . . . My flashlight picked up two glowing eyes the size of marbles. It must have been tall because the eyes were about seven feet off the ground." Police made plaster casts of footprints that were thirteen inches long. Ted Roth of the Baltimore Zoo and John Lutz of the Odyssey Scientific Research Association unsuccessfully tried to track the beast with a dog. Over the next four days, trooper Don Higgins handled four more sightings, including one incident in which a door was ripped from its hinges. Some time later the creature was spotted in the swamps around Bird River near Whitemarsh. Richard and Elva Stewart reportedly heard branches breaking as they cleared brush; they caught a whiff of gag-inducing swamp water in the area. They ran for the house, and Mrs. Stewart turned to see "something about eight feet tall with two big red eyes." A few days later the Stewarts found mysterious markings nine feet off the ground on the side of their house. Also in Whitemarsh, someone found a patch of flattened grass that looked like a spot where the creature may have slept, especially since the nearby vegetable gardens had been uprooted.

But these are just a couple of random incidents.

Washington, DC author Mark Opsasnick collected a huge directory of sightings dating back a century and published it as *The Maryland Bigfoot Digest.* And for more than forty years, an environmental scientist and local hero named Bob Chance has been investigating the sites of countless incidents. Bob is a retired science teacher, former mayor of Bel Air, and widely acknowledged as the region's Bigfoot expert. Chance ignited a huge controversy when he presented a thirteen-inch, three-toed cast he had taken in 1978 in Harford County. This flew in the face of Bigfoot orthodoxy, which stated that the creature had five toes. But Chance was not the kind of person to throw away evidence just because it was inconvenient. "I wish my cast had five toes. I really do. But it doesn't," he told *Weird Maryland.* "Perhaps they evolved differently over here to cope with the flood plains. I just don't know."

Of the literally hundreds of incidents that Chance has researched, a few stick in his mind. A chicken farmer at Winter's Run near Bel Air in Harford County found his birds killed and laid in a row. A man watching television nearby on Mountain Road noticed condensation on his picture window and looked around to see a huge apelike creature staring at his television. "Our boy likes watching the soaps!" he said gleefully. "I found tracks leading from the house down to a major streambed."

One of Chance's most reliable sightings occurred at the Peach Bottom power plant, as reported back to the station house by a Matlak truck driver. According to Chance, he said, "Man, you guys raise big men around here," and they said, "What you talking about?" He said, "I just saw this man run across my path from inside my truck. I just saw the top of his head, and it was the same height as my truck mirror." To reach that height, the man would need to be at least seven feet tall, and nobody around town was. The Peach Bottom workers made the connection because they had been hearing loud, piglike squeals from the river for the previous four days. Noises like that are often associated with Bigfoot.

While Chance has never spotted the creature, he did come close to seeing one when he investigated a sighting by a trailer parked near Deer Creek in the late 1970s. He showed us some photographs of the site.

"This is Becky. She lives in a trailer. Now, a lot of people round there can't afford neat and tidy weekly trash pickup. They chuck. And this thing would come by her trailer and forage. She didn't see it clearly, but she heard it every night, picking what it liked from her trash pile. She knew which kind of taters it preferred. I went to see her, and as I drove my truck around out of the valley, I had my lights on, and I heard a tremendous thrashing in the valley below. The following morning was when I got this cast."

Chance shows his three-toed cast with what looks like affection. He obviously loves it, despite the controversy it's caused with the West Coast Bigfoot camp. It's not just because it commemorates his nearest miss with "our boy." You get the impression that he likes it because it doesn't look like a by-the-book Sasquatch foot. With really enthusiastic hunters, things are best when they aren't too tidy and convenient and normal—even normal by Bigfoot hunter standards. The weirder, in fact, the better.

Interview with a Bigfoot Hunter

To get more perspective on the Bigfoot phenomenon, we showed up at the East Coast Bigfoot Convention to meet Bob Chance.

Weird: What got you into the Bigfoot thing in the first place?

Bob Chance: As a young man, a friend and I were trying to get a canoe out from under a waterfall when all these rocks started coming down on us. I became curious. Was it a hermit up there, or a big buck deer, or something else? Well, right around that time, a farmer found these giant footprints in the snow, next to some hog carcasses he had left out. We put it together that both these incidents were because of this Appalachian ape. He was feeding at the hog carcasses and was trying to protect his habitat and his food by intimidating intruders.

Weird: Did you take a cast of that footprint?

Bob Chance: Well, no. I didn't know how to do that in the snow. This three-toed cast I made is from another incident fifteen years later, about '78 or '79.

Weird: Between the first sighting and 1978, were you actively soliciting information about sightings and following up on them?

Bob Chance: Yes, but as a young father and breadwinner, it was a part-time hobby. I went on teaching, and gradually became known as this crazy science teacher that believes that the skunk ape was real.

In 1975, '76, and '77, I was the mayor of my town, and I tried to get a bill passed to protect this thing. Nobody would vote for it until I could prove there was something to protect. So I kept on collecting information for another thirty years.

Weird: You've spent a lot of time with other Bigfoot people examining evidence and theorizing. What can you tell us about this creature and its habits?

Bob Chance: It is a rare, two-legged mammal that's found in pockets of North America, along river valleys. It's always someplace where he can get wet, hide, not leave tracks, have some food, and just keep motoring. There are certain environmental barometers for these creatures. The first of them is the presence of mountain laurel, a second one is springheads, and a third is fish spawning and berry production.

If I'm a Sasquatch, I'm going to work the ridge, know where those back hollows are where I'm not gonna get shot or discovered, and I'm gonna keep moving, ten, fifteen, twenty miles a day, and I'm gonna know where my landfills are.

This boy hits landfills a lot. He's an omnivore. He's traveling through America, eating like a bear, using the full moons, using the new moons, knowing when he'd better lie low. Surely it's got instincts much above us Homo sapiens. He's basically nocturnal. He often smells pretty bad, but the odor is not 100 percent of the time. He only smells when he needs to, like a skunk.

Weird: Your three-toed cast didn't sit well with the West Coast Bigfoot hunters, did it?

Bob Chance: I think there are two subspecies, three-toed and five-toed, and I've gotten a lot of grief for this. Nobody gave the East Coast much credibility twenty years ago, and we still don't have much among some of the old-timers. There was some frontier snobbery. To them this is practically Europe. "Maryland . . . huh! All they have there is crabs and asphalt."

Weird: Do you think that many people have tried to hoax you?

Bob Chance: I don't know . . . as a scientist I'm quite skeptical about some things. When people come to me with a story, I look at their eyes. If they're fidgeting or don't stay with me at the eyes, at the back of my mind I'm thinking, Why are they bothering to tell me these things?

Do they just want their names in the newspaper?

I get scared when people see Sasquatch every couple months . . . even more than twice in a decade. With too many sightings, it just doesn't feel right. Every time there's a new horror movie, there's a new sighting. I hate that.

Weird: There's notoriously little physical evidence of Bigfoot. How much of that evidence is suspect?

Bob Chance: We gotta use any tool we have. I've got hair snagged from a fence he was going over. I've had it come back from testing as bovine, as primate, as "problematic." There's a lot of problematic hair out there. I've got dung. It's got fish scales and fur in it, but it's inconclusive.

I don't think hair is enough. I don't think a really good photograph is enough. But I think the Patterson film is the real deal. I know he was supposed to be connected to the circus industry. But, hey . . . where's the zipper? I couldn't see one.

Weird: You've been at this for forty years. That's a long time. What has kept you involved in this for all that time?

Bob Chance: Everybody wants to be first. The first carcass gets all the marbles. I don't want a carcass. I want a live specimen for temporary capture and then let him go.

I taught high school environmental science for thirty-five years. This thing is not in a textbook yet. It doesn't deserve to be. We're looking to come up with a whole theory and put it in a textbook. We can't do that yet. Then, collectively, we have to make sure this thing doesn't get extinct.

We need to protect it, like the ivory-billed woodpecker or the manatee. This is a piece of us. This may be really a piece of us in that anthropology tree.

Dwayyo! Dwayyo!
(Dwaylight Come and Me Want Go Home)

During the 1920s, people would say that something large, hairy, and bearlike lived in Gambrill State Park in Frederick County. And for reasons now lost to time, the name they gave it sounded like Elmer Fudd singing a Harry Belafonte tune: Dwayyo. The Dwayyo maintained a fairly high profile before the Depression set in, then disappeared for forty years. In the mid-1960s, he came back and enjoyed a brief stint in the limelight once more.

A report from November 27, 1965, describes a growling creature with long black hair and a bushy tail. It rose from all fours to attack the witness in his backyard, as he attempted to keep the beast from his wife and children. When the witness described the event to reporters later, he used an alias, John Becker. He was wise to protect his anonymity. The reporters had a lot of fun with the story.

Frederick News Post reporter George May wrote a series of articles, quoting University of Maryland students' claims that they had traced the creature's origins to the upper Amazon River and the Yangtze River plateau (a little bit of a stretch), and reported that they had seen several on campus late one night, and found them friendly and fun loving (an obvious joke).

But more credible reports came in. Several hunters saw a strange black beast roaming the woods, and a Jefferson woman said that she saw a dog-shaped animal, about the size of a calf, chasing some cows on a farm near her home. New sightings faded away by the end of the year, and none have been reported since. Perhaps the whole thing was a hoax, or perhaps the Dwayyo was a migratory creature that moved on. Perhaps it was offended by the jokes. But if it is migratory, it's been forty years since it was last sighted. It's about due for another appearance. So watch the woods, and let us know if it shows up.

Local Heroes and Villains

Even though they were a California band, the Doors described some of Maryland's residents pretty well when they released their single "People Are Strange." People really ARE strange in the Free State, and not always in a pleasant way.

Every town has its characters—some beloved and some hated—who go about their business quietly. If they attract attention, so be it, but that's not their goal. They just do their own thing, seldom if ever making headlines. It's these quiet, unusual people we celebrate in this chapter, though in some cases, the celebration takes the form of a chilling reminder of what happens when people turn bad.

Fortunately, for every villain, there's a corresponding hero. No surprise here, but many people know their hometown heroes better than they know their local politicians—and they also like what they do a lot more.

The Evil Trade of Patty Cannon

Marylanders ply many trades, not all of them entirely honorable, but none of them quite match Patty Cannon's for sheer hatefulness. Her offenses against the law and common decency were so notorious during her lifetime that her skull was preserved after her death so that her infamous acts would not be forgotten by future generations. The story opens at the beginning of the nineteenth century, when the Delmarva Peninsula was alive with tales of a kidnapping ring being run out of Johnson's Corner, now known as Reliance, on the borders of Caroline County, Dorchester County, and the state of Delaware. A large and powerful widow woman, Patty Cannon, along with her son-in-law, operated various taverns and boarding houses in the area. The two were widely suspected of all kinds of crimes, most heinous being the kidnapping of free black people and slaves. For decades, there was no evidence to support the rumors, but the tales were horrendous—including holding kidnap victims in the basements or attics of her boarding houses, and ill-treating them to the point that some of them died. The survivors would be sneaked out in groups under cover of night, transported to ports on the Virginia tip of the Delmarva Peninsula, and sold to plantation owners in the Deep South.

Patty Cannon, the wily old woman in charge, knew how to make the system of jurisdiction work for her. Whenever things got too hot in one of her houses, she'd move her base of operations across the border to another. That was how she evaded detection for decades, though everybody around knew she was up to no good.

Nobody's entirely sure where Patty came from; rumor has it she emigrated from Canada at the turn of the century after tricking a Maryland man into marrying her. When they opened a tavern, Patty immediately started in on her life of crime. She would bilk their clients, threatening or even beating them if they challenged her. She was supposedly so powerful that she could throw a grown man to the ground by his hair. When her husband died, leaving her with a daughter to bring up, Patty had no trouble

PATTY CANNON'S HOUSE
AT JOHNSON'S CROSS ROADS WHERE
THE NOTED KIDNAPPING GROUP HAD
HEADQUARTERS AS DESCRIBED IN
GEORGE ALFRED TOWNSEND'S NOVEL
"THE ENTAILED HAT". THE HOUSE
BORDERS ON CAROLINE AND DOR-
CHESTER COUNTIES AND THE STATE
OF DELAWARE.
STATE ROADS COMMISSION

It was said that old Patty Cannon corrupted Jake Purnell, who cut his throat at Snow Hill five years ago. He was a free Negro who engaged slaves to steal other slaves and bring them to him, and he delivered them up to the white kidnappers for money. . . . They marched and surrounded Purnell's hut, and he was discovered burrowed beneath it. They brought the dogs, and fire to drive him out, and as he came out he cut his throat with desperate slashes from ear to ear.

This sordid kidnapping business went on until the late 1820s, when a farmer unearthed human remains near Patty's tavern. This physical evidence was enough to get her arrested, and in 1829, she was taken into custody and moved to courts in nearby Delaware. Like the character in Townsend's novel, she wasn't going to be taken alive. After taking poison that she had smuggled into the prison under her skirts, she died in her cell.

There's a historical marker near the site of Johnson's Corner, her son-in-law's tavern, but it incorrectly labels the place as PATTY CANNON'S HOUSE. In fact, this building was erected after Cannon's death. But one gruesome reminder of Cannon's crimes remains: her skull. It was unearthed from the courthouse graveyard in Dover, Delaware, and eventually given as a gift to the Dover public library. It now rests in a back room in a bright red hatbox, but you can ask to see it.

raising money. Thanks to her fleecing of boarding house customers, she and her daughter fared quite well. Her tavern became a recruiting ground for thugs, who would do her bidding for a fee. The business she ran was an ugly one that involved agents of all kinds who had only one instruction: Bring in live bodies, and don't leave any evidence. Decades later, when the story was woven into a work of fiction called *The Entailed Hat*, by George Townsend, some details emerged that were especially sickening:

The World's Greatest Curiosity

On a hot summer night some years ago during a violent thunderstorm, in the second-floor bedroom of a red-brick row house, there would occur an event that would shock the neighborhood. . . . From the unpublished autobiography of Johnny Eck

Johnny Eck was the epitome of a local hero. He traveled extensively during his early career but returned to the house he was born in, and would hang out on the steps, spinning yarns about his travels, entertaining local kids with puppet shows and generally creating a friendly neighborhood atmosphere in the place he called home. Before he died in the 1990s, he and his brother operated a number of entertainment businesses, including a penny arcade and a fairground train ride. Yep, by any standards, Johnny Eck was a big presence in Baltimore. He was also less than two feet tall and appeared to be missing the entire lower half of his body.

Johnny Eck was born John Eckhardt in August 1911, the youngest child in a blue-collar Baltimore family. He was born only a few minutes after his twin brother, Robert, and according to one of Johnny's classic yarns, the midwife screamed when she saw his grossly undeveloped legs, declaring that he was "a broken doll," and promptly fainted. Despite this inauspicious beginning, Johnny grew up happy and secure in a supportive family where his lack of legs was taken as a matter of course. His twin brother, elder sister Caroline, and down-to-earth parents provided such a stable home life that Johnny was remarkably at ease with himself. He would later say, "It was as if God himself had chose this family to be born in." He learned to read and paint early in life and was something of a celebrity at school, where his fellow pupils would fight over the privilege of carrying him up the stairs.

By the time Johnny was twelve, his celebrity extended beyond the schoolyard. At a church magic show for poor and disabled children, he impressed a conjurer called John McAslan when he walked up to the stage (on his hands) answering the call for a volunteer. In time, McAslan became the lad's manager, touring him under the banner the Half Boy and the World's Greatest Living Curiosity, along with his twin brother. This was not just a freak show, though. Johnny was a remarkably handsome lad and, dressed in the top half of a tux, performed a skilled stage magic act on a tasseled stool. Photographs from the time show someone who really seemed to be enjoying himself.

When Johnny was in his late teens, he was performing in Canada when a talent scout asked if he wanted to be in the movies. So before he turned twenty-one, he had a speaking role in *Dracula*. Johnny's next movie, *Freaks* (1932), was set in a sideshow and starred two midgets, a man with no limbs, several pinheads, a pair of conjoined twins . . . and Johnny. The plot centered around a gold-digging trapeze artist who marries a midget for his money and then tries to poison him. The freaks in the sideshow learn of her evil plans and exact revenge upon her. Johnny has only a few lines, but he stands out in the film as just about the only person who really seemed to be having fun. He can barely suppress a grin, and in his tux and bowtie, he cuts a dashing and agile figure as he dashes up some steps to chat face-to-face with one of the main characters. It's no exaggeration to say that he's one of the most attractive people in the whole movie. He appeared in a few Tarzan movies in the 1930s, heavily costumed as a giant bird creature, and spent a lot of time in traveling shows with his brother. Taking advantage of the twins' similarity (at least from the waist up), a showman named

Director Tod Browning poses with cast members from his film "Freaks"

Rajah Raboid cast them in his variety show, *Miracles of 1937*. In a memorable lowbrow comedy sketch that's still discussed by stage magicians today, Robert Eck challenged Raboid from the audience during a performance of the classic "saw a lady in half" trick. The magician called Robert onto the stage and pushed him into a large box, which he proceeded to saw in half. Of course, Robert switched places with Johnny and a dwarf engulfed in a large pair of pants. After sawing the box in half, Raboid opened it, and Johnny chased his "lower half" around the stage.

Unfortunately for the Eckhardt twins, popular taste moved away from sideshows, so they moved back to their Baltimore row house permanently. Despite his stint in the spotlight, Johnny remained unaffected, possibly because he never made much money from his unscrupulous promoters. Still, the brothers had enough to buy a penny arcade and, for Johnny, a specially converted car and a miniature steam train he drove as a fairground ride. Johnny turned his talent in art to a sideline in screen painting, a peculiarly Baltimorean art form of painting landscapes on window screens.

Times were up and down for the brothers, though. A new business tax made their arcade too expensive to run, and rowdy fairground teenagers forced them to put the train ride into storage. They lacked the money to move out when their neighborhood began to decline, and the brothers increasingly barred the doors to some of their less savory neighbors. By the mid-1980s, although Johnny kept busy and socially active, the friendly chats on the doorstep became less frequent. When *Freaks* was released on video and people found out that Johnny was still alive, he would get a stream of gawking visitors. He was generally courteous, but found that these fanatics wasted most of his time with inane banter or rude questioning.

Things came to a head in 1987 when two burglars broke into the twins' house in the middle of the night and assaulted them during a two-hour burglary. Although they made away with only a little money, the experience affected the seventy-six-year-old Johnny very badly. For the remaining four years of his life, he was reclusive, seeing only a few old friends and staying behind locked doors. He died in his sleep on January 5, 1991, and four years later his brother joined him in the family plot in Green Mount Cemetery.

Johnny Eck still has fans and may even be the subject of a movie himself. After appearing in *Gangs of New York*, Leonardo DiCaprio signed on to act as both of the Eckhardt twins in a movie about Johnny. Several big-name financiers backed the film, but it is currently stalled in production.

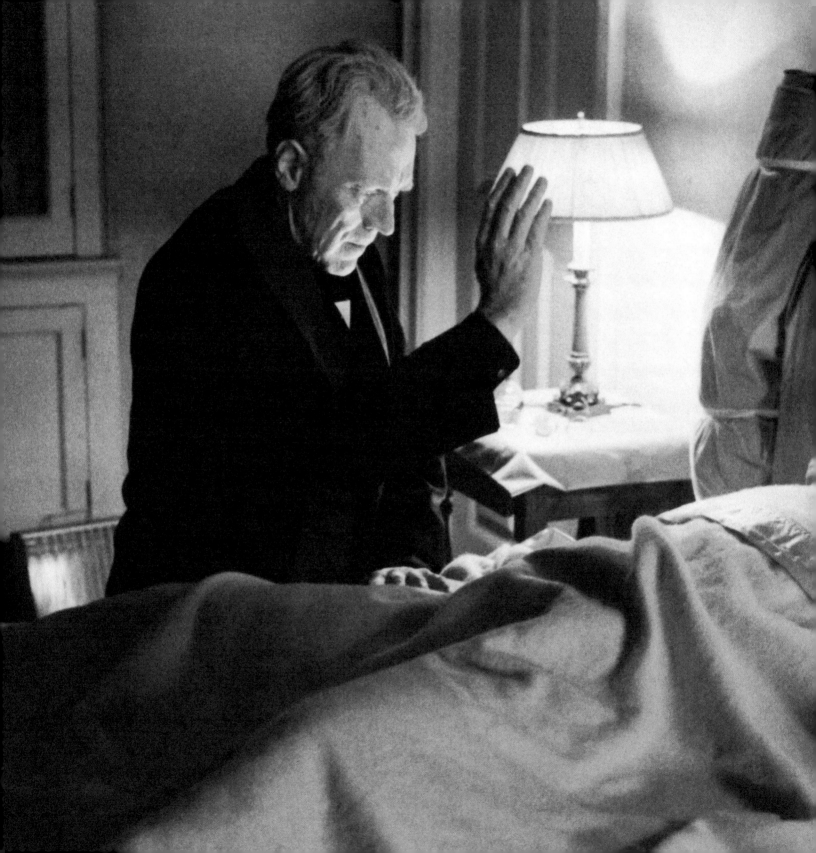

The Haunted Boy

Something beyond comprehension is happening to a little girl on this street, in this house. A man has been called for as a last resort to try and save her. That man is The Exorcist. – Tagline for The Exorcist, *1973*

Anyone who was around in 1973 remembers the phenomenal popularity of the movie *The Exorcist,* based on William Peter Blatty's novel. The film had people lining up along entire city blocks. Until *Star Wars* came along, it was the most sensational movie of the 1970s—and in some respects, was even more sensational. People were literally sickened by it. Many hated it with a passion. Some were deeply disturbed by it. Others were appalled by the film's language and debased imagery. But the one thing that sticks in most people's minds was that it was based on a true story. And that story happened not to a teenage girl in Washington, DC, as Blatty's story had it, but to a boy in one of Maryland's suburbs.

When Blatty wrote a second *Exorcist* book to cash in on the huge popularity of his novel and movie, he revealed a few details that had inspired the tale. In his 1974 book, *William Peter Blatty: On The Exorcist from Novel to Film,* he wrote that as a student at Georgetown University in 1949 he had read a series of stories in the *Washington Post* about a boy who was released from some strange forces by multiple rites of exorcism. Blatty reveals that during his research for the novel he had written to the exorcist involved and seen excerpts from his diary. A heavily edited version of their correspondence appears in the book. The actual events are overshadowed by the impact of the film and when you winnow out the details of the true story, there's very little to go on and even fewer leads for independent researchers to follow up. If you read the countless articles, documentaries, and books that cashed in on the *Exorcist* sensation, you can almost feel the gusts of wind as fantasy rushes in to fill the void left by the absence of facts.

Going back to contemporary sources, we found several newspaper reports from the month of August 1949. Three different Washington, DC, newspapers reported that a local teenage boy was "haunted" and in the care of medical and religious experts hoping to rid him of his affliction. Since the early days of that year, the boy had heard weird scratching noises in his home's walls and his bed would shake violently. Solid objects would jump to the floor in his presence. The minister first called in a doctor, who prescribed tranquilizers for the whole family. The medication didn't work, and the family went through more than two dozen rites of exorcism in three different denominations (Episcopal, Lutheran, and Roman Catholic) before the cure "took."

But the reports were full of contradiction. Some said the boy lived in Mount Rainier, others that he was from Brentwood. His age was given as thirteen or fourteen. As bits of the story were published in magazines and journals in the years that followed, he was variously referred to as Roland, Robbie, and Douglas, with a confusion of last names to muddy the waters. Even references to the eyewitness accounts were surprisingly varied. In one article in *Fate* magazine in 1975, the exorcists in the case revealed some telling details to the writer Steve Erdmann. When the boy's aunt died in January 1949, he used a Ouija board to try to contact her. In the month following the aunt's death, weird nighttime scratching noises followed the boy around, no matter where he slept. The bed or chair he slept on would jerk around. And rashes and scratches that looked like brandings appeared on his body (though the only witness to these was the boy's mother). By March, he had been

visited by many priests, some of whom he had attacked; he stabbed one in the arm and kicked another in the groin.

But details were still tantalizingly scarce. Who was this boy? Where did he live? And where did all the excitement take place? By the 1980s, youths in Mount Rainier had established that the site was a vacant lot at the corner of Bunker Hill Road and Thirty-third Street where an old "Addams Family" house had once stood. It had burned down twenty years earlier, but their parents remembered the creepy building and the reclusive old woman who had lived there. The fact that the house had gone up in flames, leaving a vacant lot, made the story all the more exciting—that's why numerous documentaries and articles have described it as the site of the *Exorcist* story. Too bad it was the wrong house in the wrong town.

People would probably be content to accept the *Exorcist* story as written and the lot in Mount Rainier as the location if it weren't for the journalism of Mark Opsasnick. He investigated the tale for *Strange Magazine* and in the process debunked many of the myths surrounding the story. In fact, he managed to track down the home of the boy, the boy himself, and a school friend of his.

The events Opsasnick uncovered took place not in Mount Rainier, but a mile outside DC's northeastern border, near the town hall in Cottage City, Prince Georges County. The family involved (whom Opsasnick sensitively refused to name) moved into a one-and-a-half-story house there in 1939, the year their son turned three.

The article (which is in issue 20 of *Strange Magazine*) includes not only interviews with many members of the church involved with the rites of exorcism but also information from the people who personally knew the boy when he was growing up and an interview with the boy himself, by then a man in his sixties.

According to the boy's school friend, there was some talk of him becoming "sick" as he entered his teens. He had already established himself as a somewhat mean-spirited mischief maker, with a skill for precision spitting. The boy grew up prone to tantrums and outbursts of aggression, personality elements that were later used to support the theory that he was possessed. He would cheerfully sic his dog, an aggressive stray he cared for, on people because he thought it was funny, and even his friends were not safe from this behavior. The family was dominated by an "obsessively religious mother and grandmother" who mixed Lutheran religion with the use of Ouija boards and spiritualism.

The combination of these two elements—a somewhat sociopathic youth in a family obsessed with fringe spiritual practices—shows a possible psychological explanation for what happened later. Though the priests with whom Opsasnick spoke were convinced of a demonic element, the things they actually witnessed—rather than heard about from the boy's mother—could be explained away as the reactions of a disturbed boy pressured by people who were supposed to care for him. The swearing, spitting, and attacks seem like the behavior of a trapped animal, but are not unnatural for an aggressive adolescent whose mother and priests kept cornering him and talking about the devil. The more bizarre elements of the *Exorcist* story—levitation, unnatural cold, 180-degree head turns, and projectile vomiting—are not from this boy's real-life story, but elements added in the movie.

Opsasnick's final phone interview with the subject is a bit of an anticlimax. He confirmed that he grew up in Cottage City, but refused to confirm anything else, especially whether he was the subject of the *Exorcist* stories. Opsasnick wrote that he seemed to be "someone who did not want to be reminded of some distant embarrassing events from his past." This is hardly surprising, given that Opsasnick's interviews confirmed he had "serious emotional problems stemming from his home life."

So perhaps it's time now to stop haunting the haunted boy with his embarrassing past, to enjoy *The Exorcist* as a work of fiction, and to celebrate the real hero of the story, Mark Opsasnick, for refusing to let sensational claims to truth stand in for good reporting.

God Is My Copilot

Anyone who's seen the movie *The Exorcist* knows that it's supposedly based on a true story. What's less well known is that the true story is about a boy from a blue-collar town in Prince Georges County. I got the street address from two of Mark Opsasnick's books, plugged it into my Copilot navigation system, and set out to find the place. Ultimately, the Copilot GPS did lead me to it, but not before taking me on a strange journey. I reached my destination in a much different mood than I had anticipated.

About five miles from the Exorcist House, I drove over the top of a hill, expecting two more miles of road before my next turn, and suddenly came to a dead-end. The only turn was into a parking lot. The road looked nothing like the road on the GPS screen. This wasn't any cause for alarm: I know that tall buildings, trees, and tunnels sometimes interrupt the satellite signal, and the software can get tricked into thinking you're one street over. So I turned around in the parking lot, took a couple of deliberate wrong turns, and waited for the software to recalculate my route. I ended up in the same lot.

It was at this point that the radio started playing the old B52's song "Devil in My Car." Now, I'm not a superstitious soul, but this sudden theme song for my travels seemed a bit more than coincidental. Was my car possessed? There were no visible signs anywhere—no cloven hoof marks on my clutch, no phantom reflections in the rearview mirror, no children with rotating heads in the passenger seat. No, I was just being silly. So I looked out the window, looking for any landmarks I could use to figure out where I was. The only sign I could see was on the building next to the parking lot. It was the Pastoral Center of the Archdiocese of Washington. It was at that point that I realized what was going on. My Copilot was looking out for the welfare of my soul.—*MJL*

Santa's Devilish Little Helper, the Anti-Claus

There is no greater hero in a child's mind than that jolly old man who comes down the chimney on the night before Christmas. But to a broad swath of Maryland residents, as well as a smattering of communities through Pennsylvania and Indiana, there's another winter visitor who's probably not quite as high on the childhood "nice" list. On the night before the Feast of Saint Nicholas (on December 5), many Maryland residents of German descent warn their children of the impending visit of the Belznickel or Belschnickel. And he isn't usually carrying a sackful of goodies.

The Belznickel is basically the Mr. Hyde to Santa's Dr. Jekyll. Clad from head to toe in fur and rags and wearing a hideous mask, he's not interested in rewarding the good kids. He's all about punishing the bad ones. To this end, he carries a chain that he rattles outside the door on the eve of Saint Nicholas, ready to tie up transgressors. He tucks a switch or whip made of birch branches into his belt ready to whack them. He may have a treat or two about his person, but more often than not it's to lull his victims into a false sense of security.

This may seem a bit harsh for holiday fare, but in the days before Xbox, it may have taken a little more than the promise of a few small treats to get your children in line for the holidays.

There's nothing like the threat of punishment to propel borderline naughty kids onto the "nice" list.

In fact, the Belznickel is only one remnant of a whole cast of nasty characters associated with the run-up to Christmas in older European traditions. The Netherlands has a malicious clown in motley clothing called Black Peter. Various other regions in Germany and Austria celebrate a threatening Santa sidekick called the Krampus, a hideous devil with a lolling tongue of Gene Simmons proportions. Compared to him, the Belznickel is positively benign.

The Free State's Belznickel buffs are tucked away in the traditional German communities in St. Marys County and the Delmarva Peninsula and a few other towns. The old man in furs is particularly hard to track down these days, because he makes few public appearances. Over the past few years, he has been seen only a couple of times at alternative Christmas events in areas with a strong German heritage. One recent example was at the Riverdale House Museum at Fort Washington, where the creepy character was sugarcoated a little for children under the age of ten. But such appearances are rare: He's not exactly a character people want to be photographed with at the mall.

Up until the 1960s and

1970s, Belznickeling was a bit more common. The folks to whom we spoke celebrated the day as a family affair. In his heyday, Belznickel often made his appearance at small house parties, usually shortly after an uncle went outside "to take care of the horses." A motley masked figure would rattle the windows with the butt of his whip and clank his chains to alert the people inside of his presence. He'd come in and either mock-threaten the youngsters or make them recite their catechism or some other lesson they had learned. If they succeeded, they would sometimes get a treat. But mostly, they were sternly warned to keep in line for the visit from the real gift giver three weeks down the line. In cultures untouched by Clement C. Moore's *The Night Before Christmas,* that figure was not a jolly old elf, but the *Kristkindel,* or Christ-Child, who came on Christmas Eve. (Over the centuries, even the German *Kristkindel* was subsumed into the Santa tradition, as his name became slurred into Kris Kringle.)

So next Saint Nicholas Eve, if you hear chains and whips rattling at your windows, batten down the hatches and don't open the door. It's either the Belznickel or some other deviant character you wouldn't want in your house.

Horrible Hermits and Heroes

Tales of crazies who live by themselves on the outskirts of town are a staple scare story in any community. Sometimes they are handy tales that parents tell to keep children from wandering off by themselves. Other times older children use them to frighten younger ones just for the sake of frightening them. Hermit tales are versatile scary stories—after all, a hermit could be sneaking around anywhere and at anytime, with only a slight rustle to give away his location. Some hermit stories evolve into full-on folklore, such as the Goat Man tales, but there are plenty of others floating around the state, and there have been for years.

Not all hermit tales are scary, however. Some strange recluses are secret heroes who brighten up the world with bizarre art and, in some cases, huge wads of money. Who knows which of these tales is true? Not us, but that won't stop us from retelling them.

Hannibal Hermit of Oxon Hill

As a kid growing up in Oxon Hill, my dad heard about an old hermit who lived in a junkyard, surrounded by old rusting cars. He lived in a Buick sedan in the middle of the lot, they said, fenced off with chain link and barbed wire, with huge NO TRESPASSING signs. Everyone was terrified of this old man because of the tales they heard about him. The teenagers would tell their little brothers and sisters scary tales about that old hermit, saying he killed children and left their hides out to dry on lines in the junkyard. If anything was flapping on the lines there, I bet it was his long underwear, but the little guys were convinced it was dry skins. And in a pre-"Silence of the Lambs" scenario, they also said that the hermit would keep all the "good bits" to eat.–*Frank*

Chillum's Drain Man

My father used to tell us about the Drain Man, who was supposed to live in the old storm drain that emptied into the Sligo Creek in the woods near Chillum. That creek used to flood terribly, and Dad said that when the water got too high, the Drain Man would move out for a while and live in a tree house in the woods. He was supposed to come out in the evening to catch rats to eat, and if any kids happened to be out playing by the creek, this mean old swine might kidnap and molest them. I assumed that molesting meant to beat them up, so I never went down there in the late afternoon. I know some other kids who never went down there at all. Thinking back on it now, I wonder if Dad used to tell us those stories to keep us from getting our shoes muddy or perhaps from some real danger of drowning in the floodwater. Too bad he's not around now for me to ask him.–*JLH*

Noah of Takoma Park

Back in the sixties, there was an old boat down by the school in Takoma Park. It was a weird thing propped up on dry land, with a crazy old man living in it. All the kids in the school said he used to have a big old shotgun to keep people away. He apparently believed that there was another Biblical flood on the way, and he was planning to be ready for it. Too bad he didn't read his Bible, because at the end of the flood story, God said he wasn't going to do that again. Anyway, the thing apparently went up in flames decades ago.–*Anonymous*

Annapolis's Trashbag Stuffed with Money

We have a guy around these parts alternately known as Trashbag Willie, Slap Happy Jack, and a few other names. He is the definition of an eccentric. He has the look of a homeless fellow: shabby clothes, massively dreadlocked hair (most likely due to not washing), and trash bags for socks.

He wanders around the downtown Annapolis area waving a trash bag and occasionally picking up trash along the way. But the honest truth is the guy's a multimillionaire. I have asked several area residents and all will tell you he's a very wealthy area man who has donated $2 million annually to the United Negro College Fund and other impressive amounts to local charities. His current condition is the result of getting hit by a car, leaving him deaf, disoriented (which gives him a bizarre walking style; imagine a marionette and you have an idea), etc. The guy's house is still around; it's a mansion, pure and simple.–*Adam Naworal*

Baltimore's Tin Can Man

There is a homeless artist in Baltimore who goes through the trash in the city and collects all the tin cans. We called him Tin Can Man. Once a year, very late at night, he lines Charles Street with tin can dolls. It's a very long street. It's neat to see in the morning.–*Jessica Myles*

A Fine-Feathered Friend

Takoma Park's local hero has a lot to crow about. During the 1990s, he had no problem scratching out a living for himself in town. Many of the townsfolk would give him a smile and a meal, especially his two main benefactors, Alan Daugharty and Alma Keating. And he was so beloved by many around town that when he passed away, they raised a life-sized statue to him right in the center of town. Not a bad deal for a stray rooster who wandered into town in the 1980s and lived there for ten years.

According to the plaque beneath Roscoe the Rooster's statue in the town square on Carroll Avenue, THE BURLY BANTAM MADE US SMILE AND BRIGHTENED OUR DAYS. He is still remembered with offerings of eggs in April.

Not much is really known about Roscoe's personal life. Rumor has it that he may have had a few chicks on the side, but that rumor has never been substantiated. Although Takoma Park is far from a barnyard, Roscoe never had a problem finding food. One look at pictures of the formidable bird is evidence his meals were not just chicken feed.

However, Roscoe's life was not without strife. He was prone to bouts of depression, and had just come out of one

of his bleak times in 1999 when he had a hit-and-run encounter with an SUV that ended his life. But not everyone believes his death was accidental. During his decade in the Washington suburb, he was not well beloved by everybody. Roosters can be a noise nuisance, and although Takoma Park is a pretty tolerant place, crowing birds can stretch the limits of tolerance. In fact, the police were called in at least twice.

One of the obvious suspects, Colonel Sanders, had an alibi for his whereabouts at the time of the accident (he'd been dead for nineteen years). But the founder of KFC is not the only person known to have it in for barnyard birds. The remains of several of Roscoe's kin have been found in the local farmers' market. Unfortunately, their deaths could not be tied to the suspect SUV. We're still waiting for evidence that will bring Roscoe's killer to justice. We hope he will fry for what he's done. As things stand now, the investigators have had to just wing it.

Today, a brass statue of Roscoe stands near the crossroads of that fatal accident. The question that remains and perhaps no one will ever really know . . . why did the chicken cross the road? –*Shara Walker*

Better the De Vol You Know

You would be hard pressed to find an adult in the Baltimore metropolitan area who does not recognize the name of Count Gore de Vol. This colorful and witty entertainer hosted a television show that aired in Maryland, DC, and Virginia in the 70s and 80s, with his uniquely distinguishable vampire garb. His show, entitled *Creature Feature*, awakened an interest in horror and campy humor in thousands of late-night TV watchers. The man who made it all happen was the Count's alter ego, Dick Dyszel. After over thirty years, he is still going strong, appearing in character at Baltimore's annual Balticon and Horrorfind conventions, and other science fiction and horror conventions around the nation. Despite the passage of time, flocks of fans continue to swarm around him, with looks in their eyes that are nothing short of adoration.

Dyszel came to this area in 1972 after two years hosting a horror show in WDXR in Paducah, Kentucky. In his first gigs at WDCA in 1972, he performed on children's shows as Bozo and Captain 20, but after six months he was able to convince the station that Count Gore would be a better outlet for his talents. So he began work as a horror host on the afternoon *Saturday Chiller* broadcast and *Creature Feature* on Saturday night. Soon, though, the two shows drained the blood of the vampire host, and he kept the nighttime *Creature Feature* broadcast, putting the afternoon *Chiller* show on ice.

His judgment was directly on target. By the mid-70s, the Creature Feature Fan Club had well over 10,000 members. In 1975, it boasted higher ratings in the area than *Saturday Night Live*. In fact, it was nominated for three Emmys, and became the longest running horror showcase in local television history. *Creature Feature* was successful not just because it showed horror films,

both classic and campy, but because Dyszel's own particular charm, inventive technique, and presentation put the shine to the diamond in the rough.

The show was cutting-edge in so many ways— Dyszel's *Creature Feature* was the first show to broadcast the entire, uncut version of *Night of the Living Dead* on television. On May 25, 1985, it was the first show in the area to be broadcast in stereo. It ran weekly from 1973 to 1980, took a hiatus between 1981 and 1983 when it ran once a year, then played weekly again from 1984 through 1987. When the show finally stopped broadcasting, many of us mourned what we thought would be the loss of a part of what made television so special. We were wrong.

The end to the television broadcast was not an end to Gore de Vol's pioneering career as a horror host. On July 11, 1998, Dyszel brought the Count back from the dead and turned him into the first horror host on the World Wide Web, where his site www.countgore.com repeatedly wins awards for its style, content, and presentation.

But where did the Count's trademark name come from? Even Dyszel himself seems to be uncertain. "The name Gore de Vol has had two origins attributed to it," he told us. "One story says it was a takeoff on the writer Gore Vidal (who I understand was not pleased with the character). The other story mentions that I passed the De Vol Funeral Home every day on my way to work."

So which one is the real origin, then?

"Maybe it was a bit of both."

Whatever the real story is, the name Count Gore de Vol is a part of the history of Maryland and will remain in the hearts of all the adoring fans who remember moving rabbit ear antennas late at night to get a clear picture of the Count working his magic on UHF Channel 20. He never failed to please back in those days, a fact that continues to this day.—*Donna Mucha*

Personalized Properties and Visionary Environments

Some people make their houses stand out from the others on the block with a spiffy coat of paint or some natty siding. Maybe they put in some interesting trees and manicure their lawns a little better than everybody else. To most folks, that's all that is necessary to make a house a home. But that's not what our kind of people do.

We celebrate a different kind of personalization project. The kind that involves covering a house with tons of foam insulation, or building a wooden wigwam as an extension, or covering the ceiling with Renaissance frescoes. We celebrate people who literally make their homes into a castle, and who fill their garages with cars covered in dolls' limbs and bicycles in the shape of giant poodles. And we suggest you give these folks a warm reception too, because you can find them all around these parts.

The House of Curves

In the energy crisis of the mid-1970s, many people retrofitted their houses with new high-grade insulation materials to cut down on heating and cooling costs. It was the smart thing to do. But most people put this insulation into their wall cavities and attics. Not so Eddie Garfinkle and his wife. When they decided to fix up their 1922 farmhouse, they put the insulation on the outside and sculpted it into a swooping pattern that changed the shape of the house completely. The only right angles on the building are at the doors and windows. In fact, except for the floors, there are practically no straight lines anywhere in the building, inside or out—just an organic set of curves.

The building would not look out of place in the *Planet of the Apes* movies of the 1960s and '70s, but it's definitely an oddity in a Maryland suburb of Washington, DC. Despite its strange appearance, Mr. Garfinkle insists that improving the house this way was a practical decision. "Our heating and cooling bills are much lower than our friends' with much smaller houses," he told *Weird Maryland.* "It's like living in a big thermos bottle."

The secret to the building's look and heat insulation is a spray-on polyurethane foam called polystucco. As most home improvers know, the compound sticks to surfaces and then expands to fill structural cavities. But it takes a really creative mind to see its architectural possibilities. The Garfinkles were riding the wave of the arts and crafts movement of the late '60s and '70s. Eddie is a sculptor, and his wife is an interior designer, and at the time, they were operating a craft supply store. They were exposed to lots of cutting-edge design in all disciplines of art, so it was only natural that they should examine some other possibilities. "We were looking for something economical and out of the ordinary," said Mr. Garfinkle. "We didn't want to live in a traditional box."

So they hired an architect for their home improvement project, and fell in love with the idea of polystucco as a primary feature in the process. The result was a three-year building project that ended up like nothing else in their neighborhood (or any other neighborhood for that matter).

"Our neighbors, well, some of them loved it, some hated it. There was a relationship between distance and appreciation. The ones closer to our house were not too crazy about it. But over the years, people would walk by . . . a number of them told us, 'You know, when you built this, I hated it. Now I love it.'"

So what makes someone push a home improvement project into overdrive? In Eddie Garfinkle's case, the answer is simple.

"In one word, what inspired us was youth. You do a lot of things in your youth that you don't do later on. It was enthusiasm. It was the '70s. Believe it or not, it was never an issue in our minds that this was out of place in the neighborhood."

Well, it may not look like other buildings, but we wouldn't say that this building is out of place anywhere. Economical, eye-catching, and weird in the best sense of the word, the Garfinkles' house of curves fits perfectly in *Weird Maryland.*

Recycled House on the Boardwalk

Ocean Gallery is the most wild, crazy and unique shop on the Ocean City boardwalk. The outside walls are a conglomeration of parts from sixty-eight other buildings from around the world. With its jumble of signs, reflectors, fences, pipes, and even a coffee mug nailed securely to the walls, the building resembles some kind of Dali-influenced nightmare.

Inside are three floors crammed with over forty thousand posters, prints, and paintings which the owner, Joe, and his staff change around every six hours. Take a walk up the circular staircase and you will see that any open space has been filled with mementoes from visits from some famous and not so famous people. Reclaimed treasures, including a wonderful crystal chandelier, add to the general "where do I look next?" feeling you get there.

But Ocean Gallery's real treasure is Joe himself. The former art and science teacher is well known for his stunts like riding a bicycle off the roof of the building, for his crazy commercials where he dresses like Batman, and for wearing his trademark tuxedo and red bow tie while escorting bikini-clad models around the shop. Besides all that, there are also Joe's cars! Since eventually it's possible to run out of room to add stuff to the building, Joe and his son Joey have expanded to adding stuff like rocket launchers, flags, flowers, old parts, or anything you can imagine, to cars.

But although he sells the work of more than sixteen hundred artists, including his own photography, being a promotional showman is really just one side of this lovely man. His goal is to make each and every boardwalk visitor smile. If fine art alone doesn't do the trick, the building, the cars, or the man himself will.–*Shara Walker*

Drinks Are on the House

Think twice before you toss away that beer or soda can if you live in Silver Spring. You might just want to save it for Richard Van Os Keuls, a local homeowner and retired architect who is giving new meaning to the term "aluminum siding."

Since 1995, Van Os Keuls has been collecting and crushing aluminum cans. What does he do with them? Well, he sides the rear addition to his house, of course! Van Os Keuls seeks out the most colorful and interesting cans—he even recruits friends to bring them back from the far corners of the world—to arrange in a fishscale-esque pattern on the outside walls of his home. He got the idea looking at a can that had just been flattened by a truck—naturally, he thought, what a great aluminum shingle THAT would make.

When he began adding on to his ranch home, he put this idea into action, beginning primarily with Diet Coke cans, since that was what he had been drinking. Unsatisfied with the uniformity of the red-and-silver pattern, he began to branch out into beer, juice, ginger ale, club soda, Yoo-hoo, cream soda, and other cans, buying them even if he didn't plan on drinking the beverages. The cans are washed, crumpled, hammered at the edges to smooth sharp patches, and affixed with nails. He estimated it will take about twenty-two thousand cans to cover his house.

The only opposition to Van Os Keuls's project thus far has been from the local authorities, who took issue when he began taking cans from area recycling bins. He was fined and told not to do it again, despite the terrific transformative use for the cans. Most people don't object, however, to the sparkly shingles, and the house was even featured recently on HGTV.

Van Os Keuls's suggestion that cans would make affordable siding for low-cost homes might suffer under the weight of impracticality, considering how long it has taken him to shingle his single home. For now, he'll have to be content that his can house is a sheer work of weird Maryland originality, albeit a recycled one.

Raters of the Last Ark

Frostburg is known for, well, just about nothing, really. Interstate 68 bisects the town at its midpoint, and cars speeding along it generally leave only a whooshing noise as proof of their passing. But there is something of interest lurking just north of the roadway. I am referring to an ark. God's Ark of Safety to be exact. And if you crack jokes about it, buster, you may very well find yourself odd-man-out at boarding time!

The story goes that in 1974, Pastor Richard Greene had a series of visions. He believes that in these God was telling him to build a replica of Noah's Ark as a sign to people. He managed to convince others and the project gained momentum. On April 18, 1976, work commenced and reports say that his faithful flock has never looked back. So what have they built for themselves? Well, a pessimist might say a close replica of an erector set on steroids. But to hear the faithful tell it, we are all currently witnessing a ringer for Noah's Ark itself; albeit only a third of the way finished. Even in its work-in-progress state, however, it is impressive. Consider: When completed, the Ark will be 450' long, 75' wide, and 45' high—the precise dimensions of the original ark.

The true weirdness of this site lies not only in its hulking unfinished presence, but also in the bizarre stories told by its flock. They claim that a man was healed of sun allergies just after visiting here, and another of his degenerative arthritis. Another unfortunate fellow dropped to the ground, seemingly suffering from a heart attack, and then mysteriously recovered shortly after the event.

When I stood beside the ark, I did appreciate it on a certain level, to be quite honest. If nothing else, there are people out there willing to create utterly ridiculous objects in gargantuan scale, simply because of deeply held beliefs. I say good for them! So drop a buck in the collection box at the site when you visit, and tell them *Weird* sent you. I'd like to see what this baby looks like when it's finished! Go Noah!—*Jeff Bahr*

Thou Shalt Not Steal from the Ark!

In my old neck of the woods, Western Maryland—specifically, Frostburg—there is a church group that is attempting to rebuild Noah's Ark—to scale. They have had the framework up for many years, right along side I-68. A few years back, a minister embezzled a good deal of money from the project, but they haven't given up.—*Kelly Gough*

Throne of the Third Heaven

By all accounts, James Hampton's life was unremarkable. Born in Elloree, South Carolina, in 1909, after serving in the army during World War II he moved not far from his brother in Washington, DC. Shortly thereafter he took a job as a janitor for the General Services Administration, which he held for the rest of his life. He had few friends and never married, and for all intents and purposes was a quiet, unassuming, religious man who spent his Sundays in various churches throughout the city because he didn't like the idea that any one sect of Christianity had a claim on God.

What few people knew during his life, however, was how Hampton spent his free time. In a rented garage (which no longer stands), near Seventh and N streets NW, Hampton labored for years—fourteen, actually—on what has since become one of this country's most celebrated examples of visionary art: *The Throne of the Third Heaven of the Nations Millennium General Assembly.* When he died in 1964, a tin-foil masterpiece was left behind—much to the surprise of his sister (who discovered the work in the garage) and probably most of the people who knew him.

Clearly, Hampton was ahead of his time: He saw nothing if not the utility in recycling. *The Throne of the Third Heaven,* a Last Judgment setting replete with thrones, altars, pulpits, and much more, is fashioned entirely out of found or reused objects covered in silver and gold foil. Consisting of 177 pieces in all, the panorama is almost two hundred square feet in size and stands three yards tall at its center. Each minutely detailed piece has been lovingly crafted out of some hodgepodge of construction paper, mirrors, jars, wooden furniture, fruit cans, shards of green desk blotters, lightbulbs, bits of plastic, and so on, and then covered with tinfoil of the kind found affixed to wine bottle tops. (The story goes that Hampton paid local winos to turn over their foil after uncorking their bottles.) Hampton used glue, nails, tacks, and pins to hold things together, making the finished product, needless to say, more than a bit fragile.

Hampton made it clear that his work is divided into two distinct sides: one for things related to the Old Testament, and one for the New, except when he entreats us to "Fear Not," which he inscribed above the central throne (this phrase appears in both the Old and New Testaments). Biblical and religious figures appear in the work—hand labeled by Hampton—including the Virgin Mary, a pope or two, and Adam and Eve. Of course they appear in the work primarily because Hampton also claimed that they appeared to him—his visions were more than likely the impetus for his work. Hampton even makes note of these visions within the Throne assemblage, on labels that make statements such as THIS IS TRUE THAT THE GREAT MOSES, THE GIVER OF THE 10TH COMMANDMENT, APPEARED IN WASHINGTON DC, APRIL 11, 1931, AND IT IS TRUE THAT ADAM, THE FIRST MAN GOD CREATED, APPEARED IN PERSON ON JANUARY 20, 1949 . . .

THIS WAS ON THE DAY OF PRESIDENT TRUMAN'S INAUGURATION."

Calling himself St. James, Director of Special Projects for the State of Eternity, Hampton also kept a notebook written in a secret, indecipherable language that he said had been given to him by God. It is possible that he considered himself a prophet akin to John, the author of the book of Revelation, who was the inspiration for *The Throne of the Third Heaven*. Speculation has been made that had Hampton lived, he would have gone on to become a preacher and used his creation as a teaching tool.

Instead, he died and left behind a mysterious, eccentric artwork that has taken its place in our weird history. Sold by the owner of the garage to a Washington couple, *The Throne of the Third Heaven* was donated by them anonymously to the Smithsonian in 1970.

The Throne of the Third Heaven has been praised by art critics as one of the best examples of American visionary art, and it wows tourists on a regular basis. So loved is the piece that for its July 2006 reopening, the Smithsonian Art Museum chose *The Throne* as the first work to be reinstalled in the renovated building.

In what seems to us like a weird epilogue to this story, no fewer than two orchestral pieces have been inspired by (and titled in honor of) Hampton's luminary artwork. In 1989, Albert Glinsky's *The Throne of the Third Heaven* premiered at the Erie Philharmonic, commissioned for its seventy-fifth anniversary. More recently, Jefferson Friedman's *The Throne of the Third Heaven of the Nations General Assembly* premiered at the Kennedy Center—commissioned by the National Symphony Orchestra and the ASCAP Foundation. Friedman explains that the piece is "the second part of a trilogy of works entitled *In the Realms of the Unreal*, each movement of which is based on the life and work of a different American 'outsider' artist." Both composers describe at length the ways in which their music pays homage to Hampton's visionary process.

One wonders what else Hampton's wonderful work of weirdness might inspire.–*Abby Grayson*

Chapel of Cheap Drinks

If you happen to crave cheap drinks and art at the same time, and also happen to be wandering near the Maryland Institute College of Art in northern Baltimore, the obvious choice is to stop in at the Mount Royal Tavern. Inside the dimly lit room you'll see a long wooden bar with ten different beers on tap and an eclectic mix of clientele ranging from blue-collar workers to art students to bikers—all under a pall of cigarette smoke. At first sight, there appears to be nothing weird about this place at all. And unless you happen to fall over on your back, you may actually leave the tavern thinking that it's nothing more than your basic city watering hole.

But our advice is to find yourself a seat and look up. There you'll see an almost perfect replica of the ceiling of the Sistine Chapel. This is indeed a bizarre sight in a cheap city bar. It's clear that the tavern is a multifaceted

place. The patron who painted this homage to Michelangelo's masterwork has apparently been allowed to drink there gratis ever since he nailed the multiple canvases to the bar's ceiling. If pressed, the bartender will probably tell you that the patron in question was a final-year student at the institute who created the work for his last project (as "the biggest portfolio he could think of") and installed it at the tavern, where he could be sure it would be visited by hundreds of receptive visitors every week. What freshly graduated artist can aspire to more? If you can tear your eyes away from the ceiling and your beer for long enough, you can also take in plenty of wall art from local artists, which in itself is pretty strange for any down-on-its-heels drinking establishment. But frankly, the real appeal to this place is the ceiling (and the cheap suds).

Futuro: The Homes of Futures Past

In the 1960s, America was having a love affair with the final frontier. Americans were so obsessed with the "outer limits" that, by the end of the decade, even rural housewives reported alien abductions. People were captivated—the possibilities in outer space fueled the imaginations of millions.

Enter the Futuro house. Designed in 1968 by Finnish architect Matti Suuronen, the "spaceship house" was intended to be the wave of the future. At eleven feet high and twenty-six feet long, the Futuro is lightweight and portable. Made of plastic and fiberglass, it was designed to break up into sixteen individual pieces for easier mobility. So if you wanted your dream house to go with you, you simply had to strap it to a flatbed, or better yet, hitch it to a helicopter. The oil crisis of 1973 brought America back to reality, though. Plastic became too expensive, and Futuro construction stopped. Fewer than one hundred homes were built.

The mobile home of the future turned out to be too far ahead of its time. But several of these out-of-this-world homes still exist today in the Delmarva area and elsewhere. Whether they're bachelor pads for Star Trekkers or just a neighborhood novelty, these futuristic houses are definitely the talk of the town, wherever they may land.

—Abby Grayson

Futuro

Finland, famed for its forests, and finely-crafted wooden structures, has produced the first well-detailed, commercially available foam fiberglass dwelling.

Now being manufactured in the U.S., the Futuro——a shiny elliptical pod——looks like it just landed. It can be dropped in by helicopter (expensive though) and requires no site preparation. It's structurally strong, well insulated, and has retractable stairs. Interior looks plastic and shiny and badly needs some madras bedspreads and non-plastic human touches.

——Lloyd Kahn

Futuro House

$10,000 for shell
$14,000 for completely equipped house
F. O. B. Philadelphia

from:
Futuro Corporation
1900 Rittenhouse Square
Philadelphia, PA 19103

Spaceships Spotted in Delmarva

Recently as I was traveling to my mother's southern Delaware home, I encountered a rather unusual sight—a spaceship. I couldn't really see because it was dark, but I was almost certain it was a spaceship. I have quite a vivid imagination, so there were a million things going through my mind at that particular second. My boyfriend was in the car and I said, "Did you just see that spaceship?" He looked at me as if I was absolutely insane. I said, "No really, there was just a spaceship. I'll back up so you can see that I'm not nuts." So I backed up the car, and he saw what appeared to be a spaceship too. It was halfway hidden behind a house and everyone appeared to be home.

We traveled back to my mother's house and said we'd get a better look at it in the morning. So the morning came and we got in the car and traveled up the street with camera in hand. We pulled up to the driveway and there it was, a beautiful spaceship that someone was living in. At this point, I didn't even care if they called the cops on me, I pulled into their driveway and we took pictures.

After that, we were traveling down Route 1 and my boyfriend says, "Turn around! I just saw another spaceship!" At this point, I could not stop thinking about how aliens probably invaded our planet 25 years ago and blended in with the American people. How hard would it be anyhow?

So I turned around and there it was: another beautiful spaceship. It was at an aerodrome, so we could get out of the car and investigate this. It was beauty to my eyes. A big, blue, round spaceship. It was all locked up, and I didn't want to harm it. Luckily there was a small window at the bottom so you could look in. Someone must have used it as an office. There was a desk, chair, and a couch that wrapped halfway around the spaceship. It looked as if it wasn't used in the past 25 years or so. I wish I could have flown it home with me. Wow, that would be very South Jersey of me to have a spaceship in my back yard!–*Autumn S., Pine Hill, NJ*

Weird Wheels

Some people soup up their cars with bucket seats and chrome. They slap on shiny hubcaps, tinted windows, and hang fluffy dice from the rearview mirror. A few flame decals later, you're looking at a personalized property. A boring one, but a personalized set of wheels nonetheless. We're not interested in these. We're interested in people who stick doll parts on the hoods of their cars or musical instruments on their roof racks—and don't forget those folks who like to build tricycles in the shape of giant birds. And we've found them all in Maryland.

Conrad Bladey's Art Cars

Drive around Linthicum or Jessup or Brooklyn for long enough and if you're lucky you'll catch sight of hundreds of red hands sticking out of a Pontiac Grand Am. Or perhaps you'll glimpse a truck with hundreds of plastic toys on its roof. And behind the wheel of these strange vehicles you'll see a Santa Claus look-alike, possibly wearing a helmet. If this happens to you, chalk it up to a close encounter with Conrad Bladey.

It's no surprise to learn that Bladey's a bit of a character. He's a sometime high school teacher, Irish studies specialist, folk artist, and musician with a penchant for playing odd instruments, such as a brass horn attached to his hat. It's not unusual to see him with a length of garden hose topped off by a trumpet mouthpiece, playing a tune through a tuba hidden among the bizarre ornaments affixed to his 1995 GMC pickup, an art vehicle he calls the Magnet Truck. He claims the acoustics are particularly good in tunnels, and the sound is much more effective for catching the attention of other drivers

than the blare of a normal car horn. We'll take his word on that.

But with a fleet of four art cars, not counting the two sticker-covered cars he lists as "dead," Bladey is clearly dedicated to strange ornamentation on his motor vehicles. In fact, he won't drive anything else. In addition to his Magnet Truck, his fleet includes his Party Car, a 1966 Pontiac Catalina splattered with paint in the style of Jackson Pollock; a 1965 Dodge Coronet painted in rectangles of primary colors with trophies on it, naturally called Bowling for Mondrian; and finally, there's the shrine to the helping hand, a 1990 Pontiac Grand Am covered with red hands he calls Handy. This last beauty won first prize in the Daily Driver category at the 2005 Orange Show, an art car festival held in Houston, Texas. Bladey drove the car fifteen hundred miles to get to that show.

During our visit to his home in Linthicum, he took us on a drive in his Magnet Truck, and it was a kick to see the wide-mouthed stares we got as we drove around several small towns between Baltimore and Washington,

DC. Smiles, waves, rubbernecking, and friendly honking from other drivers were the order of the day, and Bladey was clearly drinking it in. But not all the attention he gets is positive.

"Driving down I-95 once, I felt like I was in a presidential motorcade, with three state troopers following me," he told us. "A young officer was obviously the one who had called it in, and the other guys were his backup. He said, 'I don't think you can see.' Well, I told him that I could see anything past a yard behind the car, which is the law."

Bladey knows the laws about vehicle adornment, and he has to, because frequently state and local police don't.

"I knew things weren't going to fly off the car, but the cops didn't. I needed to prove the car was legal," he said. "Anything stuck with glue is considered a permanent repair. The windows can be blocked only up to one third the vertical height. And fenders have to be a certain distance from the wheel, but they can go out any distance . . . well, not into the next lane, but it's not limited by law. And you can have nothing sharp enough to injure on the car body."

And those specifications fit all the vehicles Bladey drives. But sometimes, it's not the vehicles' safety that officers of the law are interested in.

"I took my wife to the Mary Our Queen cathedral while I was making the Handy Car," he said. "While she was in there, I continued to take the arms off dolls. One of them had its arms connected to each other with a length of string, so I rummaged around in the car and got out a knife. I cut the string with it and put it back. It took me all of two minutes. A while later, I felt an ominous presence. Out of the corner of my eye, I saw the blue uniform. There were eight squad cars. I recognized some of the cops, and some of them were having a hard time not laughing. On reflection, cutting up doll parts in a cathedral parking lot wasn't such a good idea."

So how does Bladey transform his cars into the impressive vehicles he drives?

"You build them on a base of foam insulation. You let that dry, and you can cut it to shape. Then you have to paint over it because it's porous and the sun affects it. It discolors and turns to powder. So I put Rustoleum on it to seal it up. Then you glue things onto it with Liquid Nails. You get a lot of fiberglass artists doing that . . . building on a base of foam. The Mondrian car only has a little of that. The Handy Car and the Magnet Truck had to be done in stages."

At the end of our visit, we commented on the decor in his garden, which is something of an art environment in itself, with pink flamingos everywhere. He claims he puts up a new one every time he gets in trouble with the authorities. Is that a nod to the movies of local boy John Waters, we wondered?

"Hell, no. I see him around, of course. I was working on a car once and looked up to see John Waters and Patty Hearst watching me. I had visions of being 'discovered' so I had to tell him, 'I'm not going to be the next Pecker.' He went away."

Well, with all due respect, more fool John. We could stand around watching this guy at work all day.

Holy Art, Batman

Joe Kroart, the proprietor of the Ocean Gallery in Ocean City, doesn't just sell art. He also makes it, and sometimes the canvas he uses is made of sheet metal. Take the Batmobile, for example. He didn't sink a lot of money into this vehicle; in fact, he boasts that when he and his son adorned it, they spent less than thirty dollars in raw materials. But that doesn't mean he's not proud of his handiwork. In fact, he's been known to jump on the hood and strike a pose if he likes the person pointing a camera at it.

In addition to the Batmobile, which sits right outside his boardwalk gallery, Kroart has a decorated truck sitting in the parking lot in the back. But although he clearly enjoys bolting unusual items onto his vehicles, his real focus is on entertaining visitors and drawing attention to the boardwalk and his business. His latest promotional idea is to drive a decorated car off the pier to attract visitors to the boardwalk during the off-season. Whether he'll get permission to do that is another matter, but more power to him for having the idea in the first place.

My Art's Faster than Yours!

Every spring Baltimore's American Visionary Art Museum sponsors a race across the city. In addition to attracting attention to the museum and the city, it gives a chance for a particular breed of cyclists to show off their stuff. Unlike Lance Armstrong, the stuff they're showing off isn't so much stamina and leg muscles of sprung steel—it's the strangeness of the vehicles they pedal. This is the Kinetic Art Race, and the human-powered vehicles are . . . well, whatever the visionary artist that built them has lurking in his imagination.

To qualify for the race, a kinetic art vehicle must be human-powered, no more than eight feet wide, thirteen feet high, and thirty-five feet long. Except for that, anything goes. So you'll get dioramas featuring marine

life. You'll see quadricycles in the shape of elephants, rats, birds, and trains. And every year, you'll see the darling of the crowd, a huge pink poodle named Fifi who spends most of the year on show at the museum.

The point of the race is to travel along a tortuous route through the city, including the harbor and its muddy banks. And the goal isn't necessarily to finish first. There are polite contest rules that demand that a vehicle must yield if a faster moving cycle honks at them. The pilots of the passing vehicles must wave acknowledgment at the gesture (with a full complement of fingers). And the reason that competitors allow this is that the most prized award does not go to the first past the post. The most coveted prize is called the Mediocre Award, which goes to the person who finishes exactly in the

middle. Another highly prized position is coming in second-to-last. And the serious prizes have nothing to do with raw performance ratings: They go to the art and engineering of the vehicles.

Just in case anybody begins to take the race seriously, they should check out some of the competition's stated rules. Take Rule 1+, for example, the Personal Security Rule:

> Each Sculpture must carry at all times 1 comforting item of psychological luxury heretofore referred to as the "Homemade Sock Creature" (HSC). Homemade Sock Creature must be made in a home, from a not-too-recently-worn sock from the home, and resemble a creature homemade from a sock.

The penalty for not having an HSC is having one hour added to your race time. And the final rule, Rule 10M, mandates fun:

> All Pilots, Pit Crew members, Barnacles, Officials, Spectators, Police, Marine Posse, Timers, and Passersby must put great effort into HAVING FUN! for it is such craziness as this that keeps us all sane.

Amen to that.

iller's Castle

When people began sending us tales about a bed-and-breakfast in the suburbs of Washington that was built like a castle, we didn't quite know what to make of it. A building with turrets that sold antiques and catered to the B-and-B crowd sounded entirely too Disney to be truly weird. But then we started to hear details, and we knew it was the place for us.

This was no Magic Kingdom fairy-tale building. This was a real castle, with thick outer and inner walls, iron bars, gargoyles, and a tube-shaped inner sanctum built of cinder blocks to retreat into in case of invasion. The owner

of the B and B was a crotchety old man with a severe military haircut and a wad of chewing tobacco permanently wedged in his cheek. He named the place Bull Run Castle after the first land battle in the Civil War, and he would scare children with his aggressive demeanor and tick off women with misogynistic comments. And all kinds of weird seekers from around Washington would drive out there and pay a couple of bucks for a guided tour.

The way people spoke about this place, it seemed like a medieval-era version of

Fawlty Towers—a bizarre establishment run by a man so awful you can't help coming back for more. We were almost disappointed to find out that it was actually across the border in Virginia, but we figured, since so many Maryland residents made the half-hour drive out there from the western suburbs of Washington, it qualified as a legend in Maryland too. So we at *Weird Maryland* called up the owner, John Roswell Miller, and asked if we could stay the night in one of his suites. "No, you can't," he told us. "I've sold up, and I'm shipping out. Two weeks. That's all you got. You can come up and buy some antiques."

And he hung up on us. This clearly deserved a closer look, so we jumped into the *Weird*mobile and drove down Route 15 across the Potomac toward Aldie. It wasn't hard to find Bull Run Castle—we just kept our eyes open for anything with turrets and gargoyles, and turned down the drive when we found it. The castle is an impressive building of brick, stone, and cinder block. Even the sturdy doghouses were decorated with gargoyles. And the heavy hardwood door with its hideous knocker and dire warnings against letting the door slam was as forbidding as the rest of the place.

Pushing the door open, we discovered a spacious room where a man was throwing paintings on the fire. He looked up, growled, "That one's my mother. Sorry, Mom," and came to greet us. He asked us to pay the fee for the tour—"Two dollars, and if you don't like it, it's ten dollars. If you ask any questions, it's ten dollars"— and then he launched into a well-rehearsed routine, throwing out facts and figures so quickly, it hurt to take notes. He began the project in 1980, moved onto the property in 1986, and finished it in 1998. He had never earned more than $16,000 per year. "Never been on welfare, ate a lot of beans, but never gone hungry." The castle has fourteen closets, eighty-nine windows, and an iron-clad front door four and three-quarters inches thick. "See those beams? Solid oak. That's solid maple right there. There's nothing fake in this castle . . . including me."

Despite being one of the most accomplished outsider artists we've met, Miller has no respect for anything fanciful. This military veteran is far too down-to-earth for that. Bull Run Castle is a real castle "built so it can be defended," as he repeatedly said during his tour. The thin notches in the walls are real shooting ports, designed to repel real invaders. And he regards college graduates, liberals, and whimsical people with equal disdain. In fact, during the trip, we got the distinct impression he had us pegged for at least two of those three crimes against humanity.

"What I'm dying for is some idiot to break in here at night," he said, kicking an ammunition box in front of a heavy door to prop it open. "I've got thirty Enfield rifles and a dungeon here."

But somehow, despite his gruff monologue and demeanor, John Miller seemed to be glowing with pleasure. Grown people had told us how scary this man was, but he could barely hide a smile as he spoke. And he looked pretty good too. His white hair was well cut and groomed. If he was missing a lot of teeth, as we'd heard, he had a decent set of dentures in place. And although he was verbally challenging us, he didn't seem to have any aggression behind it. It was almost as if whatever had spurred him to build a real castle had evaporated. He was, after all, about to sell the place.

A couple of times, I risked the threat of a $10 fine for asking him a question, but he didn't rise to the bait. Secretly, though, I knew he was dying to tell us something. So after he had played a twenty-minute video to cap off the tour, he came into the room and explained everything. "I never listened to a female in my life," he

said, as if he were trying to bait us into a liberal response so he could throw us in the dungeon. "Eighteen months ago, that all changed."

He went over to a cupboard and showed us a pouch of chewing tobacco. It was only then I realized he didn't have his trademark wad in his cheek. "I chewed tobacco all my life. Haven't opened this in eighteen months. Don't want to. Why? Harriet . . . Hatty. I knew her since third grade. I walked down the road to her house and carried her books. We grew up, we kissed and cuddled, and then I got called to war. And then it was over." This was an unexpected turn to the story. But it explained a lot about this man.

"I spent most of my life unhappy and deserved it. We didn't see each other for fifty-one years. Then eighteen months ago, I met her again. And she took me back. I wore Goodwill all my life. Now it's London Fog here and Bass shoes on my feet. I used to have a flattop. She liked to see a little wave here, so I grew my hair. I even had my nails done one time."

Was this really the aggressive misanthrope we had heard about from all these people? Well, his next comment made us realize he's not entirely reformed. "A fellah in town made a comment about it, and I dragged him up by his arms. Black and blue they were. I told him, 'I'm still the same fellah!' And he believed me."

And with that, our tour was at an end. And even though he suspected we were liberal and college educated, he didn't throw us into the dungeon. In fact, he didn't even charge extra for the questions. Bull Run Castle is still standing, but John Roswell Miller has been gone for more than a year. His legacy, though, won't be disappearing anytime soon. This castle was built to last.

Aldie Mad Axe Man

I read about John Miller in the *Washington Post* or *City Paper* in the 1980s. He built a castle to withstand nuclear attack in a field about seven miles away from Dulles Airport. The armory there is a survivalist's dream. One of his neighbors was quoted as saying he was a bit crazy, and the story around town was that Miller was after this guy with an axe. I never found out if that was true, but people who visited the place believed he was capable of it.–*Virginia*

Throwing Kids in the Dungeon

I grew up in the suburbs around Washington, DC, and the single strangest place I ever went there was an antique store built in the shape of a castle. This wasn't a storybook castle, either. It had cinderblock turrets and concentric layers of walls. This was a place designed to keep people out. My parents loved shopping for antiques, but us kids hated it, so they'd pay the owner a couple of bucks to give us a tour of the place. He was the scariest man I ever met. He had a buzz-cut, not many teeth, and a big wad of chewing tobacco. He delivered his speeches in a monotone, and scared the hell out of us with his talk of locking people in the dungeon.–*No name please . . . he may come after me!*

Curious Collections

Museums Without the Mustiness

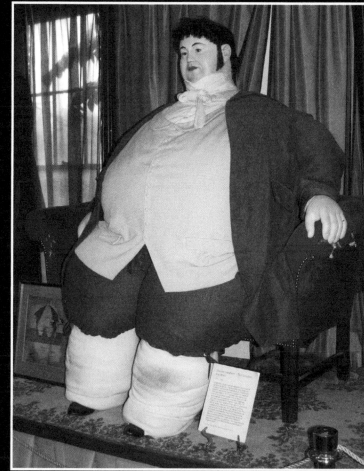

Two hundred years ago museums were often just single rooms in a person's house dedicated to a family member's collection of strange and unusual artifacts. Often they weren't even whole rooms, but just a display case that was called the "cabinet of curiosities." Some were portable and could be wheeled around and displayed as traveling exhibits or sideshow exhibits.

There was nothing stuffy or noble about these little museums—while they may have been educational, they were designed first and foremost to be interesting. Even the word "museum" was a nod to the source of all human inspiration, the divine Muses. Nowadays museums have become something less than temples to the Muses. They have become overly serious and entirely too noble.

That's why what we are looking at are the real old-timey museums, the cabinets of curiosities, and the sideshows of the museum world. And we're pleased to report that the Free State is swimming in them. One or two may have faded from their former glory; some are new and shooting for the big time. But they're out there. Trust us, they're REALLY out there.

Brother, Can You Spare a Dime?

Just when the search was finally over, the creature we had been seeking all these years slipped away from us. We had found the infamous Jersey Devil and let it get away. It turns out that the legendary flying monster that plagued New Jersey's Pine Barrens for more than two hundred years was dead and stuffed and hanging from a ceiling in a Baltimore neighborhood. And there are more wonders—in the same room, I found a Fiji mermaid, a giant mummy, and a beautiful impressionist-style landscape picture made entirely of butterfly wings. This is the American Dime Museum, the last relic of the golden age of the traveling sideshow exhibit.

Named for the standard admission fee for these private sideshows, the American Dime Museum is tucked away on Maryland Avenue, across the river from the big tourist action in Baltimore. Its three-room exhibit was one part P. T. Barnum show, one part art gallery, and one part cabinet of curiosities. In short, it is everything that weird lovers love best. There are genuinely interesting and authentic works of art cheek-by-jowl with hoax creatures and models of sideshow freaks. In addition to the butterfly wing landscape, you will find a beautiful collection of jewelry made of human hair and a bold gallery of paintings daubed onto canvas by a chimpanzee. There are some genuine historical artifacts too, including a retrospective display of American funeral customs called Good MOURNING America and the death masks of many twentieth-century American Presidents.

Weird went to check out this rare find before it shut its doors to the public. The museum's curator, impresario, and

The beautiful Jenny Haniver

chief carnival barker, Dick Horne, told us with typical carny bluster that he's always been interested in "anything obscure and in bad taste." And yet his permanent sideshow tent is surprisingly family-friendly. Some children, it's true, would not have liked the stuffed jackalope or downy ocean hunne (a fish covered in feathers), but many children don't like the dioramas in natural history museums either. Anyone who can stare into the beady eyes of a bear in a glass case at the Smithsonian would have found nothing offensive in the Dime Museum's genuine mummified cat or even the ten-foot-tall fake mummies that Horne built for sideshows decades ago. The mummy takes pride of place in the Dime Museum, with its parchment skin split in strategic places to reveal beef ribs.

Dick Horne told us that the only complaints he ever got from parents have been, in his opinion, misguided. "I've had people complain that the children will be confused by the giant mummy and the jackalope unless there's a label saying they're fakes," he said, chuckling. "The kids' parents don't expect them to be fooled by computer animation in the movies, but something like this. . . . Well, let's just say that the kids get it better than their parents sometimes."

Be it for fun or profit, there's a long tradition of faking it in these home-grown museums. And Dick Horne makes sure that the Dime Museum represents it as much as possible. Consider the Fiji mermaid. It was a classic P. T. Barnum invention, made from a fish tail and a monkey's body in the mid-1800s. The original was destroyed in a fire at Barnum's museum, but the Dime Museum has a good example in a jar, alongside several examples of an art form

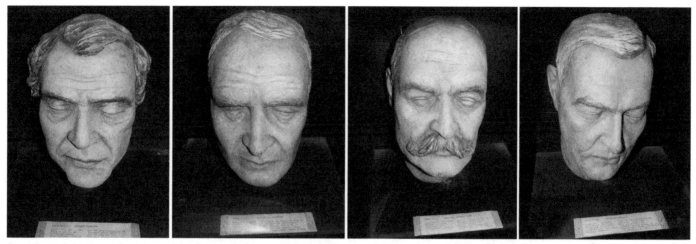

Presidential death masks, left to right: Andrew Johnson, Warren G. Harding, William Howard Taft, and Woodrow Wilson

known as the Jenny Haniver. Nobody knows where the name originated, but they have been circulating among port towns since the 1500s. Jenny Hanivers are winged monsters with incredible fangs and ghastly faces—or at least, that's what they look like. In fact, they are dead and dried manta rays that sailors used to carve up into monsters and sell as curiosities. The ray's sharp-toothed mouth is seldom seen when the animal is alive and swimming, but in the case of the Jenny Haniver, the fangs are front and center and look especially threatening. The great thing about the American Dime Museum is that you can ignore the plate-spinners that Granny and the little

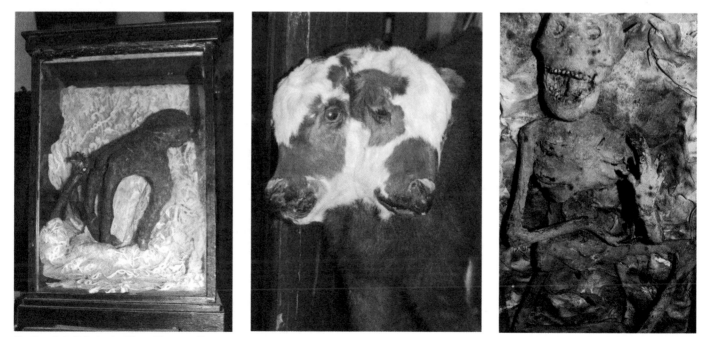

Real or fake? Only the Dime Museum Knows . . .

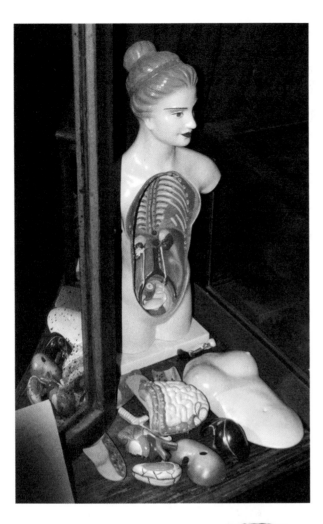

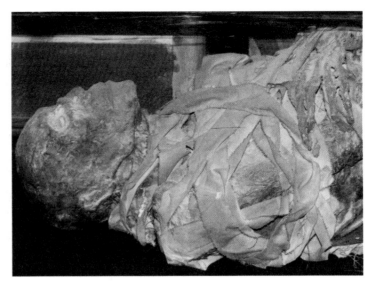

Ten-foot-tall mummy

ones enjoyed so much and walk straight over to the exhibits that really rock. And you can buy snacks there too—assuming you like to snack on worms, that is. No, they aren't fake worms. According to the label, they were real dried larvae flavored with spices. Dick told us they were delicious, so we bought a few packets to take with us. Strangely enough, we still have them, next to our other souvenirs. At the *Weird* offices, we may put our money where our mouth is, but we're not quite prepared to put worms there yet.

Old-time museums mixed sideshow masks with medical equipment in pursuit of entertainment

The American Dime Museum Closes*

Baltimore is home to the American Dime Museum. Despite the numismatic name, it has nothing to do with coins. Back in the 19th century, dime museums were private little side shows and collections where the public was charged a dime each to see just about anything of interest, including scientific curiosities, natural oddities, and a lot of weird stuff.

Back then they were a dime a dozen, but there are few left. In fact, after six years of operating in Baltimore, the American Dime Museum closed at the end of December 2005 due to a lack of funding. My husband and I are film hobbyists, and with the owner's permission, we hurried over to videotape the collection before it disappeared from public view. The owner hopes to keep the collection intact, but at this point, it's not clear what will happen to it.

We spent an intriguing day at the museum filming the amazing collection of oddities and curiosities—some real (artwork made with human hair), some fake like the jackalope, a Fiji mermaid, various furred and feathered fishes, and the small Italian pepperoni weasel. It was such a unique slice of American history. I am glad we got it on tape before it all got stored away.—*L. W. Woods, Savage Film Group*

Which animal is real? No sign will tell you at a dime museum (but it's the ducks)

*Update

The American Dime Museum is now open for small parties and tours by appointment. Call 410-230-0263 for more information.

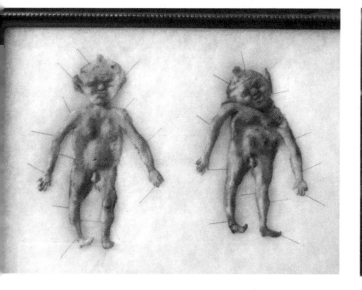

Smile, Please

To many tooth owners, dentistry conjures up a lot of negative images. A visit to the dentist is equal parts boredom and mounting tension, broken only by the occasional high-pitched whine of a drill in a distant room. And then there's the jaw-locking experience of actually sitting in the dentist's chair. Nope, it's not a favorite pastime for most of us. That's why it seems odd that the United States should have not one but three prominent dental museums. But only the one in Baltimore can proudly boast that it's a national museum: the Dr. Samuel D. Harris National Museum of Dentistry.

So what does it take to become a national museum of dentistry? It's not the hundreds of dental plates and implants on display from all over the world going back several centuries. They're interesting, for sure, but not exactly thrilling. The same goes for the life-size hanging statue of a circus performer dangling a massive weight from a strap clenched between her pearly whites. It's an eye-catching sight, without a doubt, but not exactly up there with the Capitol for cultural significance.

You get to see carved animal bones set in gold plates that people used to bulk up their shrunken toothless mouths back in the 1700s. You gawk at dental equipment used on the royal mouths of Europe and finally understand why Queen Victoria seldom looked amused in her portraits. You get to see models of the strange dental customs of other cultures, such as deliberately knocking out the front incisors or filing them to a point. If you read the captions closely, you can learn to use terms like "maxillary swaged gold partial denture" with confidence. And you get to walk past dentists' chairs. Lots and lots of dentists' chairs.

⊸ *32* ⊸
TERRIFIC
TEETH

called calomel or mercurous chloride. While this remedy was effective at abating fevers, it had a few small-print side effects. The most significant was that it made your teeth fall out.

So Washington famously wore dentures, though they were not made of wood, as popular legend goes. The set in the dental museum, made by Thomas Greenwood of Philadelphia in the late 1700s, are made of gold, ivory, and human teeth. Some of the components were held together with small hickory pegs, which may have given rise to the wooden-tooth legend, but these are state-of-the-art eighteenth-century plates, with a spring between the top and bottom sets to keep the top set in place in the days before denture adhesive. This feature also had a side effect, however: The President had to keep his lower lip in a constant state of tension to prevent his lower set from sliding out. A presidential sneeze at the wrong moment could have caused a national embarrassment. Consider that the next time you examine Washington's underbite on a dollar bill. It wasn't easy being the first President.

But the thing that most people take away from the experience is the sight of George Washington's dentures. Most people know that the Father of Our Country wasn't exactly an avid flosser. In fact, he had only two gnashers left when he crossed the Delaware, and as President he sported only ivory and gold in his mouth. It's not fair to blame the first President for his dental woes, however. Some of his problems were caused by a popular medication of the time that would nowadays be the subject of class-action lawsuits. During bouts of severe illness, namely pleurisy and dengue fever, which he suffered as a young man, Washington took a compound

If you really love the exhibits at this museum (and what's not to love?), consider scoping out the nation's two other dental museums. They are attached to the Temple University School of Dentistry in Philadelphia and the Pierre Facular Academy in Las Vegas. They too are very fine establishments, but they are hardly spitting images of the Harris museum. They can't boast George Washington's top set or an interactive exhibit about the wonders of saliva. Only Baltimore has that.

A Wee Little Place

Let there be no doubt: There is a museum for every subject under the sun, and the museum named for Bill Didusch in Linthicum, Baltimore County, is proof of this fact. Bill Didusch was an artist in the early decades of the twentieth century who shunned the smudgy impressionism and abstract art that were in vogue at the time. In 1915, he took an illustrating job at Johns Hopkins University, drawing the anatomy of the urinary tract and instruments used to treat its ailments.

His work taught doctors so well that he became a lecturer in urology and eventually a legend in the field—so much so that the university put its collection of urologic instruments on display and named the exhibit the William P. Didusch Center for Urologic History. Everything on view there was once inserted into the plumbing of patients along the route from their bladders to the outside world. We defy anybody to stroll through the Didusch Center without wanting to cross his legs and wince. There's no escaping it. The long, thick metal tubes on display are frightening in ways that beg description. There are scopes that look way too wide to examine your insides. There are lassos and nutcrackers on the end of steel tubes, designed to break up bladder stones. And there are ramrods that you won't even want to think about. The one thing that makes all this tolerable is the knowledge that to people suffering from ever painful kidney and bladder stones, these were instruments of blessed relief.

Of the many wince-inducing exhibits, the standout is Hugh Hampton Young's Prostate Punch, which looks like a massively enlarged and curved hypodermic needle. It was designed to clean out the prostate of built-up tissue and other material that might be preventing sufferers from emptying their bladders. In other words, it reamed out your tubes. Hard to believe that it actually did the job. It was so effective in the case of the hugely wealthy railway magnate "Diamond Jim" Brady that he made a generous donation to Johns Hopkins. This sum established the Brady Urological Institute and ultimately the museum itself.

A few of the exhibits at the museum seem out of place until you look closely. A set of dandies' canes appear to belong in a regular historical museum, and as for the fist-size chunk of stone, that looks like a natural history exhibit. But they all belong here. The canes contain hidden compartments for catheters and lubricant so that sufferers could discreetly open their own floodgates when dining out. And as for the large mineral sample, that once resided in some poor soul's bladder. Kidney stone disease, the buildup of minerals in the kidney, bladder, and urinary tract, is a pathology with a long history. This extraordinarily painful condition was first mentioned by name in the Hippocratic oath to separate physicians from surgeons (physicians swear they "will not cut, not even sufferers from stone"). Looking at these huge stones, it's hard not to imagine how agonizing something that rough-looking and huge would feel inside your body. Next to that, the smooth metal tubes on display, no matter how large, are easy to deal with. And there are certainly plenty of them in this museum. With an appointment, anybody can view the exhibits—they're free—or scope them out online at www.urologichistory.museum.

May the Toys Be with You

In the true spirit of the earliest museums, Thomas Atkinson houses his sci-fi collection in his own home. By appointment, he will show you around his artifacts, and on our visit he proved to be an accommodating and genial host. He's also achieved something every science fiction fan dreams of: He has crammed more objects into a room than the laws of physics will allow. Cluttered doesn't even begin to describe the state of Thomas's parlor and hallway. Every flat surface is covered with tiny models. There's barely enough floor space for normal-sized humans to walk through without losing their balance. Even the walls are obscured behind cardboard cutouts, wall hangings, and shelving. Mysterious objects hang from the ceiling. And every one of these items is a piece of *Star Wars* merchandise.

To Thomas Atkinson, the summer of 1977 was a life-changing experience. That was when this preteen science fiction fan saw the first *Star Wars* movie and, like many of us, started buying the merchandise. The first thing he bought was a $2 R2-D2 action figure. Unlike the rest of us, he kept buying, plowing thousands of dollars into his *Star Wars* collection over the years. He got some items as gifts, and some were the result of looking through dumpsters outside toy stores for a tossed *Star Wars* promotional display. Ten thousand or so items later, the collection has become the Star Toys Museum, packed into three rooms in a quiet Linthicum house the occupants call Meerkat Meade.

Small Darth Mauls line up cheek by jowl with cute little Ewoks and plastic Yodas. There are shampoo bottles, bedsheets, watches, yo-yos, kites, and key chains. There is wallpaper and furniture. A fleet of spaceships hangs from the ceiling, dominated by the most enormous Millennium Falcon ever made—a four-foot-long, seventy-pound promotional model with lights that run off a DC adapter. Thomas won it in a drawing at a local Toys "R" Us after they'd finished with it. He still can't believe his good luck and poses under it with touching pride of ownership whenever anyone whips out a camera. Off in one corner, a cardboard

cutout of C-3PO presides in his own stiff way over the proceedings.

But although Thomas is fastidious about cataloguing and displaying his astounding collection, he retains a sense of humor about the whole thing. "Now this is a weird juxtaposition," he said, holding up a Darth Vader Christmas ornament. A mental image easily comes to mind of rowdy kids at a Christmas Eve service being brought into line with the classic line "I find your lack of faith . . . disturbing." Yep, Thomas had it right: That was a strange piece of merchandise. But there are plenty of others, some of which are even more disturbing. Take the boxer shorts emblazoned with the slogan "Feel the Force." And the Jar Jar Binks candy bar, in which the plastic jaws of the horselike alien slide open and a candy tongue pops out. It's hard to imagine any creature in this or any other galaxy relishing that lollipop.

After demonstrating the tongue-popping action of the device, Thomas shrugs with a bemused grin. But other items he treats with more reverence. There were bubble bath bottles and a cardboard Death Star toy from a long ago time in a galaxy far away (Europe in the 1970s), which Thomas had jumped through hoops to find and acquire. There's a die-cast metal Tie Fighter from around 1980 in its original box that's worth at least a grand. And there's a trading card of C-3PO in a state of what looks like un-android-like arousal. "The card made it out on the market," Thomas told us. "But it was withdrawn soon after."

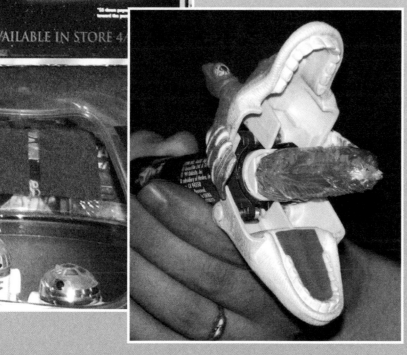

Atkinson's friends began calling his collection the "museum" long before he put it on display. But eight years ago, he incorporated it as a nonprofit organization, and he has plans to move most of his memorabilia into a new building or trailer in his spacious yard. It's also online at startoysmuseum.org. And to show that he's serious about it, he's even got some familiar names on the Star Toys Museum board of directors. Anyone who's truly steeped in star lore should recognize actor Michael Sheard's name on the advisory council: He was Admiral Ozzel in *The Empire Strikes Back*.

Weirdest Basement in Maryland . . . Period

I have to admit, the first thought that went through my mind when I heard there was a Museum of Menstruation was, Yuck. My second thought was, What kind of guy opens a museum like this in his basement? The answer is a middle-aged guy like Harry Finley, whose basement just outside Washington, DC, has displayed a collection of feminine hygiene products since 1994.

Harry Finley's interest in the subject started while he was stationed in Europe as a graphic designer for the U.S. government. He became interested in menstrual product advertisements while researching print ad layouts and found the European ads much more open and frank than those of his home country. He began collecting the advertisements and samples of products, and when he returned to Maryland he showed his basement museum to friends and then, ultimately, visitors. In due time, he began receiving donations to add to his displays. Some were simple samples or promotional materials, but some were a bit more unusual. The oddest of these donations has got to be the pink dress made out of hundreds of rubber menstrual cups.

Curiosity about Harry and his basement drove me to check out the museum's Web site at www.mum.org. Now that I had an idea of why the museum was started, I began looking at the table of contents of the Web site more closely. I settled on the Humor section, figuring I could handle that better than the Art of Menstruation, or the scarier directories of tampons, cups, or pads. Well . . . the humor proved to be intriguing, to say the least. Definitely politically incorrect at times, but certainly intriguing. From

there, I decided to check out the terms people use for those (ahem) "calendar days." Amazingly, there are hundreds of examples submitted by men and women from all over the world. I now understand what it means when the "Commies invade the summerhouse," a lady is "blowing a fuse," or "staying with Miss Scarlett at Tara."

By this time, I was still grossed out, but getting more obsessed with the site. Should I ever become a contestant on *Jeopardy* and the category up is Menstrual History, I will wow the audience because I know these fascinating facts: The first tampons were marketed in the 1920s; Lister's Towel, made by Johnson & Johnson, made disposable sanitary pads in the 1890s; Kotex comes from the words "cotton-like texture" but was first made of wood pulp. I'd even have the answers to the bonus round questions if I needed to know that it was once a custom in some European countries for women to use no protection at all during their cycles. This was where the yuck factor really kicked in.

Unfortunately for the curious, the museum is available only on the Web. The actual display space closed its doors in 1998 after only four years of service. At this time, Harry is searching for a more public location for his collection. Currently, the only visitors to the museum in Harry Finley's basement are Harry's eight cats, several who hold honorary positions on the museum's board alongside real members, most of whom are women in academia. You can tell the cats from the other board members by their names, most of which seem to be from the Padd family . . . such as Professor Mack C. Padd and Professor Minnie Padd.

—Shara Walker

More Macabre Medicine

On the second day of fighting at the battle of Gettysburg, the commander of the 3rd Army Corps, Major General Daniel Sickles, lost his leg. A twelve-pound cannonball shattered his shinbone, and because the overworked field hospitals lacked the time and facilities for delicate surgery, his only option was amputation. On July 2, 1863, General Sickles's right leg was cut off just above the knee.

But Sickles was our kind of war hero. He boxed up his broken limb and mailed it to the newly formed Army Medical Museum with a card that read, "With the compliments of Major General D.E.S." The following year, on the anniversary of his loss, the general went to visit his leg at the museum. He repeated the pilgrimage every July 2 from then until his death.

Now you can do the same thing too. The Army Medical Museum has grown from its origins as a collection of "specimens of morbid anatomy" and "projectiles and foreign bodies removed" into a full-fledged multimedia educational establishment called the National Museum of Health and Medicine.

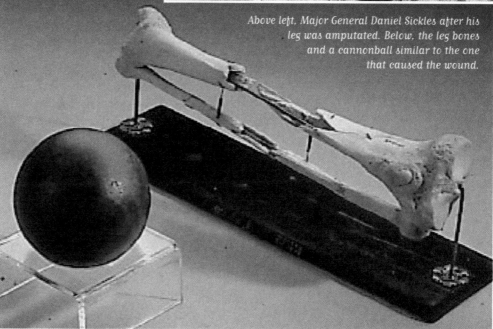

Above left, Major General Daniel Sickles after his leg was amputated. Below, the leg bones and a cannonball similar to the one that caused the wound.

But despite the noble moniker and its prestigious address in the Walter Reed Army Medical Center in Washington, DC, the museum still has its roots firmly grounded in morbid anatomy and health problems that have concerned armies since time immemorial—from shattered bones to diseases we don't talk about in polite society. There are certainly plenty of educational exhibits suitable for school field trips here, of course, but there's also a collection of medical oddities that's as macabre as anything we at *Weird* have ever seen.

This is the museum that the essayist Sarah Vowell

Right, Lincoln's deathbed scene and, inset, the probe used by Dr. Barnes to locate the ball and fragments of Lincoln's skull from the autopsy.

visited during her *Assassination Vacation* tour to view the bullet that killed Abraham Lincoln. It is on display alongside fragments of the President's bone and hair, and the bloodstained cuff of the museum's representative at the autopsy. In short, this is a morbid tourist's dream spot.

The museum also features some live examples of that staple of ancient medicine, leeches. Because an excess of blood was once believed to be the cause of a host of medical problems, leeches were applied to adjust the fluid levels. They not only suck out excess blood to control bleeding, but their saliva acts as a blood thinner. One delightful fact on display is that these nasty little bloodsuckers are back in use in some hospitals. Unfortunately, they don't say which hospitals they are, or we'd know which ones to avoid.

And then, of course, there are the things floating in jars, magnified to unnatural size by the glass and liquid they're in. The less said about them, the sooner we can go and get lunch.

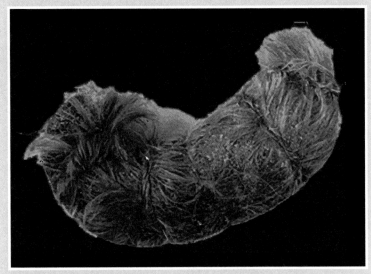

This trichobezoar, or hairball, was successfully removed during surgery from the stomach of a twelve-year-old girl. From age six she had suffered from trichophagia, an emotional disorder causing people to eat their hair.

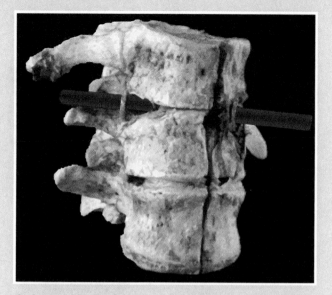

On July 2, 1881, Charles Guiteau fired two shots at President James Garfield. One shot grazed his hand the second entered the President's spine but did not exit. Garfield died on September 19 of complications from his injuries. Pathologists removed these vertebrae at autopsy to document the wound and resulting infection. The probe shows the path of the bullet.

As we have traveled through the state collecting stories for *Weird Maryland,* we've heard that the museum has toned down its exhibits quite a bit over the past few decades. Oldtimers still reminisce about going there as a rite of passage, because only real men and women could handle the sights on display. All we can say is that it must have been really grim back then, because it's not for the faint of heart (or stomach) now.

The National Museum of Health and Medicine is housed at the corner of Georgia Avenue and Elder Street in building 54 of the Armed Forces Institute of Pathology in Washington. It is open 364 days a year from ten a.m. to five-thirty p.m. Because it's on a military base, all adult visitors must present photographic ID and drivers must have vehicle registration and car insurance papers to get in.

The Green Arm of Antietam

For many years, there was a private museum in Sharpsburg in Washington County, near a pivotal battlefield of the Civil War. The Antietam Battlefield Museum had all the usual relics you'd expect to see at a war museum, but there was one that we bet you've never seen anywhere else: a severed soldier's arm that had dried out and mummified. This creepy body part had clearly not been surgically removed, but blown off its body just below the elbow: Its ragged end was just too messy to be the work of a surgeon—even one who worked a battlefield production line. But the rest of the arm was intact. Shriveled and disgusting, but intact. And it had turned a kind of gross green that made you wonder if it was a sculpture made of copper or bronze. But it was too real-looking to be a fake and just macabre enough to be stuck away in a back room of the museum, out of sight unless you went looking for it.

When the man who ran the museum, John Ray, bought the place back in the 1960s, he apparently had no idea it contained this strange relic. But when he dug it out of the box in the back room where it was filed away, he mounted it and touted it as the Arm of the Unknown Soldier. Now that's the mark of a true museum man—giving a mummified body part a cool name and displaying it proudly.

Antietam Days with Dad

I went to the Antietam Battlefield many times with my dad, who's a Civil War nut. The Battlefield Museum was the high point of our trips. While he was off looking at his stuff, I'd slip into the back room where this creepy exhibit was mounted in its own pine box, and stare at its delicate tapered fingers and well-manicured nails. They say it was the arm of a 19-year-old soldier, but nobody knows whether he was a Confederate or a Union man. When my dad found me looking at this thing one day, I asked him which he thought it was. He looked at me strangely for a while, as if he regretted exposing me to this weird stuff. Then he said, "Look at those fingernails. This was a man who took pride in himself. He's clearly one of ours. Now, let's go get ice cream." So we went. But I'd never have gone if he'd offered to take us out for Slim Jims or beef jerky.—*Les*

Roll Over! Fetch! Break the Senate Deadlock!

If Clair McLean gets her wish, her charming collection in Lothian, Anne Arundel County, will be absorbed into a new national museum in Washington, DC. We don't know whether to wish her well or hope she doesn't succeed, because in addition to breeding dogs this animal lover currently runs a neat little museum and it would be a shame to lose it to the big city.

The Presidential Pet Museum celebrates the pooches, kitties, and sundry other beasts who shared the White House with the commanders in chief of the nation. Clair McLean knows presidential pets. She used to groom Ronald Reagan's dog Lucky. And she's done plenty of research and collecting. The result is a compelling little collection housed in a gray utilitarian building down a well-manicured residential street. Amid the signed photographs, campaign buttons, and other typical political souvenirs you pick up plenty of facts about presidential pets. The Bush family's springer spaniel Spot was the first—and thanks to George W.—the only, second and third-term White House pet. Born in the White House to Barbara Bush's dog Millie in 1989, Spot died in 2003. The Clintons' Socks was a rarity among White House pets. The last cat in the White House had been Amy Carter's Misty Malarky Ying Yang. But the most unusual pets were Coolidge's bear and pygmy hippo.

Some of the more bizarre artifacts in the museum reflect how obsessive people can get about presidential pets. The Clintons' cat clearly struck a chord among ailurophiles, as you can tell from the bottles of Socks brand cat shampoo. And there's something almost shrinelike about the portrait of the Reagan family's Bouvier, Lucky. This beguiling artifact is a largish mixed-media picture coated with tufts of fur groomed from Dutch's pooch during her time in the White House doghouse. What other museum can boast such an artifact?

This is a pet lover's paradise. Not to mention the fact that as soon as you approach the museum, a troop of Bouvier des Flandres dogs, which Mrs. McLean breeds, bark out a chorus of welcomes. The museum is open by appointment from May to September and receives modest foot traffic, which gives it a personal quality that you seldom find in big-city museums. But in Clair's grand vision, it will become a 30 million dollar national pet museum in DC, where the First Pets will get pride of place. Catch this curious museum in its original setting soon before it moves to the Swamp, or check out the museum's Web site at www.presidentialpetmuseum.com.–*Rev. Dr. Bates*

This is with our new family member Lucky.

Usc 4

Ronald Reagan

Her paw print

FALA
THE WHITE HOUSE

Walking the Labyrinth

"You have to visit the Amaranthine Museum," they told me. "Don't ask why. Just go there. You won't get it until you go there."

Well, my unofficial tourist board may have consisted of art students and barflies, but they weren't wrong. This little treasure near Druid Hill Park north of Baltimore is the kind of art gallery that you won't see anywhere else on earth. That's because it covers the broad sweep of art history from classical architecture through abstract expression, and includes more than two hundred works in all kinds of media—paintings, sculpture, frescoes, furniture—all installed in a walk-through maze.

The whole thing is the work of one man, Les Harris, and this wasn't even his day job. He made each and every piece during evenings and weekends off from his teaching position at the Maryland Institute College of Art. If you're lucky, he'll be there to give you a guided walking tour through his maze on the one afternoon that his gallery is open (the first Sunday of each month). Sometimes, another member of his family will do the honors. But if you get Les, you'll be surprised at how humble he is about his artwork and exquisite installation that stretches on and on in an elaborate wooden maze. "I could not have done this; I'm not this much of a perfectionist," he says. "People ask me how I did it, and I don't know."

But the evidence is right there in front of your eyes. It's what can happen if you are extraordinarily talented and spend four or five hours every night for twenty years on a single project. Between 1976 and around 1996, Les would come home from work, hang out with his family, have dinner, and then go out to the studio he rented a few miles away. He'd start work around eight p.m. and continue until he was too tired to go on— anywhere between ten and two in the morning.

After a few years, Les's landlord wanted to vacate

the studio so he could sell the property, so Les bought huge packing cases for his canvases. When the landlord changed his mind, Les decided to use these huge cases as display walls and arranged them into a winding labyrinth-like path that literally walks you through centuries of art history. Some of what you see may be familiar, such as Les's version of Michelangelo's *David*, a Degas painting, or a beautiful pale painting of Chartres cathedral. All the time, Les chatters away, casually dropping a lifetime's knowledge in front of his audience. As you gawk at his spot-on interpretations of Egyptian art, he explains the symbolism of the snake and vulture on pharaohs' headgear: "The vulture is over the right hemisphere. They believed the vulture was fertilized by the wind, and so it symbolizes inspiration. The serpent is highest on the crown, over the left hemisphere. It eats gravel, and so it's fertilized by dust."

After an hour or more in the maze, you emerge where you began, feeling as though you've been through a time machine. To a casual fan of art, Harris's work is impressive and beautiful. To serious art students, it's a master class. But like all good things, the Labyrinth at the Amaranthine Museum may soon come to an end. The museum's Web site (www.aneventhorizon.com) casually invites sponsorship or sale of the museum. Here's hoping that it stays open long enough to inspire new generations of hard-working artists to initiate their own twenty-year projects.

Roadside Oddities

When people say, "It's not the destination that counts, it's the quality of the journey along the way," they could have had Maryland's highways and byways in mind. The state has been a driving kind of place since Route 40 first snaked its way westward. What we've learned at *Weird Maryland* is that wherever there's traffic, there is sure to be something strange on the roadside to make the journey more interesting.

Maryland has spawned many strange roadside attractions. Some of them, like Boonsboro's White Frog Colony, are no longer with us. In fact, except for a 1939 photograph in the Library of Congress archives, it seems as though nobody really knows much about the legendary home of the pale amphibian. Other dearly departed weirdness is still within living memory. The eighteen-foot-high trash can on Russell Street in Baltimore lasted until 2003, when structural defects led to its being scrapped. It lost its place in Guinness World Records as the World's Largest Trash Can, but gained its place in *Weird Maryland* as the World's Most Recyclable Monument to Irony.

Thankfully, many of Maryland's bizarre street attractions are still extant and going strong. Next time you're out and about, keep your eyes on the road, but station a lookout to ride shotgun. Because wherever you go, you'll see something strange on the way.

Land of the Giants

Giants invaded the roadsides of the United States about forty years ago, and some of them still survive to this day. Brightly painted fiberglass titans like the perky Bob's Big Boy and the provocative Miss Uniroyal began as marketing tools, but ended up in the hearts and minds of the weird-loving public.

The invasion of mass-produced giant sculptures began in 1962, when Bob Prewitt of Prewitt Fiberglass built a twenty-foot-tall Paul Bunyan for the PB Cafe on Route 66 in Flagstaff, Arizona. Prewitt was a cowboy whose real love was rodeos, so he sold his business to a boat builder named Steve Dashew, who renamed it International Fiberglass and began to diversify and ramp-up marketing efforts. By mixing and matching standard molds for limbs, torsos, and heads, International Fiberglass turned Paul Bunyan into the Muffler Man, an iconic marketing tool for auto repair shops, crazy golf venues, and pretty much any retail outlet that could benefit from a twenty-foot giant stationed near the store's door.

Some of these mass-produced statues have found their way to Maryland, where they were duly customized. But more interesting are the one-off pieces, like the carpet-laying Roland A. Remnant in Westminster or the giant His Master's Voice dog in Baltimore. The Free State has a fine group of giant statues. Here come some of them now.

March of the Muffler Men

The mass-produced Muffler Man statue has a number of distinguishing features. He's twenty-something feet high. He has a barrel chest and a Schwarzenegger jawline. He has a short-sleeved, open-necked shirt (though custom paint jobs can conceal some of these details). And he has a characteristic hand position: left-hand down, right-hand up. This belies his origins as a Paul Bunyan statue: He was designed to hold an axe.

Of course, in an auto-repair icon this hand position was used to hold up a real auto muffler. Over the years and across the nation, this lantern-jawed macho man has sometimes been given other things to hold and sometimes remains empty-handed. He has sometimes been given a different paint job and sometimes remains pretty much a lumberjack with an open-necked shirt. But he's always a towering presence.

For about forty years, a Muffler Man has stood outside an auto repair shop on the Pulaski Highway in Havre de Grace. But for about fifteen years, he's been a soldier. That's because when Ron Lynch decided to give the statue outside Lynch's Super Service a makeover, America was at war in the Gulf. The fiberglass statue had been there for years dressed as an auto mechanic, but with a fresh coat of paint he became the Desert Storm Muffler Man. His standard left-hand down, right-hand up now looks as if he was doing rifle

drills. And in a nice little touch that most people would miss, the back of his pants now bears the label Made in USA. He even had a campaign hat at one point, but it caught the wind too easily, so it's now inside the shop.

Meanwhile, a classic Paul Bunyan stands outside the Anne Arundel Fairgrounds on the General's Highway in Crownsville just outside Annapolis. He's dressed in standard lumberjack rig complete with a red wool cap. For more than a decade, this bearded monster man stood on top of a tractor store, Baldwin's Construction Equipment, holding two model trucks in his outstretched hands (both facing up, for a change). The proprietor of the store was an organizer of the fair and used to move his statue to the fairgrounds every year to promote the event. When his store closed down, the statue was taken to the fairgrounds permanently.

Over the bay and across the peninsula in Ocean City, a cutlass-wielding pirate guards the entrance to the Jolly Roger Amusement Park. He could pass for the one-eyed bearded twin of the Desert Storm Man in Havre de Grace. Certainly, his blue-striped pants, pirate boots, and jaunty hat are well-suited to a Halloween party, but the Jolly Roger Pirate is indeed the same basic model as the Desert Storm Man. It just goes to show how much a fresh coat of paint and a little imagination can change the personality of a chunk of mass-produced fiberglass.

Rollin' Rollin' Roland

One of our favorites has been rolling up a remnant of carpet for years on top of Traynor's Floors and Carpet in Westminster. He's looking a little the worse for wear these days, but carpet laying is a tough job, so we're not surprised. About twenty years ago, the owners of the carpet store ran a competition to come up with a name for this hard-working guy. The winning name is a masterly bit of wordplay that deserves a place in the annals of pun: Roland A. Remnant.

Elk Attack

Many towns have jumped on the art-statue bandwagon over the years. A while back, New York City even had an invasion of cows that were custom-painted by local artists. But in our wide research, we've found only one place whose art-project animals were a pun on the town name—Elkton's elks are unique in that respect. More than a dozen of them can be found along the main street and beyond, each with its own unique paint job. Our favorite beyond any doubt is the Wedding Elk, with its antlers adorned with a veil and bells. In the 1920s and '30s, Elkton was the elopement capital of the eastern United States, having cornered the market on wedding chapels decades before Las Vegas entered the business. The Wedding Elk stands near the last remaining wedding chapel on Main Street . . . right opposite the courthouse and next to a bail bond operation.

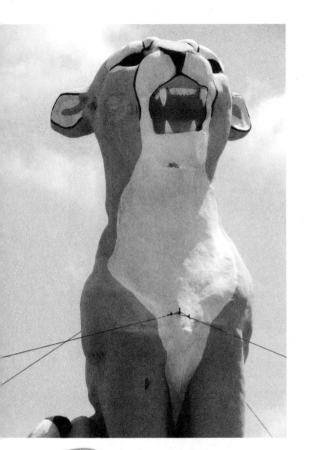

Do You Have a Tiger in Your Tank?

Well, no, but we've got a cougar on our car dealership. For the past three decades, this big cat has silently roared at the customers at Wilson Powell Darcars, a Lincoln-Mercury dealership in Temple Hills just east of Washington, DC. As with all great art, you either get it or you don't. If you don't, you just have to accept it anyway. The big mystery is why the dealership doesn't also carry Jaguars.

Here Boy! Two Dogs Have Their Day

Maryland's two most notable huge hounds are doggedly individual. One makes his home in Havre de Grace where he sits at attention on the roof of the home of a local fisherman, quietly bearing witness to the fact that his master sells fish for a living.

Baltimore's Nipper has a bit more of a story to him. This fifteen-foot fiberglass replica of the dog from the famous painting *His Master's Voice* originally sat on top of the RCA building in Baltimore. He was built by

Adler Display, the company that designed most of the Enchanted Forest in Ellicott City. After loyally representing the company for more than two decades, he was retired in 1975, when he was sold for a dollar and transported to the side of the Lee Highway in Virginia. Twenty years later he came back to Baltimore, where he sat in the yard of the Baltimore City Life Museum. Toward the end of the millennium, he was moved to his current location on Park Avenue, on top of the Maryland Historical Society building.

Of course, neither of these big dogs has nearly as impressive a pedestal as the original painting of Nipper, the perky fox terrier. His painting by Francis Barraud in 1899, *His Master's Voice*, was in fact a quirky portrait steeped in Victorian sentiment: The dog had belonged to Francis's brother Mark, and after Mark died, Francis adopted Nipper. After the dog died, Francis painted a portrait of him and the Edison-Bell cylinder phonograph, both of which appear to be seated on a highly polished casket. Yep, the original Nipper's pedestal was His Master's Coffin!

Ground Control to Montgomery College

What do roadside giants put on their desks? Why, giant globes like this one on the campus of Montgomery College. Actually, this model of Mother Earth is a water tank with a two-million-gallon capacity. It was commissioned in the late 1970s by the Washington Suburban Sanitary Commission to stabilize the water pressure supply in the Germantown area during peak usage times and to provide the emergency water needed by the fire department. The design was a compromise that the water company struck with the college, which insisted that it didn't want an eyesore on campus. This giant tank, officially called Earthoid, goes by the nickname of the Blue Marble and was dedicated in 1980 after a $1.7 million construction and painting project. The NASA-inspired image of the earth took a five-person team three months to complete, and its construction and design were so impressive that the Steel Plate Fabricators Association awarded it the Steel Tank of the Year Award. But that was more than twenty-five years ago. When we visited the site, we must admit that the paint (a urethane top coat over an epoxy base) was beginning to peel a bit at the bottom. The original paint job cost $140,000, according to a 1979 article in the college's student newspaper. Wonder what a touch-up job would run to?

Acorn or UFO?

Montgomery County's Acorn Park in Silver Spring is a little street-corner park with a disproportionately large nut in it. This bench-adorned rotunda looks pretty much like the proto-oak tree that gives the park its name, but to some conspiracy theorists (or sly wits pretending to be conspiracy theorists), it looks suspiciously like something else.

Think back, if you will, to a certain episode of the hit TV show *Unsolved Mysteries,* which addressed a mysterious UFO incident in Kecksburg, Pennsylvania, in the 1960s. All the witnesses to this incident described the object that crash-landed as acorn-shaped. Mysterious men whisked away the evidence, and the official story has been that there was never any incident or acorn-shaped UFO in Kecksburg. The Pennsylvania town erected an acorn-shaped monument to the UFO shortly after the TV special aired. And meanwhile, in a government-riddled suburb of Washington, DC, another acorn monument appeared.

Were these two monuments separated at birth? Is there some kind of cover-up? As Richard Dreyfuss's character said in the mashed-potato scene of *Close Encounters of the Third Kind,* "This means something." We just don't know what.

Mormon Temple

The Mormon Temple in Kensington was built for the Church of Jesus Christ of Latter-day Saints between 1968 and 1974. It is so huge that it rises like a phoenix out of the desolate surrounds of the . . . well, the Capital Beltway (I-495). Affectionately known as Oz or the Emerald City by area locals, it looks like a magical castle. Its six-spire design is meant to portray the church as a "light to the world," the three towers to the east representing the Melchizedek Priesthood leadership and those to the west the Aaronic Priesthood leadership. One of the six spires is topped with an eighteen-foot-tall statue of the angel Moroni, a Mormon prophet. The exterior is covered with 173,000 square feet of Alabama marble, and translucent windows of five-eighths-inch-thick marble light the interior. Situated on fifty-seven acres, it cost $15 million to build and stands 280 feet tall. It is the third largest Mormon temple in the world.

Pull up (an Enormous) Chair and Have a Seat

This giant Duncan Phyfe model chair was located on the corner of V Street and Martin Luther King Jr. Avenue, SE, until just recently when it was dismantled for restoration. Made of solid mahogany from Honduras, the nineteen-foot-tall chair was a gift from Bassett Furniture Industries. It was donated in 1958 to honor the Curtis Brothers furniture company, which was a major employer in this DC neighborhood known as Old Anacostia.

An inspection of the chair in 2005 proved it to be rotting and in danger of collapse. At the time of this writing, the phenomenal piece of furniture is being repaired and will hopefully be reset in its proper place to decorate its street corner once more.

Have a Really Big Coke and a Smile

Atop the Coca-Cola bottling plant in Frederick sits none other than—what else?—a giant Coke. It is a replica of a circa-1920 bottle, and it stands on the roof of the 1940s building as a beacon to thirsty people everywhere. The bottle was refurbished in 1998.

Drinking Big in Ocean City

Ocean City's Giant Martini sits on the corner of Coastal Highway and Eighteenth Street. The twenty-five-foot-tall martini glass was erected in 2003 next to a now closed nightclub called the Paddock. Discriminating drinkers will recognize the colossal beverage as a gimlet, complete with giant garnish and mixing straw.

Giant Cider Barrel

This gargantuan cider barrel in Germantown was built in 1926 as a roadside stand that sold locally produced cider and produce. It closed for good in 2003, and the trailer park behind it, the Cider Barrel Mobile Home Court, was razed and an apartment complex was developed on the property. In an unusual move by land developers, a decision was made to spare—and even refurbish—the landmark barrel!

It's true. Maryland's shores stretch for thousands of miles along the Chesapeake and Coastal bays and the Atlantic Ocean. It's no surprise the state has a massive maritime history. Perhaps that accounts for the prevalent nautical theme alongside the state's roads. But many of the sharks, ships, and sundries that line the roads are so far inland that it makes them anomalies. Lighthouse liquor stores and restaurants are fair enough. But perhaps less so when these marine treasures are dry-docked, like these in St. Marys County and a stone's throw from Washington, DC.

Aye, Aye, Captain

From some angles, the Captain James looks like a distinctively painted street corner diner, which is in fact what it is. But it's also a bona fide replica of an oceangoing vessel, which, for a seafood establishment, is entirely appropriate. The giant ship has been moored in Baltimore since the early 1980s, and may God bless her and all who sail in her. The last time we boarded, the establishment was open round the clock and was permanently dry-docked at 2127 Boston Street.

Flying Fish?

In a town that's widely populated with fiberglass elks, it's a surprise to see that Elkton also sports a giant fish, which appears to have been impaled on a weathervane off Main Street while flying past.

Jaws 2

Most barflies know what a shark's tooth is: dark rum, grenadine, lemon and lime juice, and soda water. Well, that may be. But to folks in Glen Burnie, the Shark's Tooth is a bar with a giant fiberglass shark's head sticking out of it. And that beats a fancy cocktail any day of the week.

Decorating the Tree, Visionary-Style

Anybody can slap tinsel, baubles, popcorn, and an angel on a tree and call it decorated. It takes a particular kind of mind to add some of the more bizarre decorations we've seen in our travels.

One of the great arboreal art centers of the East is the American Visionary Art Museum, or AVAM, in the Baltimore Inner Harbor district. Across the water from most of the Inner Harbor traffic, AVAM is a quiet corner of weirdness with a steady stream of offbeat visitors. The place really screams out its strangeness only once a year with the annual Kinetic Art Race.

The rest of the time it's content to catch your eye with quiet but compelling little details, like a glittering tree that sits by the roadside. The tree is located near a busy stretch of road, but it's hard not to notice the flashing light reflected off the mirrors and multicolored glass and plastic adorning its branches and trunk.

If you're actually on foot near AVAM, there's another tree-top delight in store. A rough-hewn tree house occupies a large part of the building's courtyard. It's a blast to walk through the building, its logs arranged in clever patterns.

Love Road Rocket

In Darlington, Harford County, a narrow stretch of country road winds off into the distance. It's called Love Road, and among its many delights is this mysterious rocket, just outside a large piece of private property filled with junked cars. What this red rocket is doing sticking into a tree, nobody can say for sure. One thing's certain: It's probably best not to disturb the owner of the property. If he's got trees that can stop rockets, we're betting that unwelcome visitors might not be so lucky.

A Tale of Two Street Names

When it comes to street names, Maryland's urban planners sure know how to pick 'em. Both Frederick and Columbia were given so much grief over a couple of roads less well named that they eventually relented and changed the names.

In 1907, a realty company based in Delaware built a little street in Frederick between West College Terrace and Lindbergh Avenue to facilitate traffic flow through its development. They chose to name the little drive with the most auspicious term they could think of: the Sanskrit word for good fortune. Unfortunately, the Sanskrit word in question is "swastika."

By 1940, there were dark rumblings about having a Swastika Road in the neighborhood. This was, after all, the national symbol chosen by Nazi Germany. Despite the obvious offense to delicate sensibilities, Swastika Road remained just that until almost thirty years after the Second World War ended. In February 1960, Frederick's mayor, Jacob Ramsburg, and his board of aldermen approved the idea of changing the name. More than eighteen months later, the street sign was removed. But it wasn't until 1972 that a new sign appeared in its place. What name did they choose? Why, Freedom Drive, of course.

About five years after Swastika Road was renamed, a delicate U-shaped residential street forty miles away in Columbia became the victim of a clerical error that would cause trouble for twenty-some households for the next twenty-eight years. The road should have been named Satinwood Drive. But one mistyped letter and an accidental space gave it a far more sinister name: Satan Wood Drive.

This name may sound like a fun gag at first, but the residents had real trouble with it. When ordering pizza or other goods on the phone, they never knew whether the order-taker would treat the call as a joke and not fill the order. Angry responses and hang-ups were not unknown. And the repetition of obvious jokes ("I bet I can guess your area code . . . same three numbers, right?") became intolerable. To crank up the irony a couple more notches, the ministers of at least three different churches lived on the road at various times.

Things came to a head in December 2004 when twenty of the twenty-one households on Satan Wood Drive petitioned the Howard County Planning Department for a name change. Three months

later the story appeared in a *Baltimore Sun* article that was reprinted worldwide. The sticking point with the process was the cost of changing signs and other official records—it would cost more than $2,000.

In the spring of 2005, *Weird* paid a final homage to the street with the wrong name by photographing the street sign. On May 3 of that year, workers finally corrected the typo from 1977 and, in the words of one of them, had "a devil of a time" removing the old signs. The road seems pretty much the same now as it was before, but we bet house values have gone up considerably now that it's Satinwood Drive.

On the subject of clerical errors: Are any towns more likely to be the victims (or results) of typing error than Accokeek, Glenelg, and Nanjemoy?

What's in a Name?

As every parent knows, picking a name can be a difficult task. When England's King Charles first signed the charter establishing the colony that is now Maryland, he did a good job . . . and a diplomatic one. Most of the Catholic refugees who settled there assumed it was named after the Holy Mother, Mary. In fact, Charles I named it after his wife. Fortunately for us, though, he gave it his wife's second name. If he hadn't, we would be traveling across Weird Henriettaland.

But having lucked out in the state-naming stakes, Maryland seems to have made some curious choices later on. For example, many towns across the world are known for their principal exports. Flintstone, Gunpowder, and Granite are good cases in point. However, it's a much rarer town that relies on its principal export's scientific name or genus. But that's what the town of Bivalve does. Yes, we mean Bivalve in Wicomico County.

Other town names are less descriptive of their main industry. The towns of Relay and Sparks are not populated exclusively with electricians. Suitland and Secretary are not entirely white-collar industrial parks. And Aquasco is not just one big water company.

Place names don't always describe the territory either. You'd be forgiven for thinking that a seafaring state's town of Delmar derives from the Spanish *del mar,* meaning "of the sea." But Delmar is in the dead center of a peninsula, far removed from Maryland's coastal borders. This is one of the state's famous composite place-names. Delmarva is the prime example, of course, cramming the names of three states into one peninsula. Many border towns truncate the state names and shuffle them around a bit for variety. That's how Marydel and Mardela Springs appeared in the mix.

Here's a bit of advice to anyone who wants to name his or her town after some topographical feature in the area. Most townsfolk who have done that try to choose a distinctive one. Perhaps someone could have explained that to the good folk of Street, Avenue, Fork, Creek, and Point of Rocks. Those are a shade too generic to be helpful, folks!

The same could also be said of towns named after names. There's Luke, Helen, Chester, and Frederick—they are fine names for your kids, but towns? At least the ill-omened name of Benedict Arnold was divvied up between two towns an hour's drive from each other, though neither had a thing to do with the famous traitor. On the subject of people names, Chevy Chase and Bowie may sound like a decent lineup for a late-night Saturday TV show in the 1970s, but they're hardly town names, are they? (Speaking of entertainers, how come there aren't any major bands from Ijamsville and Funkstown?)

It's good to have a sense of optimism when naming your town, as the good citizens of Eldorado, Fairplay, Loveville, and Friendly clearly did. There's even something confident about the rather more self-aware town name of Cockeysville. But couldn't some of this warm and upbeat spirit have filtered through the poor souls of Boring, Savage, Trappe, Finksburg, Colora, and Crapo? And was there ever a town that sounded more like it was named for a crazy shanty-dwelling hermit than Montgomery County's Cabin John?

And on the subject of self-promotion, couldn't the town fathers of Halfway, Midway, and Detour have come up with names that sound less like pit stops on a road trip?

And speaking of road trips, let's continue ours, taking care to avoid two other places, Pinto and Accident, as we investigate more things that make Maryland weird.

Roads Less Traveled

Plenty of well-traveled roads crisscross the Free State of Maryland. Route 40 and I-95 spring to mind. The Baltimore–Washington Parkway is way up in the traffic charts too. And don't even get started on that pressure cooker of canned humanity they call the Beltway.

Yes, thousands of people drive along Maryland's roads every day. But many of those roads merely provide an efficient route for traveling from point A to point B. We're interested in the other roads: the roads that wind their way across marshy or wooded lands. Roads without streetlights. Roads that carry only a few cars or none to disturb a good night-driving scare-fest. The roads with legends attached to them.

These are not the major routes that appear on a typical set of Internet driving directions. They may not even appear on some regional maps. That's one of the things we like about them. So buckle up and come with us down the shortcuts to local legend. We promise not to drive too fast.

Tales from the Governor's Bridge Road

If you're looking for a road that's soaked with creepy legends, look no farther than Governor's Bridge Road, which sets out from Bowie in Prince Georges County and heads toward Annapolis. It's astounding how quickly this road goes spooky on you. One moment you're taking Exit 13 off Route 50, and the next you're in a deserted, marshy, trash-lined track that winds off into the distance. But it's the point where the road crosses the Patuxent River on a metal bridge that attracts the most stories. The bridge has had a history of flooding in heavy rains, which is enough to make anyone cautious, but the tales go beyond sensible driving advice.

Over the years, it has been featured as the scene of all the gruesome legends you can imagine, ranging from babies being tossed from moving vehicles to traffic accidents so grisly that they turn passengers into hamburger. The stories that we have heard were common knowledge in the 1970s and had probably been in circulation for decades by then. And they are so varied that any story that's worth telling about Governor's Bridge Road somehow gets woven into its legend and becomes a part of the road itself.

Some of the stories sound very familiar, too familiar to qualify as strictly Maryland lore. We can quickly dismiss the one that tells of an escaped lunatic with hooks for hands as an almost universal urban legend. Ditto the one that insists that if your car stalls on the bridge, it will never start again.

But other tales of the road have a much stronger sense of the place. Where these stories come from is anybody's guess. Perhaps they began as teenage prank stories designed to spoil (or enhance) the fun of people who went parking or partying on country roads at night. Perhaps they were circulated by old moonshiners who operated stills in the area and wanted to keep people away from their illegal operations. Or perhaps they were made up to explain some of the peculiar events that used to take place down there. One thing that's pretty well documented by nighttime adventurers is that plenty of folks have had rocks smash into their cars along that stretch of road. Possibly the rocks were just kicked up by the car's tires, but there are those who insist they were thrown from the roadside.

Here are just a few of the legends associated with Governor's Bridge Road. Take them with a grain of salt, but be aware that somewhere in Anne Arundel and Prince Georges counties somebody swears that these stories are true.

The Beast with Five Fingers

There was a traffic accident down on Governor's Bridge Road that was so terrible that the driver was ripped to pieces. The gruesome duty of collecting the scattered body parts fell to a search team. After many hours of cleanup, they seemed to have collected everything except for one hand. The natural conclusion they drew was that it was either trapped in the mangled steel or upholstery of the car, or that a wild animal had made off with it. So they called off the search and moved on to the next accident. But the story goes that teenagers who go parking or partying down the road sometimes hear a scuffling sound of something in the undergrowth, and if they don't get out of there quickly enough, the thing will crawl right up to the car and bang on the sides until they do. Naturally, it's the missing hand, and if you're not too intent on getting away, you can see it scuffling away in your rearview mirror.

Thumbing a Ride

The bridge that gives Governor's Bridge Road its name is apparently haunted by several supernatural forces. One of them is a phantom hitchhiker. The story goes that if you

drive across the bridge at night, you may see a young woman of high school age dressed like a bobbysoxer from the 1950s. If you stop the car and open the door to give her a ride, don't expect company in your car. The place where she was standing will be empty: You won't see a trace that anyone had been there.

Weeping in the Fog

The bridge on Governor's Bridge Road is also said to have been the scene of a baby's death. Some say the poor tyke was thrown from a moving vehicle (either by vicious adults or the car's skidding). Others say that the child was unwanted and left to die by the bridge. However the baby died, it makes its presence known on some foggy nights—you can hear it crying.

Home of the Goat Man

Governor's Bridge Road is one of those roads that just seems creepy when you drive down it. It's incredibly old, windy, and has a sketchy metal one-lane bridge that goes over the Patuxent River. They say it's one of the Goat Man's hangouts. It was the site of one pretty insane happening back in March of '01. When I first went down the road with a few of my friends, the road seemed like it would just be a windy back road. We drove past a restaurant, and some car dealerships, and then past the town homes, the expensive new houses, and the paintball course. The road remains pretty open for a few yards, with lights lining it. We drove up a slight incline, and didn't expect what we hit when we got to the other side. The new pavement completely dropped off to incredibly old, bumpy, rough pavement. We drove through the first big turn and we could all tell something was weird about the road, but we didn't really know what. We got down to the bridge; nothing happened. We figured it was just a hoax.

A couple of weeks later, it was spring break, and Friday happened to fall on the 13th. One of us cracked a joke and said, "Let's go down there at midnight and see what happens." If I could remember who it was, I'd go slap him. We were piled six deep into an '85 Chevy Monte Carlo, and were at least prepared for the harsh pavement over the hill this time. But we weren't prepared for what happened after that. After the first turn where the road goes pretty straight for a good clip, we saw four random tires lining the right side of the road that hadn't been there the last time we drove by.

We pulled partway into the dirt parking area, backed up, and hit something that did not seem happy that we'd hit it. . . . It kinda looked like a goat, but definitely wasn't a goat.

Right after that the dome light of the car started to flicker. Next, we got to watch the windows fog up, which left me with pretty much no view from the backseat to see what was about to happen.

When we got down to the bridge we decided sticking around wasn't such a hot idea. We pulled partway into the dirt parking area, backed up, and hit something that did not seem happy that we'd hit it. I personally didn't see it, but from what the driver and the person riding shotgun said, they saw a creature that had hooves. It kinda looked like a goat, but definitely wasn't a goat. We didn't stay there long enough to find out what it was. We just peeled out and up the road back to normalcy.

On the way out, two of the tires were gone, the dome light was still flickering, and we saw pairs of red dots throughout the woods (with what little we could see through the windows). When we blasted back onto the newer pavement, the dome light shut off and the windows began to defog. We went to a gas station and got out to check the car. Outside the car we found what looked like a bullet hole in the left rear fender near the wheel well, tentacle-like marks on the bottom of the right rear fender, and what looked like handprints trailing down the outside of the rear windows. Our only conclusion is that we hit Goat Man, but the rest of it we can't explain. I've only met about three people who believe me that it happened, other than the six of us in the car. One of them was this guy who was afraid of nothing. He said he was in those woods on his dirt bike and something started to chase him, and he had his bike full throttle and whatever it was somehow kept up with him. As soon as he hit the pavement, whatever was chasing him disappeared. He didn't leave his house for two weeks. –*Marcus*

Terror on Tucker Road

Back in the 1970s, Tucker Road had its heyday as the creepy road of choice. This road runs just north of Andrews Air Force Base in Fort Washington, but folks from towns all around seem to have been attracted to the place. Night-driving adventurers from Oxon Hill used to love it. Back then it was heavily wooded and narrow enough to be blocked by a car coming in the opposite direction. It's a different road altogether now, widened and developed. But ask any kid's parents or grandparents about how it used to be, and you'll get a different story.

The road was not only dark and disturbing, it was at one time littered with an inordinate number of abandoned cars. Apparently, one or more hermits who liked to come out at night used to live just off the road. In short, Tucker Road possessed all the ingredients for a grade A set of local legends. And that's exactly what it had. For one thing, it was widely held to be one of the haunts of the Goat Man; on those nights with a full moon, or after a lunar eclipse, you could find him scurrying around on the bridge, frantically looking for something. Whenever a car came by to distract him, he would become annoyed and chase or attack the car.

When *Weird Maryland* went to examine the area, we were disappointed to find a well-paved road with only one very modern concrete bridge. A well-tended athletic field lies just beyond the bridge. Surely this couldn't be the place, we thought. But a man out jogging stopped when he saw our cameras and puzzled expressions, and told us how it used to be.

"When I was a kid in the 1960s and early '70s, it was a bitch to drive down here because it was so narrow," he said. "There were no shoulders, but there were lots of trees—so many that you couldn't even see the moon. Kids my age and older would tell me that an old fellah with the head of a goat and the body of a man stationed himself at the old one-lane bridge. As cars approached, he would throw bricks at them and scurry across the bridge. If you had your windows rolled down and listened carefully, you would hear bleating."

And with a chuckle, he himself scurried across the bridge.

Tucker Road may have lost some of its creepiness with creeping real estate development over the past thirty years, but it's still alive with legends. We didn't hear any bleating, but at the far end of the road from Andrews AFB we found a great graveyard filled with weathered concrete memorials. If there's not enough left in the road to give you a chill, these mementoes should do the trick.

A Bridge Too Fa-a-a-aaah

Back in the Depression and right through the Vietnam War, they used to say that a weird creature guarded the Tucker Road Bridge. He was supposed to be half-man, half-goat . . . which part is which, I don't know. Some people said his head looked like an old man's, but his body was like a goat's; he was also supposed to kill people with a brick, which doesn't seem consistent. They said he drank human blood, which he got by sneaking up to cars and killing the occupants. There used to be a lot of abandoned cars around there that made the story seem more believable. I'm sure people used to sneak up on parked cars and bleat like a goat to scare the people inside. If you heard the baa-baa noise, it was too late to get away. By the time the 1970s rolled around, people were saying that he had been killed in a fire. I don't know whether the stories are still in circulation, but they were the hot ticket back in our grandparents' day.—*Paul*

Tucker Road's Ugly Hermit

Back when Tucker Road was a little country road, there was a shack off of it near the bridge. The hermit who lived there was ugly, and people used to say he had a face like a goat. They also used to say his face got that way because he was cursed for being mean-tempered and greedy, but I forget now who cursed him and why.—*Anonymous*

High on a Bridge Stood a Lonely Goatherd

This legend's an old one that my grandparents used to tell. A hermit used to live on Tucker Road and raised goats there. Some people say he'd been an air force pilot and lost his feet in a plane crash. The stumps looked like hooves, and the trauma made him reclusive and a little crazy. Because he shunned human contact, the goats were his only companions and so he began to act like them. People used to go down there at night and terrorize him, and one night a gang set fire to his shanty and killed all his goats. The next night, the hermit either started to wear a goat-head mask or his head mutated into that of a goat. Either way, he was now homeless and angry at the world, so he'd seek his revenge on anybody who drove down there.
—*Anonymous*

The Man with the Weird Beard

The hermit of Tucker Road was an old black man with a tufted little beard like a goat's. That must be why they confused him with the Goat Man. I'm pretty sure that the legends all started out because of his strange habits. He lived in a little hut and was pretty self-sufficient. He grew his own vegetables and would go out hunting for meat. People would see him crossing the bridge with whatever he'd killed during his night hunt, and it would freak them out completely.—*Anonymous*

Fletchertown Fetches the Goat Man

Fletchertown Road in Bowie has long been rumored to be another notorious haunt of the Goat Man. Though the pavement was widened in the 1990s and some new housing developments have sprung up in recent years along the once heavily wooded byway, stories of a half human monster in bloody and tattered clothing are still told along this road.
—*Tim M.*

Bridges Too Far

Bridges are an important part of our lives, and that makes them an equally important part of folklore. In the past, they have been used not just for crossing rivers and ravines, but also for suicides, murders, and public executions, and because of this, they breed legends.

Some of our favorite bridge tales concern a dying feat of engineering—the old-time covered bridge. These resemble huts on trusses and were much sought after in the 1800s as a place to shelter yourself and your horse during storms. But the odd noises that reverberate around the walls and roofs of these structures gave easily spooked horses and riders plenty to worry about. Even to this day, you can almost hear the sound of wailing or crying on a covered bridge . . . and that's no doubt what made tales of haunted bridges so popular.

More and more covered bridges have been replaced by simple reinforced concrete extensions of the road, but a few survive. And as for the legends, they go on and on.

Jericho Bridge

Maryland's most photogenic haunted bridge is near the border of Baltimore and Harford counties near the 230-year-old Jerusalem Mill around Little Gunpowder Falls. The historic site once housed the White Silk flour mill, part of a thriving Quaker settlement called Jerusalem. Now it's a visitor center for Gunpowder Falls State Park, with a quaint preserved historic area. Just outside the settlement, near the junction of Jerusalem and Jericho roads, stands Jericho Covered Bridge. Built around 1865 and refurbished a century later, this quaint old bridge is a magnet for ghost stories. According to some paranormal watchers, there's a good reason for that.

Ablaze on Jericho Bridge

There is a dark, lonesome covered bridge on Jericho Rd. near Kingsville, off of Jerusalem Rd. The story that creeped me out was a tale about a young girl who was riding with her father in the back of an old barn truck. She was afraid of the dark, so her father had left her a lantern in the back of the truck for a light so she wouldn't get frightened. Traveling on the road that the bridge was located on, the father had made a sharp turn, knocking the lantern on its side. His daughter had fallen asleep and as they went through the bridge, the hay in the back of the truck was ablaze. He had stopped to do what he could to save his daughter, but he was too late. The young girl burned to death.

A few friends and I went up there a couple nights in a row; we brought a tape recorder, flashlights and my camcorder with night vision. The first two nights we didn't get anything, but on the third when we went back to the house to examine the tape we came across voices of the ghosts (EVPs, electronic voice phenomena), that really freaked us out. The EVP was a young woman's voice. No question about that! The voice was clear enough to understand what it said: "It's the lights." So our conclusion was that it was the young girl talking about the fire, yet it was just a few flashlights.

There are other stories of this bridge too. Three young men hung themselves from the rafters underneath it. If you stop your car on the bridge late at night and look in your rearview mirror, the figure of a body dangling from the rafters will be seen.

Another story is that of a middle-aged woman who shows up as a white, faded, ghostly image. Apparently, she walks through the bridge on certain nights carrying a basket of flowers. Some have said that they've seen her as if she was a living being but if they approach her she vanishes. Underneath the bridge is a flowing river, and it's really loud after it has rained, so if you do visit this bridge, make sure it's on a day when it hasn't rained recently.*–Kevin Lowicki*

Screams of Jericho Bridge

There is a covered bridge in Baltimore County off Jerusalem Road that has been around since the days of slavery. Legend has it that the bridge was used to hang slaves who were caught trying to run away. I have been there several times. As you drive onto the bridge, you are supposed to turn off your car and your lights and you can hear screams coming from somewhere. Also, even with the engine off, your car will continue to roll down the bridge like you are not wanted there.*–MysticPrincess*

Crybaby Bridges

The legend of the crybaby bridge seems to span the whole world and settle around old bridges, usually small ones across rural creeks. The legend has a series of set elements: There's an unwanted pregnancy, an infanticide, and often a suicide too. But as with any worldwide tale, there are many variants to the story. A typical crybaby bridge tale tells of a woman who is pregnant out of wedlock. In desperation she throws herself off the bridge, killing herself and her unborn child. In a variant, the child is born and in the throes of depression, the mother throws the baby off the bridge, then kills herself. Sometimes, it's the furious father or deadbeat lover of the unwed mother who does the killing. But no matter how the deaths came about, the sound you hear at the bridge is the wailing of the infant's ghost.

Maryland's crybaby bridges seem to be in both Prince Georges and Saint Marys counties, and often the stories that surround each one are interchangeable. But we've heard some interesting variants to the story that seem unique to a specific bridge. It's always nice to know that your own local legend has something to set it apart from all the rest.

Murder-Suicide at Crybaby Bridge

The bridge in this story is within an hour of Baltimore, closer to Annapolis. I originally heard the tale from a friend of mine who has been to the bridge. She is not sure if she experienced actual phenomena or if she was unconsciously fulfilling pre-existing expectations.

Here's the story: Legend has it that a young woman, 17 years old, lived in this area in the 1970s. Her family was very conservative (in some versions, her father was a preacher), but she had a bit of a wild streak. She became pregnant. Knowing that her father would be very upset, and probably throw her out of his house, she asked her boyfriend for help. He wanted nothing more to do with her or the baby. She decided to stay with an aunt in Virginia for a while. She hoped that once the baby was born, her father would soften up and take her and the child in. All went well, and she had a healthy baby months later. One night soon after, she packed up their few belongings, worked up her courage, and left for her father's house.

There, things took a turn for the worse. He was furious that she had not told him her plans to return. What made him even angrier was the public scandal this would cause. He viciously berated (and some say beat) her until she ran from the house in fear of her life. She took her baby with her. Hysterical, she had no idea where to run, and ended up at a nearby bridge. Looking down into the cool black water, sparkling in the moonlight, she began to see an answer to her problems. At the time, it must have seemed like the only solution. She and the baby would leave this miserable life together. As they plunged into the forgiving waters, they did just that. The bodies were never found.

If you go to the bridge on a cool dark night, especially if you're in emotional pain or distress, it is said that the baby's cries can be heard. Some say they are carried by the cold wind. Others say they emanate from the depths of the cool water.
–Deena

Tears at Lottsford Vista Road

There is a legend in our part of Maryland about Lottsford Vista Road, a country road near Upper Marlboro, and its crybaby bridge. The legend has it that a woman had a baby out of wedlock a long time ago and rather than face her family, she went out to the bridge in the dead of night and threw the baby off it into the creek below. Supposedly if you went there late at night and sat still, you could hear the baby cry.

Some of my friends and I decided to go check this out one summer night. We were joking around a little, goofing off; then finally somebody mentioned that we needed to be quiet if we wanted to hear it. So we all shut up and sat there for about 15 minutes. I remember thinking, "This is so lame." Then, all of a sudden, we all heard it, clear as day. There was no question that it was a baby crying, and it sounded like it was coming from under the bridge. I should mention that it wasn't possible that someone was playing a joke. We were all in the car, and two of my friends had checked all around when we first got there to see if anyone else was there. There are absolutely no houses or buildings of any kind anywhere around. We were all freaked, and got out of there as fast as we could. I never went back.
–LH

Murderous Dreams of Crybaby Bridge

I had never even heard of anything called Crybaby Bridge until I moved to Maryland. The bridge is only 10 minutes from my house, so I gathered my digital camera and went to the bridge one night. I can remember it perfectly—it was about 12:20 a.m. and I remember noticing how everything started to become totally isolated! As I drove closer and closer to the bridge, everything began to disappear—first the stores and houses, then people, then cars, and soon enough everything was pitch black. I was left with only my car's headlights and nature . . . and whatever phenomena might be lurking about. I stood still for a while so I could get the feel of the place. I admit I did not like the feeling I got—not one bit! I began to snap pictures with my camera and as I was doing so the feeling only got worse. It was a feeling that you get when something is consuming you or sort of threatening you, and it was then I knew it was time for me to leave. I got home and uploaded my pictures to my computer and noticed that in one I had gotten a strange mist that had a sort of human-like form. I did not get this sort of image in any of my other pictures.

There are also reports of a Satanic Church in the woods where the bridge is. Not much is known at this time but one thing is for sure: I am not the only one who has captured strange mist and orbs at this bridge and I am certainly not the only one who senses dread and danger there. If you ever happen to come across this bridge late one night, do not stay too long if you can't handle the fear and some butterflies in your stomach. This bridge is bone chilling to say the least!
–Sadie

I Have Heard the Baby's Cries

I too have been to the Church of the inverted cross and Crybaby Bridge. However, the crybaby bridge we used to visit was on Governor's Bridge Road. It was a steel frame bridge and the story I remember was something about a baby being hanged there. We used to go there as teenagers and I have heard the baby crying.*–Kimberly L. Crockett*

Crybaby Creek

In Saint Marys County are two towns that sound a lot like a West Coast settlement. They are California and Hollywood, and between them and Leonardtown stretches the winding Saint Andrew's Church Road. It's been built up a lot in recent years, but there's still a stretch of land there, near a big storage facility, that's so swampy-looking that it's likely to remain undeveloped for a while.

Near the intersection with Indian Bridge Road, Saint

Andrew's Church Road is carried over a swampy patch of land by a newer bridge that's so unobtrusive it's easy to mistake for just a length of crash barrier. In days gone by, it was much creepier, and the legends about the bridge are creepier still. One tells of a pregnant young wife whose husband went off to war. She had a son before the war ended, and late one night she was awakened by a phone call. It was her husband, who had made it to Hollywood and was about to borrow a car to drive home. She was so excited that she bundled up the baby and started up the road to meet him. He was so eager to get home that he was driving at top speed. The road was poorly lit and twisted around right before the bridge, and that's where the mother and child were walking just as her husband's car took the curve. There was no way that he could stop in time. The young woman was killed instantly, and the baby was thrown out of her arms over the side of the bridge. The baby's body was never found, but his cries can still be heard from the waters below. The stream has been called Crybaby Creek for years.

The Beat Goes On

There is a small bridge in Ellicott City just off of Bonnie Branch Road that is known locally as Heartbeat Bridge. Legend has it that many years ago there was a man who lived in a house near the entrance to the bridge who went insane and killed his wife by cutting out her heart. He then threw the still beating organ in the stream beneath the bridge.

It is said that if you go to the bridge at night, stop your car, kill the engine and remain very quiet you can still hear the murdered woman's heart beating. Me and my friends tried this out once for ourselves late at night. We parked in the middle of the dark bridge in the dead of night and rolled down all of the car's windows. Unfortunately, we made ourselves so scared that we were never able to quiet down enough to hear any heart beat. One of my friends was freaking out so bad that we had no choice but to leave the scene so that she wouldn't have a heart attack. Hopefully I will be able to go back again some day with some friends who are not prone to spazzing out.—*Rachel Newsteadt*

A Truck from Hell

I wanted to let you know about a place in Ellicott City known as "Seven Hills Road" where some weird stuff goes down. The actual name of the street is College Avenue and it is located between New Cut Road and Bonnie Branch Road. College Avenue has these seven hills (hence its nickname "Seven Hills Road"). If you are driving along this road at night and you happen to hit the seventh hill at exactly midnight, this black pickup truck will appear behind you out of NOWHERE and start chasing you! I know this sounds like a Stephen King movie scenario or something, but it REALLY happens. I've seen it for myself!

One night last summer a bunch of buddies and I had nothing to do so we drove out to Seven Hills to test this legend out for ourselves. We drove along, counting the rises and dips as we went. We were going pretty slowly so that we wouldn't miss any. Sure enough, as we reached the top of the seventh hill we looked in the rearview mirror and saw two headlights appear about a hundred yards behind us. All of a sudden they started bearing down on us! As they got closer, we could see the form of a big black pickup truck silhouetted in the moonlight. At that point we all freaked and decided to get the hell out of there as fast as my crappy car would take us.

I must have floored it for about a mile, with the truck gaining on us the whole way. I really thought that we would either be run down or end up careening off the road. But then the strangest thing happened. We reached the end of the road and I made a quick right turn. Everyone in the car turned around to look out the back window to see if the truck would make the turn too and continue to tail us, praying that it wouldn't. But it wasn't there! It had just disappeared before it reached the intersection. The weirdest part is that it had nowhere to go—no turn offs, no driveways to pull into—nothing. It just seemed to vanish. I was stunned, but I have to admit, also very relieved.

I don't know if the driver of the truck is some angry local yokel just trying to scare off bored folks like myself, or if the truck is actually some kind of demon from hell. Either way, I can tell you that it does exist. I've never heard any stories of it actually catching up to anybody or what might happen if it does—I'm just glad I didn't find out personally!—*A. Wayne*

Tunneling to West Virginia

Not all roads are on land. Some of America's oldest highways are in fact made of water. The canal age spread west from Europe in the late 1700s and had its heyday in the United States between 1790 and the mid-1800s. Canal boats were the trucks of their time, able to carry enormous cargoes over great distances, and all they needed was a straight stretch of water that was deep enough. The Chesapeake and Ohio Canal was just such a watery superhighway. In 1836, an engineer named Lee Montgomery conceived a plan to bore a tunnel through an Allegheny Mountains ridge to speed up river freight traffic, and his project is now one of the weirdest, darkest canal tunnels in the Northeast. Called the Paw Paw Tunnel, it is located along the Potomac River and connects Maryland and West Virginia.

The construction project took six times longer than planned and cost more than half a million in 1850 dollars. It was not a happy project. The work was slow and hard, sometimes involving only twelve feet of tunneling per week. The workers went without pay during frequent interruptions to the cash flow. And the records of the time speak of frequent cave-ins, outbreaks of cholera, and acts of violence. Apparently, there were even murders. And after the project drew to a close, the mastermind behind it emerged bankrupt.

The heyday of the canals waned as the age of the steam train arrived, but the Paw Paw Tunnel carried on a useful life for seventy years as boats carried tons of coal, farm products, and manufactured goods between Maryland and West Virginia. The walkway along the side of the canal became a secondary traffic lane for pack animals. But it was originally put there as a towpath for the mules that dragged the boats along and also for the runner, a boy who ran ahead through the tunnel to raise the signal to any boats coming the other way that the tunnel was occupied. That's right . . . this was a single-lane tunnel.

The walking path makes for an echoing and awe-inspiring hike. It runs very straight, so that the light at the end of the tunnel is always tantalizingly ahead of you, but it's more than three thousand feet long and pitch-black inside, so it never seems to get any nearer. And if you're sensitive to spooky atmospheres, you may pick up on a downer that pervades the place.

One strange thing about this hike is the way the light changes all the time. The ceiling is lined with white brick, which reflects the light quite well at the end of the tunnel, but even with a flashlight, it gets dark pretty quickly. The route is very straight, but the path rises and falls a bit, so you're left with very uncertain footing, especially in the muddy patches. Odd sounds echo through the tunnel, usually because of drips of leaking water—and when a drop lands on you, it's enough to make you scream. Sometimes, you'll see mad cyclists trail-biking through the place.

After walking along the tunnel's three-fifths of a mile, you break out into West Virginia and see steep shale walls and cascading waterfalls. It's a beautiful view. But you have to wonder if the disturbing experience of going through the tunnel is worth it. Especially since the Paw Paw Tunnel is about twenty-five miles from Cumberland and remote enough that you should expect to hike about five miles just to get to it. And that doesn't include the half a mile in the tunnel in almost complete darkness.

You can get there by cutting through the gravel roads of the Green Ridge State Forest off I-68, about ten miles west of Hancock. The roads to the tunnel are not wide or well traveled either, so be sure to drive carefully.

Fantastic Journey Through the Paw Paw Tunnel

If you are like me and enjoy riding into the countryside, leaving the motorcycle for a while and meandering off on foot in pursuit of scenic wonders, then, boy, do I have the ride for you!

Located in the northwestern tip of West Virginia (near its convergence with Maryland and Pennsylvania)—and situated alongside the mighty Potomac River, the Paw Paw tunnel harkens back to a time when America, still in its infancy, moved at a less frenetic pace and transported its goods overland using methods and conveyances that today seem primitive and quaint. Long before railroads ushered in the industrial era, canals reigned as the supreme method for moving freight. Of the multitude of canals that existed during those halcyon days, precious few remain intact today. There are some notable exceptions, and in my opinion, one crown jewel—the Paw Paw tunnel.

Oh, how impressive it is! Fourteen years in the making, and carved from solid rock, it pierced the mountainside for 3,118 feet—the construction crews had faced adversity at every turn,

through floods, illnesses, work stoppages, and yet there it stood majestically. With its beautifully carved stonework adorning each portal, it truly was a sight to behold.

Fast forward to the present day and you might expect to find strip malls or condominiums lying where all this history once transpired. Thankfully though, you'd be mistaken. The C&O canal officially moved its last boat through in 1928. Ten years later the U.S. government acquired it. It remained dormant for the most part until 1971 when it was proclaimed a national historical park, which accounts for its protected status and subsequent upkeep. Standing at nearly any locale along its route, the feeling is one of having been whisked back to the mid 1800's, such is the remarkable condition that this marvel of human ingenuity bespeaks.

If you plan to visit, the Paw Paw tunnel is located roughly a quarter of a mile walk along the towpath from a nearby camping area. The tunnel is passable for its entire length and people routinely move through it on bicycles and on foot. The circle of light, which is the opposite portal, seems deceptively close. It isn't. Don't even think about going through without a flashlight, the center of the tunnel is much darker than it appears from the outside and the dirt surface of the towpath undulates and can be slippery. For the less (more?) adventurous there is a marked foot trail that will carry you up and over the tunnel (just the thing for those of you with claustrophobia—or scaredy cats); it offers some outstanding views along the way and, if you're riding a mountain bike, some tremendous "air" opportunities on the way down—but for less athletic folks, it may be too strenuous. The elevation gain is in excess of 400 feet, so let your degree of fitness dictate if this is a viable option for you. But trust me, you haven't lived till you haul-ass through that tunnel, preferably by yourself, and get the tar scared out of you somewhere around mid-tunnel. By the way, do you think it was by chance that I located that alternate trail over the mountain? Heck no! There was no way that I was pedaling through that sucker again, all by my lonesome. Jeepers, give me a break, I still sleep with a nightlight!
—*Jeff Bahr*

Rolling Up Gravity Road

Forget for a while what you learned in school. Newton's laws of physics don't always apply in Maryland. There are a few places here (and elsewhere in the world, we must concede) where the laws of gravity are considered optional. Such places go by the name of Gravity Roads, Gravity Hills, or Ghost Hills, and when you visit them in your car, strange things happen. Park in the right spot on one of these hills and put your car into neutral, then wait. Slowly but surely, your car will begin to roll uphill. Yes, uphill.

We've managed to track down several such places in Maryland. One is in the Burkittsville/Jefferson area in Frederick County, with another nearby just off Liberty Road outside of Walkersville. A third is northwest of Baltimore at the Soldier's Delight Park in Owings Mills. And there's a fourth in Washington County near Boonsboro.

These places have been the stuff of legend and nighttime visits since the 1960s and earlier, and whenever we go to them, it's always a kick to have our senses turned around. Using the limited science available to us, namely a level, we concluded from the way the bubble went that the uphill road was probably a downhill road—but as true believers have pointed out to us repeatedly over the years, if gravity is sufficiently out of whack to draw a car uphill, it's certainly going to push a bubble the wrong way also.

Clearly, this is a case for a surveyor to decide, and sure enough, about twenty years ago, a group of Fortean researchers in Maryland calling themselves the Enigma Project enlisted the help of a surveyor named Mike Gilbert to give a ruling on the Gravity Hill at Soldier's Delight Park. He surveyed the road with a transit and concluded that the incline of the hill was in fact a decline. In this case, at least, the gravity hill effect is actually an optical illusion. But that isn't the end of the story. The point of visiting a gravity hill is to experience that delicious topsy-turvy feeling of having your eyes deceive you. Whatever the real reason for this effect, it's a lot of fun to experience.

Gathland Park's Spook Hill

Gathland Park, on the outskirts of Burkittsville, was the site of the Civil War battle for Crampton's Gap, which took place on September 14, 1862. There is a Civil War Correspondents' Memorial Arch to commemorate the battle, but there's a more surreal experience to be had in the area. The slope there is called Spook Hill, and it's one of the nation's famous antigravity spots. As the story goes, you can set your car in neutral on this slope and feel yourself rolling uphill instead of downhill.

There have been many explanations for this phenomenon. One is that the whole thing is an optical illusion. The road only appears to slope upward because of the grade of the surrounding terrain. In fact, you're just rolling downhill, and the weird feeling you get when it's happening is disorientation between what your eyes and your sense of balance are telling your brain. Another explanation is that the area is one of those spots where gravity doesn't drag you down normally: Something at the top of the slope has a greater gravitational pull than the entire mass of the planet at the bottom of the slope. A third explanation for the phenomenon is a lot creepier but more in keeping with the area's history.

The Battle at Crampton's Gap was a decisive one in the Civil War, and the Confederate forces did not come off well in it. They were outnumbered six to one and lost almost nine hundred men. This was the first Union victory against Lee's armies and was a direct antecedent of the bloodbath at Antietam three days later. It's not a happy place for the South. And the sheer volume of Confederate dead led to some pretty unpleasant tales of mass interment.

In one account, the Confederate army, in its rush to get to Antietam, paid a local man named Wise to bury fifty of the dead soldiers' bodies. He dumped the bodies in a well, they say, and began to see apparitions of one of the dead men shortly afterward. Eventually, he had to remove all the bodies and bury them properly in shallow graves. The notion was that when the South won the war, the bodies would be exhumed and given a place of honor somewhere special like Arlington National Cemetery. In fact, they were exhumed six years later to be reinterred in the Washington Confederate Cemetery.

But around that time, people began hearing ghostly voices in the homes and the tannery in Burkittsville. They still say the site of the old tannery is haunted, and any car parked there overnight may have marks on it the following day from soldiers' boots. The antigravity effect of the hill, they say, is caused by the ghosts of Confederate soldiers, struggling almost a hundred and fifty years later to get their cannons into position at the top of the hill and win the battle. It's a good story for a nighttime trip to the slope, but it doesn't account for some of the other antigravity effects in the area.

Spook Hill's Hoofprints of Gravity

Near Frederick is a hill called Spook Hill, which supposedly contains Civil War tunnels. If you drive up this hill and put your car into neutral, it will go up by itself. If you sprinkle some powder on top of your car, you will find hoof prints in the powder from a local ghostly horseman. Spook Hill is actually located just outside of Burkittsville. From Harpers Ferry, take Route 340 toward Frederick, and take the third exit over the Maryland bridge. Turn left off the exit ramp and drive six miles to Burkittsville. At the square in Burkittsville, turn left again, and drive half a mile to the town limits. You will see a barn on the left. Slowly drive up the hill where, at the top, you will see several historical markers on either side of the road.–*Anonymous*

Feeling Gravity's Pull in Washington County

Near Boonsboro there is a place known locally as Ghost Hill. You're supposed to go there at night, turn off your engine, and put the car in neutral, and a ghost will push your car uphill. This area is rich in Civil War history, and rumor has it that the ghost is the spirit of a Union soldier who was killed when he lost control of the cannon he was pushing, which rolled back down the hill and crushed him. Supposedly the ghost is trying to push his cannon back up the hill. The legend even includes a part about sprinkling baby powder on the bumper so you can see its handprints.

I went to Ghost Hill once when I was a teenager, and guess what—it worked! It's not really a hill—more of a sloped section of road—but the car definitely seemed to be defying gravity, and it picked up considerable speed. My friend and I didn't try the baby powder, we were anxious to get the hell out of there. Some have speculated that it's just an optical illusion, or that there are large concentrations of magnetic rock in the ground nearby (yeah, right). If I ever find myself out that way I'll probably try to find it again and maybe take some measuring tools, since I'm of a scientific bent. Then again, a logical explanation might spoil the fun.

This is in the western end of the state, in Washington County, near Hagerstown. Boonsboro is a one-stoplight, county fair, good-ol'-boy kind of town. Ghost Hill is actually on a lonely back road outside of the town. It's off of Routes 34 and 65.–*Travis*

Ghosts are so common they barely even qualify as weird anymore. When the tale of four undead spirits scaring the stuffing out of an old miser is considered sentimental family fare suitable for Christmastime entertainment, you know that ghosts have gone mainstream. But what are ghosts anyway, and why have they become so much a part of our culture? Most people who study them believe that ghosts are the spirits of people or creatures that no longer inhabit the world of the living. Some trauma surrounding their death or their life makes them unable to let go of the places they lived, worked, or died, so they stay around and can be seen or heard or sometimes smelled by the living. When they're around, they seem to suck the heat out of their surroundings—hence the common observation of cold air—and they throw certain electronic sensors into a tailspin.

Ghostly Happenings, Haunted Places

Of course, talk of ghosts brings out many reactions. Some true believers feel compassion for the dead-but-not-departed. Others are more distant, perhaps because they have been spooked by the ghosts. Others are simply skeptical and dismissive. And then there are those who just want a good scare by any means possible. *Weird Maryland* doesn't fit into any of these camps. If anything, we're ghost agnostics—not prepared to dismiss them outright, but unwilling to embrace them wholeheartedly. It is hard, however, to poke your head into the catacombs under Westminster Church in Baltimore or stroll down the narrow corridor of one of Maryland's three-hundred-year-old inns without feeling something beyond reason in the air. You can feel the skin on the back of your scalp crawl even before you know about someplace's haunted history.

Some of the experiences Marylanders have had are enough to make us wonder if there's more to this ghost business than a few scary stories. You will no doubt have your own opinions on such matters, so read on and draw your own conclusions.

The Headless Dumpster Diver of Annapolis

No collection of ghost stories is quite complete without mentioning the specter of a man without a head. Luckily for us, Maryland's got a doozy of a headless ghost tale, and it's set, appropriately enough, in the capital city. Visions of a headless ghost keep cropping up in all kinds of places around Annapolis. Down by the water, in back alleys rooting around in trash cans, up by St. Anne's Church, over by St. Mary's . . . you name it, if it's a place in Annapolis, it has played host to a translucent headless guy at some point.

But no ghost story is quite good enough if you can't get to the bottom of it—or in this case, the missing top of it. And trying to figure out the story behind this walking torso has taxed the imaginations of local folklorists for quite a while. Some people with an eye toward history point to St. Justin the Martyr as a possible candidate because, in the latter half of the second century, he was beheaded by the Romans for being a Christian, and his bones now rest in St. Mary's garden in Annapolis. It is said that to spare desecration to his grave, his remains were dug up and sent to St. Mary's in 1873. As the most venerable headless man in Maryland, he seems like a prime candidate for the headless ghost, except that there is another headless man buried in Annapolis.

According to Mike Carter, who operates the Ghosts of Annapolis Tour, there is a story of an awful murder and a deathbed confession that may explain the headless ghost. An elderly woman told him that a pastor of St. Anne's parish and several other witnesses had once heard the confession of a dying man as he told a tale of accidental death and dismemberment involving him and his brother.

Back in the early 1800s, many years before the man made his confession, he lived with his brother on Cornhill Street. The times were full of hard drinking and brawling, and sibling rivalry could sometimes turn nasty.

The brothers spent one drunken night arguing, getting more and more angry with each drink. By the time they got home, the fight had escalated to fisticuffs and, eventually, swordplay. With the impaired judgment typical of heavy drinking, it was inevitable someone would get hurt, and sure enough, one of the brothers was stabbed and died.

The surviving brother sobered up quickly. He knew he would swing for his crime, so his only option was to remove any identifying evidence. In the days before fingerprinting and DNA evidence, removing the head was a common ploy to hide the identity of a murder victim, so that's what the survivor did. He lopped off his brother's head, staggered down to the waterfront with it, and tossed it into the water. It was never seen again. As for the headless body, he buried it underneath the house.

The precise location of the house where the body was buried is unknown. There have been a number of fires along Cornhill Street since the early 1800s, and it's entirely possible that the house is no longer standing. However, we can assume that the headless corpse is still buried somewhere around there, but apparently he doesn't stay put. He's out looking for his head by night. His murderer, his brother, didn't get off scot-free either. He may not have swung for his crime, but his deathbed confession tells how heavy a burden his deed laid upon his soul. Whether telling his secret eased his conscience or not, we can be fairly sure he won't be hanging out with St. Justin the Martyr anytime soon. But he did do us the favor of explaining the headless ghost, and for that small mercy we should be grateful.

Little Orphan Annie

In the 1800s, Maryland had no shortage of places where the wealthy could send their daughters to learn the skills required of a true southern lady. The Patapsco Female Institute was just such a place. Built of yellow granite in 1839, on a hill overlooking a nice little town outside Baltimore, this finishing school lasted up until the Civil War left its curriculum irrelevant. For the next sixty years, it was used as a private residence, a hospital, and even a theater. Then it served the community as a cool abandoned building, complete with collapsed roof and rotted floors. It's now stabilized and is the centerpiece of a historic park that's open on Sundays between April and October. Oh, and it's the residence of Annie, the spirit of a girl who died there in the institute's heyday.

Annie Van Derlot was a student at the Patapsco Female Institute for a short time and seems to have hated every minute of it. Like many of her classmates, she was the daughter of a wealthy plantation owner from the South, sent up to the thriving northern metropolis of Ellicott City to learn French, genteel manners, and deportment. She seems to have concentrated on her penmanship, mostly in the form of miserable letters of complaint about her "incarceration" in this cold northern mill town. The teachers were strict and unpleasant, she hated the town and its people, and the damp, cold building made her sick. Her family must have assumed that she was merely suffering from homesickness, but apparently, they agreed to come and get her during her first winter at the institute. It turned out that her malaise wasn't psychological. Before they arrived, she died of pneumonia.

During daylight hours in the tourist season, it's possible to visit the institute, and quite a few tourists say they see a young woman at the door or coming down the stairs of the now wrecked building. Many more people see a face in the windows, looking out at the world in abject misery. And those who have seen her describe her in very similar ways: She wears a long dress in the fashion of the early 1800s and has long hair flowing most of the way down her back. She's immensely sad. And more often than not, she is carrying a bag, as if trying to leave the place under her own steam, after more than a century and a half of confinement.

Haunted Houses

The real estate market thrives on multiple-occupancy residences, but in the weird world that expression takes on another meaning. Single-family homes whose past occupants still show up in shadowy form are a staple of the ghost-watching world and here in Maryland we're blessed with an unusual selection of them. Most of these are private places, whose owners don't want a lot of publicity, so we've had to keep some specifics vague. But the details that really count, the ones that relate to the otherworldly visitors, are intact.

The Most Haunted House in Maryland

Anyone who has enjoyed a trip through Fell's Point in the Baltimore harbor area will have heard a ghost story or two about the place. Most of these stories often are repeated and embellished, but one of them has twists we never expected.

The majority of the stops on ghost tours of the city are saloons or hotels, but on a side street in Fell's Point there's a private dwelling about which sensitive people feel particularly uneasy. It's a three-story building that tour guides like to call the most haunted house in Maryland, and according to people attuned to paranormal activity there are five ghosts there, including one of a particularly angry cat.

When Donna Carpenter went on the Fell's Point Ghost Tour, she heard the tales of the specters: two young ghost women, an angry male ghost, and an older woman who lived on the third floor. But she intuited a lot more to the story than the guides were telling. Normally, we prefer hard evidence over intuition, but Donna knew details of the stories behind several places on the tour before the tour guide mentioned them, even though she'd never been to that part of town before. So we were intrigued by what else she could tell us. One of her intuitions related to animal bones discovered recently in the basement.

"They were doing some remodeling on the house," Donna explained. "And they broke through a wall in the basement. They found bones there, animal bones, and by breaking the wall down, they let out the cat . . . or at least the spirit of the cat."

Donna's take on the situation was this: The angry man whose ghost still haunts the building was a mean drunk who despised his wife's pet, a large cat. He kicked the creature whenever he could, but unlike his submissive wife, the cat fought back. An atmosphere of mutual loathing grew between the two until the man finally took his lead from Montressor in Poe's tale "The Cask of Amontillado" and walled the cat up in the cellar. Like Fortunato in the tale, the cat died behind the wall. People still talk about an angry presence that will violently shove those who stand on the doorstep of this house. That's the old drunkard. But they talk less often about an almost feral ghost animal that bristles at the presence of men in and around the house. That's his wife's pet, understandably ticked off at anything on two legs with a Y chromosome.

The old woman on the third floor, though, is a much calmer character—much sadder, but still calm. "She died there, in an attic back room," Donna told us. "Her spirit is an unsettled, unhappy spirit. She scares people only because she's there and she shouldn't be."

The house in Fell's Point used to be more accessible than it is now, but the current owner dislikes publicity and requests for ghost hunting at her home. Because of that we're keeping the exact location of the place secret. But any ghost tour of the Fell's Point area will take you discreetly to the place, as long as you don't get too near the front step. Of course, we wouldn't recommend getting too close anyway—not with the ghost of an angry drunk man waiting there to kick you.

Step, Tap, Step, Tap . . . Slam!

When I was ten, we moved into a Victorian house in Prince Georges County near Upper Marlboro. The house was built around 1886. I lived there for seven years, over which time small but weird things would happen. For instance, one night the tub got filled up to the brim with water on its own. Things would disappear, like pens off the desk. Every now and then, the door in my room that led to the storage area would be hanging open when I went up there. Our cats would sometimes freeze and stare at nothing, then turn and go a different way. We had a hand bell in the kitchen that sat on a shelf, and sometimes if you were alone in the house and upstairs, you would hear it ring. There was a side door that opened onto the wraparound porch, but we never used it, so it was always locked and in fact had been painted shut. We came home from vacation one time to find it standing wide open. Our neighbor had just checked the house a few hours earlier and it had been closed then.

There were also weird noises. We all heard someone walking up and down the stairs after everyone was in bed and assumed it was another family member until one of us mentioned it at breakfast one day. My dad did a lot of research on our house after all this freaky stuff started happening. It was built by an old sea captain named Captain Reid, who died there. We then realized the noises on the stairs must have been the Captain. You could hear the distinctive step, tap, step, tap—he had a wooden leg, apparently. This only went on for about three weeks, after which I guess he thought we were okay.

The freakiest thing that happened to me was about the door. There was a closet door that never quite stayed shut—it was always open about an inch or so. One night I came home late, around 1:00 a.m., when everyone else was upstairs sound asleep. I had the attic room. As I was getting ready for bed, I heard a loud banging. Feeling like the doomed heroine in a horror movie, I forced myself to go downstairs and see what was going on. It was apparent that someone had slammed the door open with great force, so that it hit the TV cabinet, bounced back against the door frame, and then banged open again. The closet door was standing open about half way. The hair on my arms is standing up thinking about it! I said out loud, "I'm sorry if I upset you," then went upstairs but left my light on and didn't sleep a wink! Things did actually seem to calm down a bit after that, and I never heard the door slam again. However, I wasn't sorry to move out when I did. —LH

A Hearth Without a Home

My summer camp, Camp Conowingo in Harford County, is probably the scariest place I've ever been to. There's this abandoned chimney on the side of the trail to our cabins. The story is that a mother and her three kids lived in a cabin during the Civil War. The father was away at war. One night, the mother looked out the window and saw Confederate soldiers marching up the hill. She knew they were coming to kill the family because her husband was a Northern soldier. She wanted her children to live, so she put her daughter, 9, and her son, 7, in the stone chimney. Then she gave the daughter her 8-month old baby. The children heard the mother being killed by the soldiers.

When they were sure the soldiers were gone, the children started to cry for help. But no one heard them. Nobody searched for the kids because they thought the whole family had been killed. Eventually, the kids died of starvation. They say that if you shout up the chimney on an extremely dark night, the children will scream back at you and haunt your dreams. *–Mary Beth McAndrews*

For Whom Belle Manor Tolls

There is a house called Belle Manor. It was the home of a mother, her husband, and adult son. Her husband and son went to war and the mother was upset. She was scared she would lose her family. Several months later, the lady got a letter saying her husband had been killed in battle. She was devastated. She wrote to her son and told him the news. She was glad she at least had her son left. Three months later, she got a letter saying her son had been killed. She was overwhelmed. She had no family. After two months, the lady had been driven so mad with grief that she hung herself. On a moonlit night you can see her ghost hanging from the window with a rope tied around her neck. There are many other stories about Belle Manor, too many to tell. *–Mary Beth McAndrews*

Haunted Hostels

Hotels and drinking establishments seem to be havens of paranormal activity — or at least, of tales of paranormal activity. Perhaps people feel more sensitive to an otherworldly presence when they're spending a night away from home or when they've knocked back a few drinks. Or perhaps the spirits of the departed like to belly up to the bar just as they did in life. Who knows? But there's no denying that as far as Maryland's ghosts are concerned, inns are the in place to hang out.

Haunted Hotel of Port Deposit

Port Deposit is a long, thin town perched on the rocky slope along the north bank of the Susquehanna as it runs along Route 222 between the Conowingo Dam and Route 95. It's a great old boating town with a long history, and one of its historic points is the Union Hotel Restaurant, which has been taking care of water-faring folk, dam builders, and people on the road since 1790.

The Union Hotel is now run as a tavern and restaurant, but for more than a century it was a hotel, and for a while in the 1920s, when the Conowingo Dam was being built, it served as a brothel. Along the way, it has played host to all kinds of ghost tales.

Truly strange things have gone on there. The servers at the restaurant, who walk around in period costume, told us about an

old clock case that sat on a shelf for show, and how, for about four months, it would chime even though it contained no clockwork. A cedar box on the mantel moved as one of the waitresses watched. And against the rules of physics, the door to the kitchen, two inches thick and solid as a safe door, would unlatch itself and swing open. At times when only two people were working in the building, there were almost comical incidents of misdirection, when the sound of footsteps and opening doors would have one person going in completely the wrong direction looking for the other.

Former employees tell tales of haunted Valentine's Day parties, visits by creepy ghost children, and the spirits of dead babies in shoeboxes (perhaps a reminder of the hotel's brothel days). So if you want a side of paranormal with your pub fare, visit the Union Hotel Restaurant.

Tales of the Admiral Fell

The Admiral Fell Hotel in Fell's Point has two hauntings, a woman and a man. During our trip to the area, we were across the street, and at one stage I had such strong feelings about the hotel that I had to turn and walk away. My companion asked if I was okay, but I wasn't. There's a young woman on the top floor, and she walks up and down the hallway. According to our tour guide, if I remember correctly, she was a chambermaid and she died. Now, this isn't written in anybody's history, but I knew that she had been killed because of jealousy. A woman thought she was stealing her husband away and made sure she was taken out of the picture. The guy's more fun. He's on the second floor, and he's a partier. People will hear him in a meeting room. They'll hear parties . . . all the noise of parties, music, and so on . . . that's where he is. He'll do silly pranks—blow people's hats off, come up behind them and pat them on the bottom, that kind of thing. He's a fun kind of ghost.—*Donna C.*

Whistling Oyster

The second floor of the Whistling Oyster bar isn't used. They say it's because they just don't need the space, and so they removed the stairway. But the real story's different. They tried to store things there, but the boxes would get moved around and smashed. You can sometimes see a young girl looking out of the window. She was about ten or twelve during one of the typhus epidemics that used to go through the area. She looks out of the window as she did when she was sick and dying, watching the carts go by filled with dead bodies and knowing that she is next. But there's someone else in the room there who throws things around. I never got a bead on this person. The girl is sad that she's going to die, but the other person there is angry. That's why she moves everything around.—*Donna C.*

Baltimore's Bar District

Fell's Point has two proud boasts: It was the birthplace of the Baltimore Clipper and, at one time, had more than fifty bars and saloons. If the walls of these buildings could talk, they would tell tales of hard drinking, outbreaks of disease, and the drugging and kidnapping of strong young men to serve as unwilling deckhands onboard ship. Such was the way of things in port towns in centuries past. And with this kind of history it's no surprise that some unwilling souls are still being spotted along these brick-paved streets around Aliceanna and Thames.

The Horse You Came In On Saloon boasts several things, all with great conviction. It's the oldest drinking establishment in Fell's Point, dating back to before the Revolution. It's the last place in which Edgar Allan Poe ever took a drink—they say he fell facedown in the gutter staggering back from a night's bender here. And they say a ghost that everyone calls Edgar makes his presence felt here all the time.

They also relate that cash register drawers fly open at random. The chandeliers swing for no good reason. And sometimes, to appease the ghost, the staff will leave a glass of whiskey out for him at closing time. Those are the rumors, and when we asked Mike the barman about it, he confirmed another: One night after closing time, something slammed shut the heavy door of the safe in the office. This heavy metal door was hard enough for a barman to move; it seemed unlikely that gravity or a gust of wind could do it. With a laugh that wasn't entirely mirthful, Mike told us he closed up pretty fast after that.

The Cat's Eye Pub at one time could have been more accurately named the Cat House. During renovations to the place, workers discovered a system of switches wired to the upstairs rooms that indicated which of the occupants was ready to receive customers. This had clearly been a fast-turnaround operation. Naturally, the switch system hadn't worked for longer than anyone could remember, and by the end of the renovation it was safely hidden behind wallboard. But many insist that it's possible to hear clicking behind the wall, as if the ghosts of the former working girls haven't quite shaken their work ethic even in death. But the weirdest tale of all is one that the co-founders of Fell's Point Ghost Tour tell. Amy Lynwander and Melissa Garland spent years pulling together the tales they relate on their tour, and during the research phase Garland visited the Cat's Eye and bought a T-shirt from a barman there. When she returned to the bar a few years later to tell him he would be mentioned on the tour, the staff looked very disturbed indeed. The barman she described and named had died six years earlier, a clear four years before she claimed she had bought the T-shirt from him.

Bertha's Restaurant, with its famous, if uninventive, slogan "Eat Bertha's mussels," is a favorite haunt of paranormal watchers. This tends to make the tales of the place a little unreliable, since people looking for ghosts tend to find the evidence they want. The number of photographs from Bertha's we have seen with orbs in them is huge . . . and after the event, it's hard to tell whether these faint circular blobs are ectoplasm or dust or some strange refraction in a flawed camera lens. But the sheer volume of Bertha's stories is hard to ignore. A few years back, when the Maryland Ghost and Spirit Association had a dinner at the restaurant, most of the people present were getting dozens of cloudy flaws in their pictures, swearing that these were spirits in transit lacking the energy to take on their human shape as they moved.

For those who aren't impressed by such evidence, there's a stained glass window in the restaurant that responds very strangely to electromagnetic field detectors; it can elicit wide EMF detector readings that swing from the edge of the red back to a normal ambient green without any apparent electronic interference. Like most places in Fell's Point, Bertha's used to lodge people in upper rooms in times when yellow fever and typhus were rife in the port towns. People who hear strange noises on second-story floors or see the owner's cats hissing down the hall or feel strange presences in the rooms (and these people are many) like to pin their experiences on victims of some nasty outbreak who aren't yet ready to quit the vibrant bar district. After all, it's much cleaner and safer now than it was in centuries past. And all the really interesting characters seem to have stuck around.

With Maryland's pivotal position near the centers of government during the War of Independence and its strategic position during the Civil War, this state has seen a lot of war. And to anyone with a bent for the paranormal, that means there's a strong possibility that some military ghosts still walk the earth here. Here are just a few of the thousands of places where old members of the armed forces continue to march the earth.

I Didn't Do It

One of the most celebrated tales of the Naval Academy at Annapolis concerns the death of Lieutenant James Sutton a century ago. The official verdict was that in the early hours of October 13, 1907, he placed a loaded gun to his head and pulled the trigger. Normally, the death of an officer would be announced to the family in the form of a telegram. However, this is not how the Sutton family back in Oregon heard about James's death.

James told them about it himself, and his story didn't jibe with the official report. James's sister and mother saw his ghost the same day he died, telling them that he had been beaten to death by his fellow Academy members. The family, incensed at the news, demanded that their son be exhumed and given a proper autopsy. The body was a mess because of a gunshot wound to the head, but a close examination revealed that the young man had received a serious and probably fatal beating before death.

Ghost tourists and cadets alike love to swap this tale when they are around the Academy, and some people insist that after his trip home to talk to his folks, James's ghost took up permanent residence in the Academy.

Lookout, It's Smallpox

At the southernmost tip of Saint Marys County, at the convergence of the Potomac River and the Chesapeake Bay, lies Point Lookout State Park. Mention this area to any local and talk of the paranormal will result. The area has a tragic history. In the 1600s, when the first settlers arrived, an entire family was killed at the point by Indians. In 1860, a lighthouse was built, which is often called the most haunted in the world. In 1863, the Government started a hospital to treat wounded Civil War soldiers and shortly after, a prisoner of war camp was opened with room for 10,000 Confederates. It ended up housing 20,000. Next a smallpox hospital was established. All in all about 4,000 people total lost their lives on the point, and about 3,000 are still buried there in unmarked graves. Ghost stories are rampant, but the weirdest was when a wall in the lighthouse glowed green for ten minutes. That's pretty darn weird!
–Sean Myers

It Wasn't Me!

One night last fall, a few of us amateur ghost hunters went out for a drive to Point Lookout at the southernmost point of Maryland. It is a very scenic ride with a lot of straight and curvy roads for us to enjoy. We arrived at the park around 11 p.m.; it's open 24 hours because of the night fishermen on the piers.

Fort Lincoln is still there: It's the main fort that was on the peninsula. It was a Union prison and hospital for the Confederate soldiers. At one point there were supposedly 10,000 soldiers there. Many who died were buried in unmarked mass graves.

So we pull in and pay and head down to where the lighthouse is. The lighthouse is very old and supposedly very haunted as well. It's right on the very end of the peninsula. It was very dark and very windy and we could feel the mist from the Chesapeake's choppy waters. My wife got cold and wanted to go back to the car so I said I'd walk her back. Now our five-month-old Chihuahua, Thor, seemed to be very uneasy in this area, not wanting to leave Alicia's side and seeming to sense something in the direction of the water.

I left the two of them in the car and began walking back to the group who had slowly walked down to the restroom area. When I got down to them, my friend Evan said, "It took you forever to walk down here!" I looked at him, very puzzled, and said, "I just started walking down here 15 seconds ago." Evan looked at me like I was crazy.

He said he saw the outline of a tall figure walking very slowly in the dark from the lighthouse to where

they were all standing about three to four minutes before I walked down to them. The individual seemed to be in no hurry to get anywhere. No one else besides us was out at the lighthouse area.

As soon as Evan and I realized that it wasn't me he saw, we all split up real quick and had a quick look around. Nothing. We got back to the car and my wife hadn't seen anything, but the dog was still very, very antsy. I have done some searching on the Net and found out that others have had similar experiences, with some even getting close enough to make out the Confederate uniforms. Others will see whole brigades march across the road in their rearview mirror, only to turn around and see nothing. To this day we're not 100 percent sure of what Evan saw. You can draw your own conclusions—I know I have.—*thestereogod*

U.S.S. *Constellation*

One of the centerpieces of Baltimore's inner harbor is the U.S.S. *Constellation,* a hundred-seventy-five-year-old ship rebuilt from the timbers of the first frigate in the U.S. Navy. The original *Constellation,* built in 1797, had a bloody history that some believe stuck to the material of the ship after it was rebuilt into the frigate in 1849, and still clings to the ship, even after it was renovated in 1995.

Legends have surrounded this ship ever since it was docked in Baltimore, with dark tales of moaning noises below decks and a nebulous apparition on the forecastle deck—the space at the bow of the ship, just below the main deck. In December 1955, a lieutenant commander on the neighboring submarine, the U.S.S. *Pike,* was the first to photograph something on the deck. Around midnight, Allen Ross Brougham was waiting with his camera set up and pointed at the forecastle. At a few seconds before twelve, he caught a faint odor like gunpowder. Directly afterward, he

USS CONSTELLATION
37 USA
2004

saw a "phosphorescently glowing, translucent ectoplasmic manifestation of a late eighteenth-century or early nineteenth-century sailor, complete with gold stripe trouser, cocked hat and sword." He took the picture, and the apparition vanished suddenly.

It didn't take long for professional investigators to appear. The international darling of ghost hunting, Hans Holzer—along with his right-hand psychic, Sybil Leek—gave the vessel a thorough going-over; he published his findings in two books, *Portal to the Past* and *Ghosts: True Encounters with the World Beyond.* In his accounts, he tells a tale from the early 1960s, when a Catholic priest arrived

for a tour, found nobody on deck, and went below to find his hosts. He met an old sailor down there who showed him around, pointed out features, and instructed him in the proper names for various pieces of equipment. On the priest's return to deck, members of the Maryland Naval Militia apologized for not being there when he arrived and offered to give him a tour. They had no guides below-decks. When they rushed down to find whoever had shown the priest around, he had vanished.

Once Holzer and Leek had given the place a thorough investigation, the stories behind these spirits emerged. The well-decked-out spirit in the forecastle was most likely the Revolutionary War captain and first commander of the *Constellation,* Captain Thomas Truxtun. He was an experienced tactician and stickler for discipline who wrote drill manuals and tactics for the fledgling navy. The shimmering mass on deck is probably a shell-shocked sailor who left his post during a battle with a French frigate in 1799. Neil Harvey by name, this sailor got the traditional punishment for leaving his post during battle: He was run through with a sword, strapped—bleeding but still alive—to the front of a cannon, and blown to pieces. Sybil Leek also intuited a third spirit of a young surgeon's assistant, an eleven-year-old boy, who was stabbed to death in the early 1820s.

It seems odd that spirits would stick around on a ship that was so heavily renovated and that moved around so much, but who are we to argue with these tales? Strange things, they say, happen at sea.

Andrews Air Force Base

Andrews AFB has a few ghost stories. In the Air Force One hangar, a man was spotted on the security cameras between the two security fences. A patrol was dispatched immediately to intercept him and was told that the man was right in front of them, but the patrol saw nothing! The man then suddenly vanished and the patrol was at a loss as to where he went, let alone how to enter this in the blotter.

The far side of the base had two hangars that had been built before WWII. One was used to store German officers' bodies, and in the other, a maintenance worker named Chuck died. The first has its share of very strange noises that can be heard all the way from the flightline outside and that's when nothing is in there.

The story of Chuck is a sad one. Chuck was a single guy, without a lot of friends outside of work. He lived by himself and had no family in the area. The night that he died, he was working on the tail of an airplane. The old scaffolding they had was not very sturdy or wide to stand on. As the others were preparing to leave, one asked if Chuck was working late and he said, "No, I'll be gone before you guys come out of the locker room." Well in the time that Chuck said this and his fellow employees went into the locker room, Chuck fell from the scaffolding and broke his neck and was knocked unconscious bleeding on the floor.

When his fellow workers returned from the locker room, they saw that Chuck wasn't on the scaffolding but did not see Chuck laying there because he was hidden behind a piece of machinery. Thinking he went home, they shut off the lights and locked up. Well, when he regained consciousness supposedly he tried to pull himself to the phone but he had lost too much blood and died there on the floor. This was also on Friday, so no one would find poor Chuck till Monday.

Since Chuck lived alone, no one realized that he was missing. Now supposedly Chuck's ghost can be heard walking through the hangar late at night. And his ghost has played with some people's minds. A few friends of mine one night went into the hangar to try to put this Chuck story to an end. Now these were all Security Forces Military policemen. One blatantly yelled, "Chuck, if you're here, we're not afraid of some dumb ghost!"

At that moment, it sounded as if someone ran down a set of metal stairs in the hangar. The guys dropped their flashlight and ran for the door. Since we have to pay for anything we lose, the one cop had to go back in to get his flashlight, searching for a few minutes. They eventually found it, turned off and sitting nicely on the 4th step of the metal stairs!—*thestereogod*

Haunted Local Government

Maryland is constantly haunted by the realization that it borders Washington, DC, but that's only a source of horror to a few of us. The real government terror is the rash of local government buildings that are haunted by mysterious entities. We've got them here in Maryland, make no mistake about it. But are they as real as the national debt? And are they as scary?

Buggin' in the Courthouse

In 2004, the Associated Press described a mysterious cloudy object picked up by the security cameras of the Kent County Court House in Chestertown. It was built in 1860 and has recently been renovated and a new wing added.

The security system was less than a month old when security officers saw a round object in the stairwell of the new wing on the timed-delay footage. They later watched live security camera footage of a round translucent object hovering up and down the stairs for more than an hour. Security officer Philip Price walked up to investigate and saw nothing, but a group of people watching the live footage from the camera in another room saw the orb flying ahead of him. Despite the muggy summer conditions, Price felt a chill descend on him at one stage during his climb.

Ghost hunters clamored to see the footage and turned up plenty of history that seemed to show the place could be haunted. The wing where this all happened had been built in the 1960s over an old graveyard. The courthouse had been a hanging site since the 1700s. And many courthouse employees confirmed that they heard strange noises when alone in the building, such as doors opening and closing. It all seemed to be a cut-and-dried case of orb infestation until Atlantic Security, which installed the cameras, explained the anomaly away. Brooke Eyler, the company's general manager, said it was a flying bug, distorted by the camera's lens and out of focus.

"I've seen it so many times, it's not funny," Eyler told reporters. Kent County's sheriff was satisfied with the explanation and closed the book on the subject, refusing to allow paranormal investigators in to test the area with night-vision cameras, temperature gauges, and electromagnetic field detectors. Some people took this as a local government cover-up. Although the law did deliver a verdict of natural causes, not everybody agrees with that judgment.

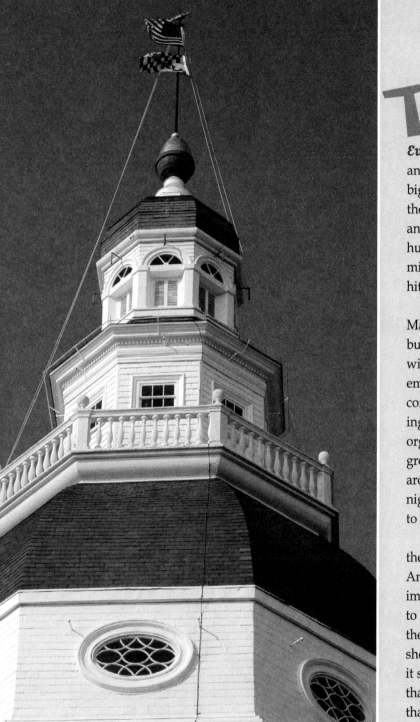

The Phantom Plasterer of Annapolis

Even a master craftsman can make a mistake, and on February 23, 1793, Thomas Dance made the biggest one of his life. While plastering the dome of the State House in Annapolis, he lost his footing and fell off the scaffolding. Since he was almost a hundred feet off the ground, this was the last mistake Thomas Dance would ever make. When he hit the ground, he died instantly.

But it wouldn't be his last appearance at the Maryland State House. Not by a long shot. The building Thomas Dance helped to construct echoes with strange footsteps at night, even when it's empty. And in the heat of summer, icy blasts of air come from nowhere (nowhere near an air-conditioning vent, at least). The Ghosts of Annapolis tour organization likes to announce that people in their groups have reported seeing a man wandering around the dome of the State House by day and by night, even though the dome is locked and off-limits to everybody.

The only time anyone goes up there is to set the flag to half-mast. And whenever the Ghosts of Annapolis group hears a report of the death of an important official, they check with the State House to see if the person lowering the flag saw anyone up there. The response is always no. Perhaps the flag should be flying at half-mast permanently, because it seems as though a death that happened more than two hundred years ago was more significant than anybody thought.

Churchyard Chillers

We all know that churches are places of worship and celebration, but the fact that most old churches are also surrounded by the bones of their dead parishioners adds a peculiar piquancy when sensitive souls pay a visit to them. Churchyard tales of terror are commonplace throughout the world, but Maryland has a few that are hard to pass over.

Meet Joe Morgue

Annapolis's Church Circle surrounds St. Anne's Parish Church and has a burial ground that's been used for hundreds of years. Many of the tombstones there were originally made of wood and have long since rotted away, leaving the precise location of the dead open to some debate. One person who kept track of such things was its sexton, Joseph Simmons, who died in 1836 at an almost unheard-of age for that era: a hundred years old.

No doubt one of the reasons for his hale disposition was his vigorous exercise regimen. He spent almost seventy years digging graves. He dug them for the recently dead. But he also dug in places where the grave markers were missing to make sure that coffins were still there. St. Anne's was probably the most aerated burial ground in the world. As the story goes, Simmons was so intent on his task that he didn't stop piling the dirt on the coffin of one Jeffrey Jig even after everybody heard banging inside the coffin. It

was clear that Jig was still alive, but old Joe kept piling the dirt on, saying, "He has to die sometime!"

No surprise that Simmons was referred to as Joe Morgue. He was apparently a grouchy man—dirty and tired from digging—and was often teased by the local children. But he had a well-practiced retort that soon shut them up: "I'll have you one day!" Given his extraordinarily long life, he must have often made good this threat.

When he finally died, Joe was buried in a less crowded graveyard in Spa Creek, but people insist that his slouching form still hangs around the area, causing streetlights to flicker, blow out, or explode. He often sits in the back of the church in the pew reserved for the sexton. People who enter the church early in the morning or later at night see him there and assume he's a vagrant looking for a place to relax. If they approach him, he'll rise, scowling, and make his way out without saying a word.

Chills in the Catacombs

Baltimore has a history of residents who found it, to use an overused expression, "a nice place to visit" — so nice they wanted to live there forever. And it seems that they did. There is a veritable condominium of those who made themselves comfortable for the long haul at the Westminster Church and Catacombs, where I unexpectedly experienced the most terrifying afternoon of my life.

I was working on an article on Edgar Allan Poe. I found myself at Westminster Church speaking with a Poe expert, LuAnn Marshall, who also happens to be a tour guide of the Westminster Catacombs. Poe was buried behind Westminster Church in a pine box, but when crowds made the cemetery impossible to manage, a new tombstone was erected at the front of the cemetery, where passersby did not have to enter the gates to view his grave.

My interview went as planned until I turned around and saw the rusty gates of the catacombs. LuAnn Marshall mentioned that the church was in fact built over the catacombs, which housed many of Baltimore's founding fathers and was filled with numerous bodies (and soon, I was to find out, souls). She then noted that she had often felt a presence in front of the largest mausoleum, and that various "mediums" and "psychics" have also felt and heard things that suggested it was a hotbed of paranormal activity. I stood there, skeptical, feeling nothing abnormal as we stood and talked.

Then, all of a sudden, I felt myself drawn—actually, yanked—to the right side of the catacombs. (Ms. Marshall later told me that psychics usually gravitate there as well.) It did not get cold, but I suddenly felt frozen to the spot. I had the overwhelming sense that, though Ms. Marshall and my photographer hadn't gotten to me yet, I was not alone. I sensed children. A lot of them. First, I had an overwhelming urge to laugh, followed by the need to cry,

then scream. But nothing would come out. It was every nightmare I had ever had. The air got so heavy I felt my breath being sucked out of me and I had to get out of that place or I knew I would be crushed with the weight of this presence.

I am usually not meek, nor am I easily frightened, but I got away from that area as fast as I could, and almost felt as if I were being mocked for giving in. It was an evil game of cat and mouse, and I was the mouse.

Once we got outside, my photographer wanted to tour the rest of the graveyard, but I had to get out of there so I made a beeline for the gate. But I couldn't. I found myself standing frozen directly next to the same spot I had run from, with the wall of the church between that horrible place and me. Bile in my throat, hysterical, I made it clear to my photographer it was time to go.

After I was well away from that place and caught my breath as much as I could, I looked at the digital photographs. It was then that I lost all sense of reality again. Though no other photos were remarkable from the catacombs, the one taken in that area I was chased from had orbs everywhere in the rafters, and even appearing to "sit" in pews. These photos were taken in daylight, I was certainly not up in the rafters causing dust, nor did any of us sit in the pews, so I have no explanation for them.

What I do know is that I am not a professional paranormal expert, nor was my photographer professional. I was not on a mission that day to find proof of the existence of spirits there—but I found it, and it still leaves a bitter taste in my throat. I could not find orbs in the other photos. Whatever they were, the camera picked them up in that location alone on that day and in no other place in the catacombs where we took photos. Skeptics, believers, it doesn't matter to me. I can only relate what I experienced, and leave it to you to decide for yourself.—*Donna Mucha*

ROBERT C. HALL
BORN DECEMBER 31. 1830
DIED AUGUST 19. 1908

"IN AS MUCH AS YE HAVE DONE IT UNTO
ONE OF THE LEAST OF THESE. MY BRETHREN
YE HAVE DONE IT UNTO ME."

MARY R.
WIFE OF ROBERT C. HALL
BORN JANUARY 24, 1833.
DIED SEPTEMBER 26. 190?

HER CHILDREN ARISE UP. AND
CALL HER BLESSED."

Cemetery Safari

*"Show me first the graveyards of a country and I will tell you
the true character of the people." — Benjamin Franklin*

Let's get this straight from the outset: There is nothing
morbid about visiting graveyards. Since the mid-
1800s, cemeteries have been a tourist destination
and even a place for townsfolk to take pleasant Sunday
afternoon strolls. That's when overcrowding in churchyard
burial grounds led to an innovation called the Victorian
garden cemetery — beautifully landscaped graveyards in the
countryside that looked more like parks than cemeteries. In
fact, these cemetery gardens became so popular that some
families relocated their dead from the old churchyard out
to the country. That's right, a full century before live
people had the idea, dead bodies began to move to the
suburbs. And the result was a revolution in cemetery art.

Old flat slabs of stone with names, dates, and terse
epitaphs were overtaken by a new wave of memorials. As
people came to stroll around the tombs, the bereaved
began to commission something for visitors to behold:
sculptures, art, and sometimes witty expressions of what
their dearly departed stood for while they were still alive.

So don't feel embarrassed about scoping out
graveyards. You may find people there trying to come to
terms with their loss, but you will also find celebrations of
life. And some of those lives were very weird indeed.

The Hanging Sailor of Perryman

It was one of those research trips: At noon, you're in the reading room of a historical society, and two hours later, you're lying facedown in a cemetery. Stories like these don't come up every day, but when they do, you have to ride them through to their natural conclusion. And this tale begins like a variant on a well-worn joke theme: A genealogist, an author, and a rock star walk into a historical society. . . .

I first became aware of their conversation when a man I later knew as Hank Peden uttered the words, "Perhaps he wasn't soaked in rum. Perhaps he just had a bottle of rum with him when he got buried." His comments were directed at a younger guy with cool hair and a soul patch beard, who said; "You've seen the pictures. The coffin looks like a boat made out of sailcloth. I just wish I could see some evidence of the chains."

Now, you can't let a conversation like this pass, so I had to join in. And after an hour's conversation over

lunch, the elements hung together into a great story. The younger guy, local rocker Kevin Johnston, had been fired up to finally learn the truth about Harford County's most storied grave site, and Hank, a genealogist who's a fixture at the Harford County Historical Society, was helping him. The grave was the final resting place of John Clark Monk, better known as the Hanging Sailor of Perryman. You could say this old sea dog is buried at the Spesutia Church of St. George's Parish in Abingdon, Harford County, but he's not buried in the traditional sense of the word. Before he died, Monk made it clear he didn't want his body to touch dry ground. So the story went that his crew members lowered their captain into an underground vault and suspended him from the ceiling by chains. To ensure that the casket didn't rot away, it was made of metal (some say it was a lead shroud) and he was soaked in rum. And because the underground vault was topped with four spaced-out stone slabs, the coffin was open to the elements and would swing in the breeze. On top of the slabs stands a six-foot stone sarcophagus containing the remains of the sailor's daughter. To get a good look at the seaman's plot, however, you need to lie facedown at one of the gaps between the stones, shield your eyes from the glare, and wait until your eyes get used to the darkness. Down there beneath the ground are two stone shelves reaching across the chamber, about halfway above the leaf-strewn floor. Perched on both shelves is a

Perched on both shelves is a strange container that looks like a sculpture of sailcloth wrapped around a canoe.

strange container that looks like a sculpture of sailcloth wrapped around a canoe. It's impossible to see the whole thing at once, but by sliding along between the cracks, it becomes clear that it's roughly coffin-shaped and coffin-sized. But what it's made of is anyone's guess. The weird thing is that you can see bones on the floor of the chamber. Amid the rusting flashlights dropped by nighttime visitors and sticking up from the leaves that nature contributed to the chamber floor, there are ribs and what looks like a skull.

Kevin Johnston is so taken with the story of the land-fearing sailor that he's been in touch with surviving descendants of John Monk to restore the swinging coffin to its original subterranean glory. There are no objections to the project from the church or the cemetery caretaker,

but as yet, the plan is only in its initial stages. So perhaps the swinging sailor will rock once more in his underground lair. Until then, the only thing about John Monk that rocks is the song Kevin wrote about his legend, called "The Swinging Sailor of Perryman," which his band, the Captain Quint, performs. Given that they are trop rockers (as in tropical), we're not sure whether their audiences are soaked in rum or just carrying a bottle.

The Mystery Visitor at Poe's Plot

The tiny burial square attached to Westminster Presbyterian Church at the corner of Fayette and Greene streets in Baltimore is home to one of the most beloved characters in weird-dom: Edgar Allan Poe. The master of the macabre died a suitably mysterious death, discovered insensible in the gutter outside a Baltimore bar on Lombard Street. He was taken to the Church Hospital at Broadway and Fairmont, where he died a few days later at the age of forty.

The cause of Poe's death is a matter of raging debate. Many people assumed his lifelong heavy drinking had finally killed him, but many of his fans found this explanation dismissive. They suggested that the rats that ran riot in the harbor town had given Poe rabies. One of the more creative explanations for his death cited poisoning by corrupt political factions. The author of some of the scariest stories on earth was found dying in the gutter on an election day in an era when some shady politicos pressed people into voting at every polling place. Some of the voting gangs recruited voters in the same way that navies used to recruit sailors: by slipping drugs into their drink and dragging them away. In Poe's drink-ridden state, being slipped a Mickey Finn would have been enough to induce coma and death.

But whatever way the beloved author of the haunting poem "The Raven" met his end, he wound up in the Westminster Burial Grounds, a suitable Gothic church complete with crypts. Initially he was buried around the back of the church, but twenty years later he was moved with his cousin-wife Virginia and aunt–mother-in-law Maria Clemm beneath an impressive monument at the entrance to the yard.

That would be pretty much the end of the story except for a strange visitor who began appearing at Poe's grave on the centennial of his death. On Poe's hundred and fortieth birthday, January 19, 1949, a cloaked man in black appeared at the grave in the early hours of the morning. He raised a glass and murmured a tribute to his hero, and made his way off as quietly as he came. He became known as the Poe Toaster, and he appears at the site almost every year at the same time. His appearance has certainly been witnessed every year since 1977, when the curator of the Poe House and Museum, Jeff Jerome, began keeping an annual vigil with a group of whoever is willing to join him. On some visits, the Poe Toaster leaves a tribute of red roses, a half-full bottle of cognac, and a letter at the monument. Whether this man's the macabre equivalent of a department store Santa or a bona fide mystery, nobody can say.

Green Mount Cemetery

In a city with more than its fair share of memorable graveyards, Baltimore's Green Mount Cemetery is the only one that can boast not one but three conspirators in a presidential assassination. It also has some of the most marvelous and well-preserved statuary we at *Weird Maryland* have ever seen in a Victorian garden cemetery, including grave markers shaped like furniture. Really, what more can you ask for?

The Lincoln Plot

One of the great features of Victorian garden cemeteries is the fact that they attracted famous families. Unfortunately for them, some of the famous families weren't necessarily desirable. Take for example the great Booth acting dynasty of Harford County. Junius Brutus Booth got his start on the stage in London and settled on a farm in Bel Air. He had ten children, several of them actors, including his ninth child, John Wilkes Booth, who was also a presidential assassin. Junius and many of his family, including John, are buried at Green Mount. Except for a few conspiracy theorists, most people believe that some time after John Wilkes Booth assassinated President Lincoln, he himself was shot and killed in Port Royal, Virginia, on April 26, 1865, and buried in a horse blanket near the Old Penitentiary at Washington Arsenal Grounds. Two years later the body was exhumed and placed in a pine box, and two years after that, re-exhumed and transported to Green Mount, where it was buried in an unmarked grave in the Booth family plot on Saturday, June 26, 1869. The seriousness of Booth's crime was so great that the minister who presided at the reburial was shunned by his congregation after they learned about the service.

It's appropriate that Booth should end up in Green Mount, where two of his co-conspirators, Michael O'Laughlen and Sam Arnold, are also buried. And it's inevitable that the graves attract the attention of people who take a fringe view of the Lincoln assassination. The unmarked grave in the Booth family plot, taken by most to be John's, frequently receives floral tributes. People sometimes stick pennies on the marble, because of the President whose head is on the coin. And according to staff at the cemetery, cards, letters, and banners also appear by the grave, but usually whisked away in the interest of good taste.

. . . at the Table

I often wonder whether this table-like arrangement is deliberately near the famous Fulton chair-on-a-pedestal monument at Green Mount Cemetery. I'm sure that the ghost of Mr. Fulton (if there is one) would pull up his chair to take a meal here. Too bad the cemetery is so secure and well managed: That's something I'd like to see. –*Tapho*

Pull Up a Chair . . .

In most Victorian houses, Father's favorite chair was a powerful symbol of the patriarch: When he was out of the house, the little ones would see the empty throne as either a welcome reprieve from a stern disciplinarian or the absence of a cherished parent. Either way, they'd never have the nerve to sit in it. So when Charles Carroll Fulton died in 1883, his children erected a monument to him in the form of an empty chair. And just so there was no mistake about what kind of father he was, they inscribed on the pedestal: HE HAS LEFT US A PRECIOUS MEMORY OF ALL THAT WAS LOVEABLE, GENTLE AND GOOD.

Take a Bath

For years, people believed that this bathtub memorial was designed to celebrate a family that made its fortune in the plumbing business. Even the cemetery staff used to tell that story, but in more recent years an even more interesting story came to light. *Weird Maryland* heard about it from several staff members in the Green Mount offices. The woman buried beneath the tub was an avid bather whose husband insisted that bathing wasn't healthy. In our age of daily showers, it's easy to forget that cleanliness isn't the only way to

An Absolutely Divine Memorial

A truly larger-than-life celebrity is forever at rest at the Prospect Hill Park Cemetery in Towson. Born Harris Glenn Milstead in 1945 to Diana and Harris Milstead, the child would grow up into the notorious drag queen "Divine." When Harris was twelve years old, his family made a fortuitous move from Towson to nearby Lutherville—down the street from young John Waters. Harris and Waters became fast friends in high school, and as Waters went on to film-directing fame, he helped transform Harris into Divine and cast him in roles as women in most of his early films. Probably best known for a turn as Edna Turnblad, mother to 1960s dance-crazed daughter Ricki Lake in Waters's 1988 movie *Hairspray,* Divine was branching out to nondrag television roles when he died—likely of complications due to his weight—in March 1988, a week after the film opened.

A visit to his grave will prove that although outlandish in life, in death Divine is almost understated. Inscribed simply with his name, stage name, dates, and the phrase OUR LOVING SON, Divine's headstone is a solemn tribute to the actor. Much weirder than the grave itself are the trinkets often left behind by fans. From trees made of fake fingernails to bras draped over the headstone and kiss marks left in bright lipstick, Divine devotees pay homage to their hero(ine). Unfortunately, it was reported in 1998 that one such fanatic had defaced the gravestone by writing in marker, "Make Heaven Flashy!!!" and using a garish shade of pink to color in

stay healthy. Back in the days before central heating and adequate insulation, being wet led to getting cold. Getting cold could run down your body's defenses and lead to illness. And illness could develop into pneumonia and lead to death. That's what happened to the woman who lies beneath the bath in Green Mount Cemetery. But if any kids happen to be reading this, don't try that as an excuse for skipping your bath tonight: The germs that killed the wife had to come from somewhere, and our money is on her unwashed husband.

the fingernails on the stone's hands in prayer. Perhaps Divine would have reveled in these additions, but there are better ways to pay tribute than by defiling a grave site. On a more recent visit to pay our respects, *Weird Maryland* was happy to find the monument clean and graffiti-free, so it seems the grave has been lovingly restored. The diva is likely pleased by all the attention.

Bleeding Tombstones

One of the favorite items in folklore is a bloodstain that won't go away. These stains remind the living of a terrible event in the past—usually a violent or sudden death, often a murder, and sometimes an unpunished crime. And there's no more chilling place for this old legend to raise its head than in a graveyard.

The bleeding tombstone is a staple of local legend, but all too often it's hard to find out exactly where the stones actually lie. Marbled or weathered tombstones can look awfully like bloodstained ones after a century or two, and the difficulty most people have navigating cemeteries often leads to false-positive identification of the stones in question. Nevertheless, here are some of the tales we've heard on the subject. See if you can find the stones.

Thurmont Thanatophobia

There's a tombstone in a cemetery near Thurmont that's said to bleed at certain times of the year. A man named Tobias Matthews was in a terrible bad accident in the late 1800s. He was taken for dead, and buried. They say around here that he wasn't really dead when he was buried and that's why the stone bleeds. They say that he tried to scratch his way out of the casket and that he broke off fingernails and wore his fingers down to the bone and bled to death finally. They say the stone bleeds on the day that he died. I don't know, but they say that there are dark stains on the stone all the time.*–JT*

Somerset Cemetery Shocker

Out in the woods between Princess Anne and Snow Hill in Somerset County, there used to be a little Nazarene church. This was right in the middle of Pocomoke Forest, and the church house is now part of Iron Furnace village. But there's still a graveyard on the old site, and tucked away in this woodland bone yard there's a tombstone that they say is covered with bloodstains. It's a popular haunt to visit at midnight on Halloween or the night of a full moon (or both if you can manage it). I've only been there at night, and I can't tell what the stains are by flashlight, but they're there alright. The story about the grave varies a lot depending on who's telling it, but most of the stories involve murder. And they all say that the place is haunted. One of the creepiest stories I heard was that you'll see the flashes of light that look like they're being reflected off eyeglasses, but you can't see who's wearing the eyeglasses.*–Quakerboots*

Rocky Hill Horror

The legend behind the bleeding tombstone of Rocky Hill Cemetery in Woodsboro could have been ripped out of the pages of the Brothers Grimm. It has a widower, a cruel stepmother, and a mother who grieved from beyond the grave. The woman who is buried at the gravesite made her husband swear on her deathbed that if he remarried, their children would still be the most important thing in the world to him. Well, he remarried, and sooner or later, his new wife started to work on her husband so he would forget his promise to his first wife and transfer all his affections to her. The children were sidelined and eventually neglected, but not forgotten. Their mother grieved for their sad situation from The Other Side. The woman's tombstone broke out in a sweat of dark beads of liquid that looked just like blood. They say that it still does. Rocky Hill Cemetery is on Coppermine Road in Woodsboro, Frederick County, and the tombstone is located three rows back in the middle of the row in the left hand corner of the yard. The stones adjacent to the bleeding stone bear the names of George and Mary Fox. I couldn't read the name on the bleeding stone the time I went there.*–Gracie*

Cedar Hill Cemetery: Lost and Found

Following the railroad tracks out of Havre de Grace toward the Susquehanna River, you come to a patch of wooded scrub on a dead-end road called Elizabeth Street. Beneath the leaves and brush lies a missing piece of Havre de Grace history: Cedar Hill Cemetery, a final resting place of Civil War veterans, nameless vagabonds, and the victim of a bloody murder more than one hundred and fifty years ago.

A short scramble up a grassy hill and into a thick scrub of woods and weeds, a deer trail leads first to a simple gravestone in the ground and then to about a dozen more, but only a handful remain standing and fewer still are legible.

Some slate stones have survived the weathering of the last century and look as if they could have been carved a year ago and not one hundred and fifty. A heart-shaped stone sat awkwardly tilted, but now rests beneath soil and brush — much like the occupant of the grave. One stone is eerily engraved with the Latin phrase MORI VINCENT OMNES, which means "Death Conquers All."

Another headstone bears the name of a Mary Elizabeth who died August 21, 1874, at the age of only three months and four days. Eight headstones have some kind of markings on them, and a half-dozen more are just crumbling stone. Most unsettling is evidence of more graves in the numerous sunken pits on the property, indicative of collapsed coffins.

While most of the tombstones have toppled or crumbled with time and weather, the government-issued headstones of two Civil War veterans remain standing and contain valuable information that answers some questions, but asks volumes more.

One of the soldiers seems to have lived the simple life of a musician and shoemaker before dying of consumption in 1871; his story is modest when compared to that of his comrade resting a few feet away.

Born in Ireland, Casper Smith enlisted and became a private in Company H, 2nd Regiment Eastern Shore, Maryland Volunteer Infantry. His first brush with death occurred July 18, 1864, during a battle at Snickers Ford in Virginia, where he was shot in the lower abdomen. Amazingly, Smith survived the gunshot wound, only to die nearly two

Some slate stones have survived the weathering of the last century and look as if they could have been carved a year ago and not one hundred and fifty.

decades later, the victim of a sinister plan and a vicious crime. The January 13, 1882, edition of the *Aegis and Intelligencer,* an ancestor of today's *Aegis* newspaper, trumpeted the deed in its headline HORRIBLE MURDER OF HAVRE DE GRACE CAPTAIN.

On Christmas Eve 1881, Captain Smith left Havre de Grace aboard the schooner *Shelldrake,* which carried guano to Baltimore. The ship was expected to arrive back in Havre de Grace on December 28 but on December 31,

Richard Moore, a deckhand on the *Shelldrake,* returned to the city alone, without the schooner or Smith.

When the owner of the ship went to Baltimore to investigate the disappearance of the *Shelldrake* and its crew, a grisly scene awaited him. The ship was found docked and covered in snow, which indicated it had not been moved or tended to recently. Smith was found dead, facedown with holes in his temple, bloody handkerchiefs stuffed in his mouth as a gag, and two small kegs of powder — perhaps to blow up the ship and destroy evidence of the gruesome murder.

It was determined that the death blow came from an iron marlinespike, a pointed hand tool used to separate strands of rope, and was delivered by Moore. Moore, who at the time lived with his mother and three brothers in Havre de Grace, was arrested and convicted of second-degree murder, for which he was sentenced to eighteen years in a penitentiary.

Captain Smith, who during the war had taken a gunshot to the stomach and lived to tell about it, was dead at the age of forty-five at the hands of his own deckhand. Now Smith lies forgotten on the wooded hill.

The cemetery is believed to have opened in 1832 and was abandoned only a decade later, but there are stories that, even as late as the turn of the twentieth century, it was still being used as a paupers' plot. It disappeared from city maps after 1945 and at present doesn't show up in any city land or tax records.

Few ever set foot these days on the once sacred soil — leaving the dead alone with quite a view over the living below. *–Brian Goodman*

The Name's Bond. Cemetery Bond.

An integral part of every ghost tour of the Fell's Point district near Baltimore harbor is a stroll down Shakespeare Street to peer through the iron railings of the grandly named Bond Cemetery (or "Cemetary" as the stenciled sign has it). It's a grand name because it occupies a single house lot and contains a single granite sarcophagus that marks the final resting place of four members of the Fell family. The brothers Edward and William Fell, who gave their name to the area in the early 1700s, lie there, and so do William's son Edward and Edward's son William. But they're not actually inside the sarcophagus. That was erected in 1927, long after the Fell brothers and their children and grandchildren had passed away.

The reason this place is a staple of ghost tours is the tale of a well-dressed apparition who is reportedly often seen walking along Shakespeare Street but who fades away the closer he gets to the Fell graves. Because of his outdated clothing and the apparent destination of his walk, people say he's probably one of the Fells, but who knows the real story?

Granite Graves

As you approach the old Nike missile base in Granite, near Patapsco Valley State Park, you drive past one of the small roadside graveyards that pepper the countryside throughout the state. This particular cemetery has about a dozen stones, all pretty well cared for, in a little grassy area in what is now a residential street. Most of the graves belong to members of the Smith family, and it's a fair bet that the non-Smiths named on the other stones are relatives.

Island of the Dead

Pooles Island has been many things over the past four hundred years since it was first mapped and named by adventurer John Smith. The two-hundred-acre pocket of land in the Chesapeake Bay marked the entrance to two shipping channels, the shallow Gunpowder River to the west and the deeper Bush River to the east.

It staked its claim to weird fame in 1855, when it established the most isolated micro-graveyard in Maryland. Now prosaically named Private Cemetery P-PI (well, it is part of a military base), it is a single grave commemorating two brothers who died at sea during a snowstorm in the bay on February 24, 1855. Captain Elijah Williams and his elder brother James, also a captain, died that day, and almost four months later Elijah washed up near the lighthouse on the northeastern point of the island. The lighthouse owner buried

him, and shortly afterward a headstone and footstone commemorating the brothers were placed at the grave site. The footstone is labeled with the brothers' initials. The headstone reads

IN MEMORY OF CAPT. ELIJAH WILLIAMS, AGED 24 YEARS WHO WAS LOST IN A SNOWSTORM FEBR'Y 24TH 1855 NEAR POOL'S ISLAND. HIS BODY WAS FOUND JUNE 14TH 1855, AND INTERRED IN THIS PLACE.

ALSO TO THE MEMORY OF HIS BROTHER, CAPT. JAMES WILLIAMS, AGED 26 YEARS LOST WITH HIM AT THE SAME TIME; HIS BODY HAS NOT BEEN FOUND.

NO FRIENDLY HAND DID CLOSE THEIR EYES
THEY SAW NO TEAR, THEY HEARD NO SIGHS;
BUT IN THE WAVES THEY LOST THEIR BREATH,
AND THEY ENDURED A WATRY DEATH.

It's too bad that nobody can get to the graveyard without military clearance. We certainly couldn't gain permission, though Harford County historians were granted access a few times in the 1990s to record details of the site. One thing they noted is that it's not the actual burial place of Elijah Williams' body; the stones were moved to protect them from coastal erosion, and Elijah's bones weren't moved with them.

Just Plain Weird

Some odds and ends in cemeteries are SO odd that they defy any attempt to file them away in a category. We're not even going to try. Read on, and see if you agree.

Anyone for Chocolate?

Tucked away in the corner of Green Mount Cemetery in Baltimore is a Pavlov's corner for cocoa lovers. Perhaps we just have chocolate obsession, but the memorial to Robert C. Hall and Mary R. Hall looks like a a Hershey Kiss to us. Actually, the Halls' blob-on-a-column, erected somewhere between 1908 and 1913, looks a bit more like a Wilbur Bud than a chocolate chip. The Wilbur Bud first appeared in 1894, and many people believe it inspired Milton Hershey to manufacture Kisses, which came along in 1907. Okay, so the memorial is probably just modeled on the Middle Eastern architecture that inspired so many Shriner memorials. But our money's on the chocolate.

X Marks the Spot

It's possible that the two strapped-together logs on this grave in Baltimore are actually supposed to symbolize Christ (like the X in Xmas). But the rather cheerless biblical verse under the X is hardly the usual hope-of-resurrection theme: WEEP SORE FOR HIM THAT GOETH AWAY FOR HE SHALL NOT RETURN NOR SEE HIS NATIVE COUNTRY. Nice way to comfort the bereaved.

Comes in Handy

You frequently see hands pointing upward on grave markers. It's a symbol of hope (as in, we hope that's where the departed's soul is going). It's not as common to see such a hand stuck on top of a huge column, as in Joseph Carty's 1867 burial marker in Mount Olivet. Even less common is what's going on in Hannah Truscott's grave at Mount Olivet. Is that hand raised in a military salute? Is that a tiny crown at one o'clock? Are those clouds, mashed potatoes, or a flouncy hairdo? And what does it all mean?

Ghosts in the Graveyard

There seems to be no getting around it — whenever people are discussing cemeteries, the topic of conversation always seems to turn to ghosts. And why not? Graveyards are, after all, not only where the mortal remains of the deceased are interred for all eternity, they are places where people go to honor and remember the dead. Throughout Maryland, there are tales of spirited cemeteries filled with spooks and specters that cry out to be remembered, sometime in the most hair-raising ways. Here now is a tour of just a few of our state's many ghostly graveyards.

A Ghostly Prankster in the Graveyard

There is a strange ghost in Cresap-Wilson Cemetery in Rawlings, Allegany County. This ghost likes to appear and take the belongings of the people who come to visit the graveyard. People do not know who the ghost is or why it likes to take items. If you visit this graveyard, lock the doors to your car and do not set down your belongings or you may not get them back. Several cemetery visitors have set down items such as jackets and bags, only to have them vanish without a sound or trace. Back in 1986 a man I know named Al was writing a book and stopped to take pictures of the cemetery. He laid his camera case on the ground right next to him when he started shooting pictures. He felt a slight tap at his right back shoulder. Startled, he quickly turned around but no one was there. Instantly chilled, he reached down to grab his case before fleeing, but it was plain gone. Two years later he went back to take more photographs. He went back to the area where the strange incident occurred. Just before he took a picture something knocked his baseball cap off by its brim. Again, no one was there. He took one step forward and tripped over his camera case that had disappeared two years earlier! —*Beverly Litsinger, MarylandGhosts.com*

Brother Against Brother in Finzel Cemetery

This story unfolds in the town of Finzel, which is located north of Allegany County. The town has one road with the old Finzel cemetery located at the end of it on the outskirts of town. During the Civil War two brothers took up arms on opposing sides — talk about a family feud! One brother fought for the South and the other brother fought for the North; both fought tirelessly. Nonetheless, the two brothers met often in secret inside the small, secluded graveyard to discuss the war and to catch up on stories about the family and various goings-on. However, late one night the brothers got into a heated argument in the cemetery. Having broached the dangerous topic of politics, they argued about which side was morally right. It was an argument that ended tragically. Push led to shove, which led to concussion when one of the men fell and hit his head on a tombstone. The Northern brother, who lay bleeding and begging God for his life, looked into the eyes of his Confederate brother and told him that he would remain there and await his brother's return with help. He told him they could later finish the battle to see who was correct. The Southern brother ran off, presumably to summon assistance. Whether he just kept going, or met some unexpected fate, no one knows, but the help never arrived and the Yankee brother died.

People say that to this day he is still waiting in the cemetery for his brother to return. Witnesses report that if you walk to the rear of the cemetery, near the largest headstone, you may come eye-to-eye with the baleful stare of the now long gone Union Soldier. —*Beverly Litsinger, MarylandGhosts.com*

Big Rover Is Watching You

Some people find the sentimentality of pet cemeteries just a little too much to swallow, and names like Ling-Foo, Stinky, and Spee de Bozo hard to take seriously. And there are only so many statues of Saint Francis one can take. But although you may feel on the verge of mocking when you enter a pet graveyard, your attitude changes when you actually get in. It's hard to dismiss the depth of feeling that pet owners feel toward their departed four-legged friends. A stroll around one of Montgomery County's finest cemeteries serves only to underline that depth of feeling. The Aspen Hill Memorial Park in Silver Spring has been laying pets to rest since 1920, perhaps even earlier, and continues to do so to this day. Although much of the multi-acre site is overgrown with ivy and creepers, it's a vibrant and contemporary place with more than its share of strange memorials.

Among the dear departed are upward of forty thousand animals ranging from the usual suspects, dogs and cats, to a whole section full of horses, a monkey, and a pile of fur coats (more about those later). Stranger still, at least three humans also made it into this hallowed ground. When *Weird Maryland* got a guided tour from the caretaker, James Thompson, he pointed out the grand mausoleum to a truly beloved dog, Mickey, and then brushed clear the pervasive undergrowth to reveal the plaque to his two owners, George and Gertrude Young, who died in the late 1960s and had their ashes interred with their adored pet.

Like most grave sites in

Maryland, Aspen Hill has its fair share of celebrities. Fans of old RKO movies make pilgrimages to the cemetery to see the final resting place of the Little Rascals' dog General Grant, a.k.a. Jiggs. That's not the terrier with the weird ring around its eye, but the butch little bulldog. Just to make that point clear, there's a picture of the jowly beast on the front of the stone.

And then there's Rags, a veteran of World War I, who was the mascot of the 1st Infantry Division. The creature was found by a private who had celebrated Bastille Day in

July 1918 a little too vigorously and was discovered by military police stumbling around in Montmartre. When the MPs were about to arrest him for being AWOL, he picked up a stray dog he saw and told them he had been looking for his division's mascot. That's how this mixed-breed terrier joined the army, but he quickly lived up to the spurious role Private James Donovan had given him. Donovan and Rags moved up to the front, where Rags acted as an early-warning system for the troops and would even carry messages back along the lines. On October 9, 1918, Donovan and Rags were evacuated to the military hospital at Fort Sheridan in Chicago, where Donovan recovered from wounds he had received. The daughters of Major Raymond Hardenberg adopted the dog and traveled around the various bases where the major was transferred. He was so popular with the troops that in 1930 he became the subject of a book, *Rags, War Hero,* by Jack Rohan. He eventually died in the spring of 1936 at the age of about twenty.

Aspen Hill observes the time-honored tradition of putting the pet's names on the front of a memorial stone and the family name along the top. And it's this factoid that adds some luster to the otherwise out-of-the-way and overgrown plot dedicated to Spee de Bozo. The name along the top of the stone is Hoover. That's Hoover

as in J. Edgar Hoover, the infamous director of the FBI. Spee isn't the only Hoover bulldog in the plot either. He buried all seven of his dogs at Aspen Hill, but as the first, only Spee warranted a headstone.

So what about the fur coats buried in their own plot? Well, that was the brainchild of the people who bought the cemetery in 1988—the animal rights activists PETA. Before donating the property to the Chesapeake Wildlife Sanctuary in 1996, they used the site to raise awareness for their cause by erecting a memorial to the animals that died for fashion. While that's a typically controversial tactic for PETA, it's not really out of place to be confrontational in a cemetery. Like the old inscription from the 1600s that reads AS YOU ARE NOW SO ONCE WAS I, it's a reminder of what cemeteries are there for. And it's just one of the reasons why you can't leave this cemetery unmoved.

Among the dear departed are upward of forty thousand animals ranging from the usual suspects, dogs and cats, to a whole section full of horses, a monkey, and a pile of fur coats.

Abandoned in the Free State

There is no feeling more chilling than being alone in an abandoned place. As you wander through a site that was once beautiful, or at least bustling with life, you feel the emptiness of abandonment more keenly. Visiting places that were once hives of activity but are now unnaturally quiet, still, and empty makes for some very weird adventures. Sometimes, it's a scary experience to visit such places. Other times, it just feels sad, as though you're looking at a huge monument to human achievement that has fallen to wrack and ruin because of some cosmic entropy. Whether you're looking for the chill of existential angst, a little nighttime ghost terror, or the indescribable kind of beauty you can find in a great place in decline, Maryland's abandoned places really deliver. Just be sure that you don't break any laws when you visit these places—especially trespassing laws. This is a thrill that doesn't come cheap if you're fined for it!

The Enchanted Forest of Howard County

Anyone who grew up around Baltimore between the 1960s and 1990s will have heard about the Enchanted Forest. This wooded fairy-tale theme park was about twenty minutes' drive from Route 695 and sat just off Route 40. Its celebration of Mother Goose, Cinderella, the Three Bears, and other childhood favorites permeated the minds and hearts of residents and visitors alike, so that even after it had become hopelessly out of date, it managed to attract people because of its kitsch factor. In fact, it was featured as a set in a movie by the least fairy-taleish of all directors, John Waters. When you see a pumpkin-laden park in the 1990 movie *Cry-Baby* with Johnny Depp, you're catching a glimpse of the Enchanted Forest.

That's about the only glimpse you'll be able to catch nowadays. The only public evidence of this old favorite is a barred and crumbling front gate, and the Enchanted Forest shopping mall. The mall sign touts retail favorites like Petco, Blockbuster, and Safeway in their corporate lettering, but features a fancy scrollwork ENCHANTED FOREST sign topped with the rotund statue of a fairy-tale king. As you stroll along the standard strip mall, past incongruous names like Enchanted Forest Family Dentistry, if you look beyond the dumpsters behind the stores, you can see brightly colored buildings. Dimly, through the chain-link fence and untrimmed undergrowth, you can make out gingerbread and ice-cream-cone houses. And someone with an excellent sense of humor has lined up gingerbread men behind the iron fence, so that their uplifted arms look as though they are holding the bars of a prison cell.

The Enchanted Forest opened in 1955. Ever since it closed in 1994, various local organizations have tried to reopen it. Apart from a few scout-sponsored cleanups, though, most of their efforts have come to naught. The site seems likely to remain closed to the public for a while. But some of the exhibits won't suffer the same fate. A local farmer has acquired a few of the old attractions and relocated them to his place. Clark's Elioak Farm on Route 108, 10500 Clarksville Pike, now displays old Forest favorites—Cinderella's mice, the Three Bears, and some giant toadstools. In November 2004, Cinderella's Pumpkin Coach also moved to Clark's (presumably before midnight). The castle and shoe house are unlikely to join them, though, since these huge structures are made of concrete. So on your way to the Enchanted Forest Sherwin-Williams store, you still have something to glance at behind the dumpsters.

Old School Ties

Perhaps it's because schools are so busy during the day and you only get to see them nearly empty when you're serving after-school detention that the idea of poking around in an empty school brings out the naughty schoolkid in all of us. It's certainly that way with the two great empty schools in Maryland—the DC-area National Park Seminary and the abandoned St. Mary's College near Ellicott City in Howard County. True, most people who visit these places actually risk detention in the big house for trespassing, but from a tantalizing and legally safe distance, these are some of Maryland's great treasures.

Refinishing the Finishing School

With the demand for housing around Washington, DC, it's almost inconceivable that a whole town could stand largely abandoned for fifty years just inside the Capitol Beltway. And yet that's exactly what happened to Forest Glen, a Victorian resort town near Silver Spring. But even more bizarre than the fact it exists is the way it looks. The site's two-dozen buildings include a pagoda, a Greek-style temple, a scaled-down castle, and Mediterranean villas, with statues scattered everywhere. That hardly qualifies as your average DC suburb.

But how did such a strange place come about in the first place? Forest Glen began life as a suburban resort, attracting the new class of permanent government workers created by the 1883 Civil Service Act. The prevailing opinion at the time was that city life was unhealthy and it was imperative to take frequent breaks to country resorts. Silver Spring was far enough out to qualify as the countryside, so a consortium of developers built Ye Forest Inne there, a quarter mile from the Forest Glen station. For about seven years, it eked out a declining business until in 1894 two teachers bought it up and turned it into a girls' finishing school.

John and Vesta Cassedy renamed the site the National Park Seminary and touted the school's creed of "soul training." Their brochure read, "A daughter needs, above all, that the windows of her soul should be thrown wide open to the universe of beauty." The Cassedys decided to ornament the area's natural beauty with some man-made attractions. Inspired by the 1893 Chicago Fair, they embarked on a building spree between 1894 and 1916 that added sixteen "international" buildings—everything from

a Swiss chalet to a Japanese-styled pagoda. These newer buildings were designed as sorority houses. The rolls were filled with the daughters of prominent families—Chrysler, Heinz, Kraft, and Maytag—and the school remained active until 1942, under two changes of ownership. That's when the army invaded.

Under the War Powers Act, the army was empowered to commandeer buildings it needed, and it decided that the National Park Seminary was exactly what it wanted. The Walter Reed Army Hospital bought the place for $859,000, put in some utilitarian buildings, and left the rest to slowly fall apart. For decades, it was a great place for urban explorers—some of whom hastened the decline of the buildings by vandalism. During this time, locals liked to walk through the place and came to regard it as a public park. By the late 1960s, the buildings were crumbling so much that the army drew up a demolition plan. By the end of the 1980s, the army wanted to level the place. It was then that Maryland residents began the call for preservation. In due time, the National Register of Historic Places and a preservation society called Save Our Seminary came on board and stopped the army. But the decay continued. They held back the United States Army until a truce was finally reached in 2005.

The sequel to the Forest Glen story as an abandoned site ends sadly. A group of developers are in the process of turning the ruins into prime residential real estate. The old inn and its grounds will become rental units, condos, and single-family homes. The place will retain its historic integrity (the preservationists will see to that), but it will no longer be the eerie abandoned place so many hundreds of people visited from the 1960s onward.

The True Story of Hell House (St. Mary's College)

The little town of Ilchester on the border of Howard and Baltimore counties is home to the most storied ruin in the Free State. This massive series of stone buildings has been the subject of countless local legends, most of them so dramatic that the place goes by the name of Hell House.

If the stories are true, it is the site of a cruel murder and suicide. The tales surrounding the building are varied—in some, the hall is a school, in others it's a seminary for young men. However, at one point, they say, a crazed priest who taught there killed five girls in a fit of madness and then took his own life. They say the ruins echo with the sounds of their voices to this day.

Of course, these stories aren't true, but that doesn't stop people (including us) from retelling them. They have become such an integral part of the property that it would be wrong to withhold them just because they're fiction. But it would be equally wrong to hide the real story behind the building. Hell House started life in the mid-1800s as a stone building owned by a member of the Ellicott family, which eventually gave its name to Ellicott City. George Ellicott hoped that the local B&O railroad line would erect a station at Ilchester, so his building could serve passengers and railway men as a tavern. But the town was at the bottom of a steep incline, and the trains needed all the momentum they could muster to climb it, so they never stopped at Ilchester.

The isolation of the place better served a Roman Catholic religious order called the Congregation of the Most Holy Redeemer. This group, which was commonly referred to as the Redemptorists, acquired the building and the

surrounding 110 acres to establish a college for training in their order. George Ellicott Jr. took the money, moved down the road a stretch, and became the first mayor of Ellicott City. Two years later, in 1868, St. Mary's College opened as a seminary for young men and continued in that vein for a century.

By the late 1960s, however, the enrollment had dwindled to about a dozen students in the graduating class. A fire destroyed the original stone building on June 14, 1968, and the order saw no reason to rebuild it. The college closed for good in 1972 and was sold off to the state of Maryland and private investors in 1987. Most of the grounds are now part of the Patapsco Valley State Park, but the remains of the college's upper and lower houses are located on private property, behind NO TRESPASSING signs. The impressive stone staircase is also in a no-go zone.

Anyone interested in seeing what's left of the building without breaking the law can hike to an overlook in the Patapsco Valley State Park, on the Baltimore County side of the river. You can get to the trailhead from a parking area on Hilltop Road and along the path, catch sight of the ruins of the upper house.

The Cold Spot at Hell House

There is one creepy set of stairs that leads up to Hell House. A lot of people have commented on a cold spot at the top. The stairs continue after many brambles and overgrown grass. Close up, you can see evidence of the fire on the crumbling façade of the building. Another side of it looks like it was destroyed by a wrecking ball. Over the entrance on the marble above the columns are the letters GE. There is a strange pit in the foundation of the site. It looks like some sort of subterranean entrance or hiding place that leads to tunnels under the property. For some reason, correct historical information is very hard to obtain about this place, and maybe that is one of the reasons it fascinates so much.—*Betsy Earley*

Feeling the Chill

I went with my friends to Hell House and searched all over the grounds and found the pool and greenhouse, but then when we went back to the actual school house to get a second look, something kind of weird happened. We found this cold spot under the stairs.

We didn't say anything to each other about it. Then my girlfriend started crying uncontrollably for no reason. When I put my arms around her she was really freezing cold. We looked around a little more. I began to feel these cool spots going through me. I began to feel anxious. We went back to the car and talked about what happened. I told them about the cold spots, and they all felt them too. My friend told me that when we started searching the school again he felt really dizzy and cold.—*Steve Hart*

Mad Priest of Hell House

There is a legend about an insane priest who killed five girls. He hung them up each facing one another around a pentacle and then he shot himself. People believe the building is haunted by the girls. Sometimes at night you can still hear their tortured screams, and there is a cold spot at the top of the huge stairs. This may be an urban legend but the story refuses to die. People also believe that the Cugle family, who worked for the college for many years, is still haunting the college.—*Beverly Litsinger*

Hellish Priest Dabbled in Black Arts

Here is the story of Hell House, the old St. Mary's College in Ellicott City: supposedly a priest started dabbling in the black arts. In one of the rooms he hung five girls, students of the school, and then himself over this pentagram on the floor. Supposedly this is a true story, and really happened, but records or articles about it are hard to find.—*Holly*

The Army's Leftovers

The U.S. Army has done sterling work in preserving Maryland's most appealing abandoned sites. They also did their fair share of creating sites and abandoning them. During the Second World War, when the Delaware Bay was considered an open invitation to Axis forces to destroy the United States's oil refineries and shipbuilding centers, the army maintained a system of watchtowers and gun batteries that you can still see when you drive north from Ocean City. And during the cold war, when missile attack was dreaded most of all, they created rings of defense around Baltimore and Washington that went way beyond the duck-and-cover mantra of the era.

Nike Missile Bases

Before she was the patron saint of overpriced footwear, the Greek goddess Nike was best known for embodying victory in battle. That's why she lent her name to a cold war missile defense program that began in Fort Meade, Anne Arundel County, and spread across the eastern seaboard. The Nike project drew up defensive rings of missile bases around key areas in the United States, including a series of major bases in Maryland around Baltimore and Washington, DC.

By design, these sites were in suburbs of major cities, so everyone in the burgeoning suburban culture of the cold war era knew about them. They even proudly dubbed them "supersonic rings of steel." But few people in the era of nuclear paranoia knew that within a few years of the project's inception most of the missiles had nuclear warheads.

Each of the bases had a similar design, with two sites per base. The command-and-control center contained radar towers and communications officers, and at some distance underground silos housed the batteries of Nike Ajax and Nike Hercules missiles. The program ran until the late 1960s, when it slowly began to wind down until 1974, when the last base was closed.

After that, many of Maryland's two dozen sites found new purposes for a new era. Some were repurposed as FEMA and MEMA administrative buildings, and others went to different government or military purposes. Several were sold off for redevelopment. Some of the aboveground buildings now house retirement homes, community centers, and school district facilities. But other sites were just decommissioned and left to fall apart. Their bunkers were filled with building rubble to make them inaccessible, and their entranceways were capped and welded shut. Chain-link fences were erected and the properties patrolled. That's why Nike could equally be

the goddess of abandoned sites.

This was the fate of Nike base BA-79, on Hernwood Road, less than a mile from the town of Granite. Next to footpaths and fields stands a huge chain-link fence topped in places with barbed wire, with signs loudly proclaiming the area as a government property, with no trespassing allowed. Through the fence you can see crumbling concrete buildings, an abandoned guard post, and concrete pillars that once housed radar and tracking equipment. A little farther along are the magazines that held the forty-one-foot-long, two-stage missiles, with their kilotons of defensive power tucked away in their tips.

The bunkers lie empty and unused, filled with pools of water, with their retractable metal roofs welded shut and overgrown with weeds, but with cracks that allow light to filter through. If you could get onto the site (and

that's not likely in this day and age), you could see bolts on the floor that once secured elevators that lifted the 1,200-pound, telephone-pole-thin missiles to the launching pad. You'd also see bizarre structures that look like concrete barstools with square seats. These are the plinths that once supported the radar towers.

While they were still operational, these suburban bases provided peace of mind. Now, they are at best an idle curiosity. But that doesn't stop us from wondering, if only we could unweld the metal caps to those access tunnels and remove the rubble that blocks the way, maybe we could see just how deep the rabbit hole goes.

Bunkers in the Bay

Just across the Maryland border lies Cape Henlopen State Park in Delaware. And if the huge number of Maryland license plates there is any indication, it's a cherished destination for Free Staters as well as those First Staters. Youth groups stay in bunkhouses and wander with clipboards, examining the rugged dunes and bay life, as well as taking dips in the Delaware Bay and Atlantic Ocean. But it's the series of concrete towers and bunkers that really pique their interest.

Two concrete cylinders with slots for windows rise above the park's maritime forest. The steps leading to the door have been removed to prevent easy access, but through a hole in the plywood that covers the entrance you can glimpse the ravaged interior of what once protected the Delaware Bay against the German navy.

Those in the observation towers scanned the bay for enemy ships that might attempt to sail up the Delaware to the oil refineries, manufacturing plants, and shipyards in Philadelphia and New Jersey. They relayed information to a central control area, which could in turn command the big guns to open fire. There were two twenty-inch guns and two sixteen-inchers concealed in concrete bunkers beneath man-made dunes at Henlopen, capable of sending even the largest battleship to the bottom of the bay. And for any U-boats that might have tried to take a stab at sneaking by underwater, there were thirteen sets of mines each ready to dispatch its thirty-five explosives.

As it turns out, the base saw very little action until the war ended, at which point a U-boat surrendered to the forces there. But the army's presence still did some good for the cape. They kept developers out, while nearby Lewes and Rehoboth and Ocean City became meccas for beach buffs. So it retains a thriving and relatively unspoiled beach ecosystem. Since 1964, when the army gave the cape back to the state, fishermen and students alike have delighted in the place. But fans of abandoned military facilities get their kicks from the concrete buildings half hidden behind dune pines and undergrowth.

Empty Hospitals

The huge mental hospitals and tuberculosis wards that used to be in vogue during the Victorian era often suffered decades of neglect before they were eventually deemed even unhealthier than their patients and closed down. The nation is dotted with hundreds of places like this, and Maryland is no exception. The massive Glenn Dale Hospital complex is the state's prime example.

All of these hospitals weren't abandoned because they had served their health-giving purpose: They were left for dead.

Abandoned and Haunted: Glenn Dale Hospital

Glenn Dale Hospital is a sprawling abandoned complex that sits on 216 acres of Maryland's Prince Georges County. It was originally built in 1934 as a tuberculosis hospital with two main buildings—one for adults and one for children—plus many smaller outlying facilities. After the discovery of antibiotics and a TB vaccine, tuberculosis epidemics were largely curbed. The complex remained in operation as a general hospital and then a mental hospital until 1982, when questions of structural integrity and the presence of large amounts of asbestos finally forced its doors to shut. Among the still standing buildings are the original children's hospital, the massive main adult hospital, as well as laundry buildings, guard buildings, and nurses' quarters. And what's more they still contain furniture and equipment left over from the facility's years of operation. Many of the buildings are connected by underground tunnels that were used to transport patients and materials over the vast complex without having to go outside, especially during the cold winter months.

In the two decades that the buildings have been abandoned, dozens of legends have cropped up about them, especially since during its later years Glenn Dale was used as a hospital to house the criminally insane. Stories are told that upon the hospital's closing, some of these deranged lunatics were simply released to the outside world. With no family to speak of and no idea of where to go, they found their way back inside the abandoned buildings and now call them home. In the darkest recesses of these ramshackle structures reside some truly insane individuals—or so the stories say.

Another tale claims that the hospital had to be abandoned due to an overwhelming epidemic of tuberculosis that killed most of the patients and staff and infected the very building itself. Explorers should be careful, the story goes, because touching any of the remnants of the building's past could expose them to this deadly disease. While this is untrue, it is once again worth mentioning that the buildings are in fact rife with asbestos and do pose a threat to the health of adventurous visitors.

Many late-night explorers to Glenn Dale report hearing strange noises and even seeing ghosts. Many say that the

spirits of those patients who died while residents of the hospital haunt the halls of the now abandoned buildings. Not surprisingly, many people report experiencing odd occurrences in the vicinity of the morgue, located in the basement of the main adult hospital building.

Glenn Dale Hospital is a no trespassing area regularly patrolled by Prince Georges County police as well as park police who live in a facility on the grounds.

Upside-Down Crosses at Glenn Dale

Inside the buildings of the Glenn Dale complex, there are still gurneys in the storage areas, a chair at the solid wood reception desk, prosthetic limbs, sanitizers for surgical instruments, toys in the children's ward, a reel-to-reel film machine complete with screen located in the theater, pews in the church, trash that never made it into the incinerator, and the board of trustees plaque in the facilities building. One local researcher was even lucky enough to locate a new patient booklet handed out to all new tuberculosis patients of the hospital. It reads like a 1950s Soviet propagandist pamphlet: "A healthy tuberculosis patient is an active tuberculosis patient."

Rumor has it that Satanists used to worship down in the basement of the main building. I have seen evidence of that—there are plenty of spray-painted upside-down crosses. At one point I even saw an upside-down cross spray-painted with an arrow pointing towards the hospital on top of an enclosed children's bus stop at the intersection of Glenn Dale Rd. and MD Rte. 450.

The buildings are now very unsafe. Broken glass and debris are everywhere. Asbestos hangs from the ceilings, there are holes in the floor, the stairs are coming loose from their supports, the elevator doors are open and one could mistake that for a doorway. The basement is always flooded, so there is very little chance of ever finding the tunnels. Also, hundreds of bats nest in it, so there is the distinct chance of walking into a room, feeling your foot sink in something and hearing a lot of fluttering overheard.

The area around the hospital is starting to be developed. But the word is that it would be too expensive to redevelop the 200-plus acres that Glenn Dale sits on. The buildings would have to be cleared of all that asbestos. The government has started talks on what to do with it all.—*Pete Monaghan*

Old Hospital Just Left for Dead

I grew up in Bowie. Just down the road from Bowie there's an old hospital referred to as Glenn Dale Hospital. It's an old abandoned hospital that used to be owned by the District of Columbia. I've heard that it was a tuberculosis center and later became an insane asylum as TB cases became uncommon. Supposedly in the '70s they just shut the hospital down. If you go inside you can still find medical files and equipment, like the workers were rushed out of there. There are tunnels under the buildings. Prince Georges County owns the land now and has an on-site security guard to keep the kids from wandering on the property. Be careful. Most of the buildings are falling down.—*Shane Nordvik*

Memories of the Mental Hospital

Growing up, my brother always spoke of Glenn Dale Hospital and how he and his friends would hang out there. It was the weekend hangout for many teens. Most would party outside the broken down building, but those brave enough would venture inside. The stories I heard of what they found inside were really scary—blood stained walls, body parts still in jars, screams as you walk down the dark hallways, and of course the "Morgue" stories. The buildings were never torn down, but left to rot. The eerie feeling I always got driving down that road and passing the old hospital was horrible—no one in sight, just the darkest sky you could imagine and the thousands of souls that were tortured. Recently, I ventured back and decided to take a ride down the infamous creepy road. To my surprise, guess what was still standing? The old Glenn Dale Mental Hospital, surrounded by mini-mansions and huge pricey houses. So I asked my brother about it and he told me that the buildings are filled with TB and can't be torn down.—*Shannon Lawrence*

Silence of the Glenn Dale Morgue

I will never forget the 3 a.m. adventure to this hollow graveyard of empty wards and endless hallways. We approached from dead on with many options on where to enter. There was a heavy door slightly ajar that had stairs heading straight down. We headed down and soon found that water had covered over 3 inches of the floor. The air had a chill to it. As we went through the lower level there were hidden tunnels to go even further down. Then we stumbled upon the morgue. There were slabs pulled out as if to tempt you into laying on one. Old tables that held the body as it was emptied of fluids were turned over. I have never been more afraid.

Aside from the main hospital, there are other small buildings for those patients who were quarantined. One of these buildings happened to be more creepy than the hospital itself. We didn't stay long enough to see all there is to see here, but we were here long enough to watch the sun peek over the horizon and get a real glimpse of how huge and intimidating this place is.—*Melissa F.*

Henryton Center

Glenn Dale isn't the only abandoned medical facility in the state. Between 1923 and 1955, the state's department of health and mental hygiene built twenty-three buildings, known as the Henryton Center, in Carroll County. The center was built to serve the state's African American population as a tuberculosis hospital. In time, TB vaccinations reduced the number of patients, and the center was repurposed as a home for the developmentally disabled of all races. Like many mental institutions, it was closed down in the 1980s, when the prevailing philosophy was to integrate the disabled into society at large.

This has left a large abandoned hospital off Marriottsville Road in Marriottsville, right next to Maryland's historic railroad. The place is prominently marked as private property and is often patrolled by police, who not only arrest trespassers but ticket cars parked on the property. Beginning in 2005, the state began actively soliciting developers to redesign the buildings into something that would serve the community, but for now it's just a big, empty complex of buildings that are beautiful by day and menacing by night.

We do not encourage anybody to trespass on such properties, because it's just not right to do so. But some people who wrote in to *Weird* have furnished us with some other reasons to avoid Henryton. Their stories follow, and if you're still keen on visiting the place . . . well . . . don't say you weren't warned.

A Smashing Time at Henryton

One night, three of my friends and I went to explore the Henryton Center. One of my friends considers herself psychic. She constantly gets bad premonitions about things, and she is usually right. But, the whole time we were walking around, she didn't have any. The largest building is sort of "E" shaped and there are many lampposts so that everything is lit up around the building at night.

My friends and I went around to the back of the building and stood looking up at the huge structure. It is about 4 or 5 stories tall and brick, with rows and rows of windows on each level. I made a comment about the dark windows: "Isn't it funny how if someone were looking out one of those windows right now, they could see us, but we could not see them?" We laughed and proceeded into the building. Most every door and window is boarded up, but because this is a common place for thrill-seekers, one of the lower doors had been un-boarded.

We walked through a creepy kitchen and into a long hallway. On one side of the hallway were the long lines of windows we had seen from outside, and on the other side were doors to many small rooms. We walked to the end of this hallway, and there was a very large room and a stairwell. We walked up the stairwell to the next level, where the hallway was similar to the first floor. The whole time, my psychic friend had not commented on having any bad feelings. In fact, she led the way. We got to the end of the second hallway, and climbed the stairwell to the third floor hallway, which was similar to the first two.

This time I stopped at one of the windows about halfway down the hallway, and peered down to the area where we had been standing outside looking up at the windows. Then I said, "Isn't it funny that now I could see someone if they were down there, and they can't see me!" And I laughed. Right then, my psychic friend freaked out and said, "We have to leave now, I don't want to be here!" She started running down the hallway, down the flights of stairs, through all the doors we came through, and back out to the parking lot we had been standing in. We tried our best to keep up with her, but she beat us outside. When we got out there, she was standing staring up at the rows of windows where we had been standing on the third floor. She had a horrible look of terror on her face. So, we turned around to see what she was looking at, and almost right where we had been standing, the large window was completely shattered. It was not broken when we were up there.–*Carly L.*

Lights Go on at Henryton

Everyone who has been to the Henryton Center at night knows that when you go, you feel like you're being watched. At night, you can see faint lights in the windows. Or perhaps that creeped-out feeling you get is because the place is a haven for bats. Maybe you can see them out of the corner of your eye and subconsciously register that they're there without actually consciously seeing them. But whatever the explanation, there's something about that place that just isn't right.—*FineTime*

Perryman Mansion

On the Perryman Peninsula in southern Harford County, there exists an old and crumbling manor house. Once the estate of the Boyer family, the sprawling mansion lies on the coastline of the Bush River.

The once extravagant multi-level mansion was abandoned by its longtime tenants decades ago when Baltimore Gas & Electric Company purchased the home along with two hundred and fifty acres of land on which to build a regional plant.

The home and property were cut off from civilization for years because of their unique location and situation. Surrounded by water on three sides, the peninsula is accessible by only one road, which is closed off to the public once it reaches the BG&E plant. On one side of the peninsula runs an active railroad line, and on the other side is the Aberdeen Proving Ground—the heavily guarded and fenced U.S. Army post.

Situated as such, the mansion was literally cut off from human contact. Naturally, rumors began to spread and its legend grew. Any Maryland ghost hunter worth his salt has heard of the Perryman mansion and its strange goings-on.

There are stories of ghostly green lights moving in patterns along the walls. Visitors say they have heard voices and other unexplained noises. Many get chills just gazing at the imposing structure and refuse to enter its doorway. Maybe that's because the ground outside the mansion is littered with small bone fragments. And animal carcasses are commonly found along the road leading back to the house.

Historical records also point to an old graveyard on the property, which is now covered in weeds and shrubs. Most investigations of the mansion have uncovered death—in one form or another.

Photographs taken in and around the mansion routinely capture orbs or other mysterious lights and objects. One recent investigation of the Perryman mansion did result in the positive identification of one of its reclusive inhabitants. A strange crying spooked the team and led its members upstairs, where they were able to definitively pinpoint the shrill whine—a baby raccoon!

Those brave enough to venture into the attic—the highest point in the mansion—are greeted by the putrid smell of decay where coal-black turkey vultures have been found silently guarding clutches of bloody eggs.

There is little left of the mansion now. A fire destroyed much of it. The suspected cause of the fire was arson, but no one was ever charged.—*Brian Goodman, acurse.com*

Perryman Memories

The Perryman mansion has been almost a playground to my friends and I for more than six years. Every time I have been there something or someone has made itself known. It starts with the hike to the house. The first 10 minutes are ducking the lights of the electric company, BGE, and staying close to the sporadic trees to hide in the shadows from any disgruntled workers. This is the only area you will feel safe.

As the large lights disappear you are surrounded by thick woods to your left and the train tracks to your right. Even if you feel you are brave enough and nothing can keep you from venturing on . . . a train goes by and drowns out all the noise around you. You can't hear if you are being followed in those brief seconds.

At the end of the paved trail you hang a left and become swallowed by woods. A long walk and you can see far enough ahead to trick yourself into thinking there is someone waiting beside the tree lines. As you approach the mansion itself, there are rhododendrons near the stone entrance. A fence surrounds the house but there is a hole cut out to squeeze through . . . or get caught up in while trying to escape.

There have been more than three occasions when I have heard women speaking as I made my way left of the fence. I am not the only one who heard them. Left of the house you can go to the old pier that sits sideways over the river. You almost forget that you are about to go into a haunted mansion and will more than likely have some sort of unexplainable experience. Let me just tell you of a couple.

A group of us went into the house. Outside were bones of some sort of animal. There are always bones. We stuck together in a uniform line and decided to go through the living room and upstairs. One of us stayed behind due to fear of seeing something. I had been there so much I honestly wasn't worried about it. Until we began to walk up the steps . . . one by one pushing each other to go faster. I heard someone whisper in a very stern and serious tone, "LOOK."

We all turned our heads at the same time as if in a bad

Robert Palmer video and on the wall behind us leading up to the stairs a green glow seeped through. At first it was still . . . then slowly moving up. Then back down. Then up, down and side to side. A cross shape? Needless to say, we didn't go upstairs or in the basement. We ran out of there. Another adventure also included a large group of people. We made our way to the basement. All of us going our own ways. As we explored, many of the group talked to keep their spirits up. All of a sudden a loud thump came from the first floor. My friend and I stared at each other wide eyed. Only three of us heard it. As I saw my friend's mouth open to warn the others I demanded her to not say a word. The last thing you want to do in an old building that is literally falling apart is to give reason to freak out and run. We kept our secret until we were safe outside.

There is nothing special about the way the mansion looks from the inside. It is the sight of it from the fence that makes you shudder. The blank gaze of hollow windows seems to warn you.–*Melissa F.*

INDEX
Page numbers in **bold** refer to photos and illustrations.

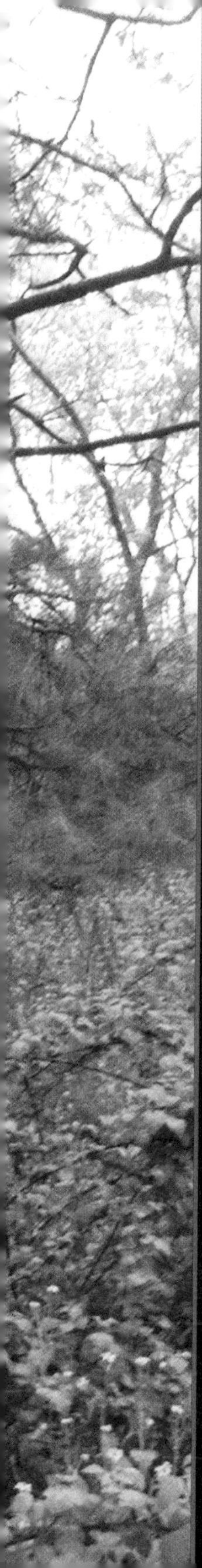

WEIRD MARYLAND

By
MATT LAKE

Executive Editors
Mark Sceurman and Mark Moran

ACKNOWLEDGMENTS

More than most books, the *Weird* series is the work of many people. Naturally, huge credit is due to the Marks, Messrs. Sceurman and Moran, who launched the whole project with more than a decade's worth of dedication to chronicling their home state of New Jersey. I still don't know what you were thinking, guys, but don't stop now! Cracking the editorial whip and keeping me honest were the Barbaras, Morgan and Chintz. Corralling the individual stories and photographic elements into a cohesive unit was the work of Emily Seese, Gina Graham, and Richard Berenson. And making sure I got to some of the more obscure locations were my satellite navigators, Mary Kelly and Nicole Tiedemann from ALK. Thanks, everyone, for keeping this thing in line. And further credit goes to the following researchers, polymaths, and sundry good eggs:

Brian Goodman
Shara Walker
Bob Chance
George Reynolds
Julia Lake
Henry Peden
Linda Hassett
Donna Carpenter
Christopher Lake
Beth Alvarez
Joel Rickenbach
Donna Mucha
Ronald Pilling
Caroline Craig

Publisher:	Barbara J. Morgan
Managing Editor:	Emily Seese
Editor:	Marjorie Palmer
Copyeditor:	Alexandra Koppen
Production:	Della R. Mancuso
	Mancuso Associates, Inc.
	North Salem, NY

PICTURE CREDITS

SHOW US YOUR WEiRD!

Do you know of a weird site found somewhere in the United States, or can you tell us about a strange experience you've had? If so, we'd like to hear about it! We believe that every town has at least one great tale to tell, and we're listening. It could be a cursed road, haunted abandoned site, odd local character, or bizarre historic event. In most cases these tales are told only in the towns in which they originated. But why keep them to yourself when you could share them with all of America? So come on and fill us in on all the weirdness that's lurking in your backyard!

You can e-mail us at: Editor@WeirdUS.com,
or write to us at:
Weird U.S., P.O. Box 1346, Bloomfield, NJ 07003.

www.weirdus.com